MW00560334

The Sage Returns

SUNY series in Chinese Philosophy and Culture

Roger T. Ames, editor

The Sage Returns

Confucian Revival in Contemporary China

Edited by

Kenneth J. Hammond and Jeffrey L. Richey

Cover image from shutterstock.com

Published by State University of New York Press, Albany

For information, contact State University of New York Press, Albany, NY
www.sunypress.edu

Production, Diane Ganeles
Marketing, Anne M. Valentine

Library of Congress Cataloging-in-Publication Data

The sage returns : Confucian revival in contemporary China / edited by Kenneth J. Hammond and Jeffrey L. Richey.
    pages cm. — (SUNY series in Chinese philosophy and culture)
Includes bibliographical references and index.
ISBN 978-1-4384-5491-7 (hardcover : alk. paper)
ISBN 978-1-4384-5493-1 (ebook)
    1. Confucianism—China—History—21st century.   I. Hammond, Kenneth James, editor.   II. Richey, Jeffrey L., editor.

BL1853.S24 2015
181'.112—dc23   2014009551

10 9 8 7 6 5 4 3 2 1

Contents

PART THREE. CONFUCIANISM AND POPULAR CULTURE

Illustrations

Foreword

On December 9, 2010, China awarded the "Confucius Peace Prize" to Lien Chan, Taiwan's former vice-president, for having "built a bridge between the mainland and Taiwan." The prize was awarded one day before the Nobel Peace prize honored the imprisoned Chinese dissident Liu Xiaobo. Outside China, the "Confucius Peace Prize" was widely derided as a crude attempt to counter the Nobel Prize. The Confucius Peace Prize also set off alarm bells that Confucianism is being officially promoted to justify an authoritarian form of government and to counter growing calls for political liberalization, similar to the way the "Asian values" discourse was used by the Singaporean government in the early 1990s to counter its pro-democracy critics.

Whatever the truth of such accusations, it would be wrong to indict Confucianism in China on the grounds that it is nothing but a slogan used to justify the political status quo and to counter social critics. This fascinating book demonstrates that the revival of Confucianism is taking place at different levels of society, often outside the government's sphere of authority. For example, Robert Moore shows that the Confucian ideal of harmony strongly influences family dynamics in China (in contrast to the United States).

Chinese media, as everybody knows, are subject to government control. But Anthony DeBlasi's chapter shows that government interests must be increasingly balanced by consumer needs. And it turns out that there is substantial market demand for Confucianism, which helps to explain why it increasingly featured in the media. Several contributors discuss the Yu Dan phenomenon: a charismatic female academic who has sold millions of copies of a book on the *Analects* of Confucius. Julia Murray shows that new representations of Confucius have proliferated in a variety of media, including movies and animated cartoons. Murray adds that ordinary people prior to the twentieth century were not likely to encounter representations of

Confucius, and Confucius himself did not have a popular following. In some ways, Confucianism may be more deeply embedded now than in Imperial Chinese history, when it was the official ideology of the state and promoted by male elite intellectuals but did not always impact the ordinary life of the "masses."

This book also shows that the political uses of Confucianism are not always as conservative as they seem. While Yu Dan's "feel-good" version may deflect attention from social problems, more politically minded Confucian-inspired critics pose substantial challenges to the status quo. In Imperial Chinese history, Confucianism served, as least intermittently, as a challenge to and check upon the abuse of power. Ken Hammond's contribution shows that Confucianism also serves similar purposes today. Hammond argues that there is a convergence between socialists who draw on China's political culture to promote a more just and equitable society and Confucians who seek to revive Confucianism as a basis for public life and political ethics within a modern socialist state.

Another important contribution of this book is that it sheds historical and comparative light on some of the reasons for the revival of Confucianism. Jennifer Oldstone-Moore shows that political leaders in Nationalist China drew on the language of scientists to promote Confucianism in the 1920s and 1930s. In the same vein, the Chinese Communist Party today has deemed Confucianism to be an appropriate working partner with scientific socialism that serves to promote a "rational" form of ethics. Robert Foster compares official support by the Chinese government to the promotion of Confucianism in Meiji Japan. However, what Foster calls "popular Confucianism" is driven more by psychological than political factors. Concern over moral decline that accompanies economic modernization motivates many social reformers. Jeffrey Richey shows that popular Confucianism is also supported by a growth in national pride and a search for identity that differ from Western-style ethics.

In short, this book deepens our thinking on the revival of Confucianism in China. It also opens up new questions. One of Confucianism's strengths is that it has demonstrated an amazing flexibility in assimilating the challenges of other value systems, from Daoism, Legalism, and Buddhism in the past to socialism, liberalism, and capitalism today. Obviously, Confucianism has changed via these repeated encounters with other traditions, but what exactly are the core values that underpin and survive these encounters? How precisely can core Confucian values help with educational, social, and political reform in China today? And what can Confucianism offer to the rest of the world today? This book provides the historical and sociological material that helps us to think about the answers in informed ways.

Daniel A. Bell
Beijing

Introduction

The Death and Resurrection of Confucianism

KENNETH J. HAMMOND AND JEFFREY L. RICHEY

In 2006, Yu Dan 于丹, a professor in Beijing Normal University's Department of Cinema, Television, and Media, published what became a runaway best-seller in China, *Yu Dan Lunyu xinde* 于丹《论语》心得 (*Yu Dan's Insights into the [Confucian] Analects*), which transcribed the contents of her very popular television lecture series on China Central Television.[1] In 2007, the Wang 王 brothers' 265-day quest to carry—on foot, in a custom-built carriage that they dubbed *Gan'en* 感恩 ("Thanksgiving")—their aged mother to famous sites all over China riveted Chinese media audiences.[2] In 2008, the publication of a volume titled *Rujia shehui yu daotong fuxing* 儒家社会与道统复兴 (*Confucian Society and the Revival of the Orthodox Way*), which called for a revitalization of Chinese society and politics through an embrace of Confucianism, met not with jeers or indifference, but rather attracted serious engagement and even praise by political thinkers and public intellectuals in China.[3] In 2009, the traditional springtime rite of tomb-sweeping (*Qingming* 清明) at Confucius's grave in Qufu 曲阜 was enhanced by the revival of animal sacrifices to Confucius by his descendants, more than a thousand of whom gathered later that year to celebrate their ancestor's birthday by sacrificing three large animals on the altar before his image.[4] Finally, in early 2011, a thirty-one-foot bronze statue of Confucius weighing seventeen tons mysteriously and suddenly appeared in Beijing's Tian'anmen 天安门 Square, only to be removed under the cover of darkness some four months later.[5]

1

Why did a professor's commentary on the teachings of Confucius sell upward of 10 million copies (in both official and pirated editions) in less than a year? Why did two middle-aged men willingly endure the hardship of carrying their elderly mother more than 4,500 kilometers (about 2,796 miles) on foot? Why does animal sacrifice to a long-dead Chinese sage play any role whatsoever in contemporary life? Why would the Chinese government erect a gigantic icon of the ancient thinker whom Mao Zedong 毛泽东 once condemned as "a feudal mummy" just across from a fifteen-by-twenty-foot oil painting of Mao himself— and in China's largest public space, to boot? And why is all of this happening now, in the early twenty-first century, when Confucianism long ago was pronounced dead by China's Communist regime, not to mention a half-century of progressive-minded reformers who preceded Mao's Communist revolution in 1949? The answers to these questions lie in the story of Confucianism's revival in contemporary China, which this volume seeks to tell as well as to understand.

For more than two thousand years, a sset of ideas, institutions, and practices commonly known as Confucianism formed the basis for Chinese intellectual and religious culture and for many aspects of Chinese and East Asian culture more broadly. Rooted in the texts and teachings associated with a figure (ca. 551–479 BCE) known as Kong Qiu 孔丘 to his contemporaries, Kongzi 孔子 ("Master Kong") to his students, and Kong Fuzi 孔夫子 (Westernized as "Confucius") to millions thereafter, what we now call "Confucianism" began as a loose set of master-disciple networks in a China divided by civil war between the collapse of the Western Zhou 周 dynasty in 771 BCE and the brutal unification accomplished by the Qin 秦 dynasty in 221 BCE. During this time, Confucianism and Confucians enjoyed no special privilege and appear to have been regarded as minor, even countercultural figures by most Chinese elites.[6]

Confucianism's fortunes changed dramatically when the Han 漢 dynasty (206 BCE–220 CE) adopted Confucian thought as a tool for legitimizing its power and controlling its subjects. In 136 BCE, the Han government established Confucian texts as the basis of its civil service examinations, making Confucian thought a mandatory subject for all who wished to obtain official employment. During this period, Confucian thought took on many recognizably religious aspects, including the ritual worship of Kongzi in state-sponsored temples.[7] Once Confucianism acquired government support, its teachings, texts, and traditions formed the basis not only of court ritual, bureaucratic procedure, and administrative ethos, but gradually of community and family life as well. Over time, Confucianism both absorbed and countered influences from other traditions, especially Buddhism, and became well established as the dominant worldview of Chinese elites. While elites propagated what Robert W. Foster, in Chapter 1 of this volume, calls "ruler's Confucianism" (the use of Confucianism to promote social stability, obedience, and faith in authority), the permeation of Chinese culture by Confucian values also made possible what Foster calls "popular Confucianism" (the use of Confucianism to promote checks on rulers, such as the necessity of moral government, accountability to Heaven, and the right to revolt against unjust authorities). Thus, at both elite and popular levels, Confucian ideas formed an ongoing dynamic field of discourse that came to encompass most areas of knowledge and behavior and that continued to be developed and adapted by thinkers and activists as the social and economic conditions of Chinese life themselves changed over long spans of historical time.[8]

As the imperial era in Chinese history approached its end in the late nineteenth century, Confucianism began to be subjected to new kinds of critique, not simply in an effort to revise and adapt it to further changing circumstances, but to an increasing extent as a repudiation of both its form and content and what was more and more seen as its negative role in contemporary life. Throughout much of the twentieth century, Confucianism was subjected to thoroughgoing rejection by many young Chinese across the range of political perspectives. From the antimonarchist revolutions of the first decade through the rise of liberal Nationalism and then the emergence of Marxist radicalism, Confucian ideas, institutions, and practices were seen as retarding China's modernization and as fundamentally unsuited to the needs of a progressive, forward-looking nation. Educated, politically engaged people in China turned to a variety of alternatives to seek a path of wealth and power for their country.

By the middle of the century, the Chinese Communist Party (*Zhongguo Gongchandang* 中国共产党, or CCP), espousing the theory of Marxist dialectical materialism and proclaiming its dedication to the construction of a socialist New China (*Xinhua* 新华), had come to power, and it set about the tasks of transforming China both in political economic terms and in the cultural sphere. Confucianism remained a target of criticism, rejected not only for its adverse practical effects, but for its putative basis as an ideology of reaction and repression.

However, the CCP was deeply divided over how best to pursue its goals of developing the New China, and the political struggles between leadership factions generated repeated intense campaigns of popular mobilization. These culminated in the Great Proletarian Cultural Revolution (*Wuchan jieji wenhua da geming* 无产阶级文化大革命) of 1966–76, by the end of which many Chinese, both urban and rural, were exhausted and frustrated, felt alienated from political engagement, and were deeply skeptical of the claims of socialist ideology, especially its moral dimensions. The early 1970s campaigns to criticize CCP-identified villains as widely separated in time as Kongzi and Lin Biao 林彪 (Mao's second-in-command until his mysterious death in 1971, after which Mao branded him a traitor) were in some ways the final exhaustion of both the fratricidal struggles of the CCP leaders and the trashing of the country's classical tradition.

With the consolidation of power by Deng Xiaoping 邓小平 by November 1978, China finally settled on a clear path of development, the policies of opening to the outside world, and the use of market mechanisms to advance economic growth. The 1980s became an era of rapid change, with many positive economic effects, but also with the spread of corruption and abuse of power. The values of socialist morality were further compromised, yet there was no clear alternative to replace them. The upheavals of 1989—before, during, and after the government-repressed protests in Tian'anmen Square—further eroded lingering faith in the established order, and a cynical materialism seemed increasingly pervasive.

Yet already some people in China were beginning to look back into the country's traditional culture to seek bases for moral values and for ways of understanding the world around them. By the 1990s, this process of searching for foundations for values and "new" ways to ground moral action was becoming much more widespread. Buddhism, Daoism, and other forms of traditional spirituality experienced popular revivals. Many young people turned to Western thought and religion, from Christianity to postmodernism.[9]

Within this turbulent and dynamic ferment, it is not surprising to note that the ideas and values of Confucianism also have been rediscovered. Beginning in the 1980s and accelerating through the 1990s and into the twenty-first century, ideas, images, behaviors, and attitudes associated with Confucianism have been discussed and sometimes acted on by a wide range of groups and individuals. Especially in the earlier stages of this process, much of the activity was either academic in nature or sponsored by government agencies, and dominated by men. But as time has gone by, the Confucian revival has become a much more broadly based phenomenon, and the variety of agents involved has gotten increasingly diverse, both in terms of social position and in the particular views or interpretations of Confucian thought being presented.[10] Women, non-academics, and nongovernmental organizations have become some of the most prominent spokespeople for the revived Confucianism expressed in popular best-sellers and other media, as well as major contributors to the revision, reimagining, and revival of Confucianism.

Now, at the end of the first decade of the twenty-first century, it is possible to look at the contemporary Confucian revival in China as a complex and multivalent field of cultural production. Confucian revivalists are both transmitting ancient traditions (and thus maintaining continuity with their cultural past) and innovating new interpretations of them (and thus creating new meanings that keep these traditions relevant in an ever-changing, uncertain modern China). This volume examines aspects of this process, primarily within the People's Republic of China (PRC), but also in the context of the larger East Asian region. Unlike previous studies, it expands the critical focus on contemporary Confucian revival in China beyond the fields of ethics and politics and addresses the revival's relationship to China's long history and the abundant historical precedents for such a revival. Its chapters are divided into three sections: (1) Confucianism and the State, (2) Confucianism and Intellectual Life, and (3) Confucianism and Popular Culture.

Part I begins with Robert W. Foster's comparative analysis of the role played by Confucianism in Meiji 明治 (1868–1912) Japan and post-Mao (1976–present) China. Each is a case of a modernizing East Asian state attempting to balance rapid economic development with the maintenance of political control. During these periods, both Japanese and Chinese turned to Confucianism to define a distinctive identity based on "civilization" (*J. bunmei, C. wenming* 文明) as a way to promote national unity in the face of social change, with rulers using Confucianism to build support and critics using Confucianism to voice dissent. Jennifer Oldstone-Moore's chapter builds on Foster's analysis by documenting how Confucianism has been promoted as a universally valid, if culturally specific vehicle for modernization in progress in Lee Kuan Yew 李光耀's Singapore, Taiwan 台灣, and the PRC by being presented in terms of scientific rationality (as opposed to religious superstition, a label that earlier modernizing opponents of Confucianism attempted to foist upon the tradition). The striking contrasts between the regimes that have appealed to Confucianism for legitimacy—imperial Japan, Nationalist China, postcolonial Singapore, and the CCP—not to mention the diverse uses of Confucianism to mobilize opposition to such regimes, point to its persistent flexibility and appeal as an East Asian ideology.

Part II concentrates on the intellectual dimensions of the Confucian revival in contemporary China. Anthony A. DeBlasi discusses the marketing of Confucian values beyond official (i.e., academic and governmental) circles in China. His chapter examines how Confucianism is presented in works aimed at a popular readership, which in turn reveals much about the appetites and interests of China's emerging literate public, to say nothing of the complex interactions now under way between academic discourse, state power, popular culture, and the market economy. Kenneth J. Hammond's chapter focuses on the ongoing conversation between "New Leftism" (*Xin Zuopai* 新左派, the ideological critique of capitalistic reforms and advocacy of Mao-era socialism inaugurated in the 1990s) and what he calls "Left Confucianism": a movement based not on Marxist thought, but on Confucian values, whose exponents nonetheless are (like "New Leftists") equally concerned with the social and human costs of China's rapid modernization and economic development. Finally, Jeffrey L. Richey discusses how Internet discourse in the PRC reveals the resurgent power of Confucianism as a conceptual resource for articulating in-group morality, critique of youth culture, and the value of native norms vis-à-vis Westernization. All three chapters in this section explicate different ways in which Confucianism is being deployed to articulate a revitalized humanism that is rooted deeply in the Chinese past, but that can restrain the centrifugal social forces unleashed by the market economy of today.

Part III turns to the fascinating and myriad ways in which Confucianism increasingly plays roles in Chinese popular culture. While Confucianism was a prominent target of the first two of China's massive youth movements during the twentieth century—the "May 4th Movement" (*Wusi Yundong* 五四运动) of 1919, which protested consequences of the Versailles Treaty that favored Allied powers, including Japan, at China's expense, and the aforementioned Great Proletarian Cultural Revolution (1966–76)—the third great youth movement has drawn strength from Confucian traditions. This is the subject of Robert L. Moore's chapter, which investigates the relationship between Confucian values and China's "millennial" youth (the post-Mao generation born after 1980, or *baling hou* 八零后). His anthropological fieldwork reveals that most young Chinese today view the values of harmony (*he* 和), filial piety (*xiao* 孝), and respect (*jing* 敬) for tradition and education as paramount and as constituting the culture to which they feel they belong—or, in other words, that most young Chinese today articulate their sense of cultural identity in terms of Confucian values. Julia K. Murray concludes the volume by chronicling the proliferation of images of Kongzi in contemporary China fewer than forty years after such images were ritually desecrated and destroyed by zealous youth during the Great Proletarian Cultural Revolution. Through a broad range of media ranging from monumental public statues to feature films, paintings, and animated cartoons, the image of Kongzi and thus the tradition for which he stands is taking on meanings and performing functions that would have been unimaginable in China at any prior moment in the past century.

In the early twentieth century, the Chinese author Lu Xun 鲁迅 likened the social impact of China's Confucian traditions to cannibalism, arguing that it led to the destruction of the nation's social health and cultural vitality.[11] Many other Chinese intellectuals followed Lu's lead, so much so that China could be described as having adopted a strict anti-Confucian cultural diet for most of the next hundred years. Now it seems that China is reviving its ancestral cultural recipes. At the same time, China is tinkering with old ingredients and cooking methods; this is not "your father's" Confucianism, but rather one adapted to modern tastes and dietary concerns. No one knows precisely what the future holds for Confucian traditions or Chinese society. At the banquet of Chinese culture, however, one may be certain that Confucian dishes will continue to be served, even if they are distributed across a variety of courses. Whatever the future of China may be, it—like China's past—will continue to be intertwined with the fate of Confucianism.

Notes

1. See Sheila Melvin, "Modern Gloss on China's Golden Age," *New York Times*, September 3, 2007, http://www.nytimes.com/2007/09/03/arts/03stud.html, and Chapters 3 (Anthony A. DeBlasi, "Selling Confucius: The Negotiated Return of Tradition in Post-Socialist China"), 4 (Kenneth J. Hammond, "Left Confucianism and the New Left in Early 21st Century China") in this volume.

2. See "Fueled by Filial Piety," *China Daily*, March 10, 2010, http://www.china.org.cn/china/2010-03/10/content_19573827.htm, and Chapter 5 (Jeffrey L. Richey, "Jackie Chan as Confucian Critic: Contemporary Popular Confucianism in China") in this volume.

3. See Chapter 4 (Kenneth J. Hammond, "Left Confucianism and the New Left in Early 21st Century China") in this volume.

4. See "Descendants Attend Memorial Ceremony for Confucius in Qufu," *China Economic Net*, March 31, 2008, http://en.ce.cn/National/pic-news/200803/31/t20080331_15010653_4.shtml, and Chapter 8 (Julia K. Murray, "The Sage's New Clothes: Popular Images of Confucius in Contemporary China") in this volume.

5. See Andrew Jacobs, "Confucius Statue Vanishes near Tiananmen Square," *New York Times*, April 22, 2011, http://www.nytimes.com/2011/04/23/world/asia/23confucius.html.

6. Valuable studies of Confucianism's early development include Robert Eno, *The Confucian Creation of Heaven* (Albany: State University of New York Press, 1990) and Michael Nylan, *The Five "Confucian" Classics* (New Haven: Yale University Press, 2001). David S. Nivison provides a useful account of early Confucianism's wider cultural and intellectual context in "The Classical Philosophical Writings," in *The Cambridge History of Ancient China: From the Origins of Civilization to 221 B.C.*, ed. Michael Loewe and Edward L. Shaughnessy (Cambridge: Cambridge University Press, 1999), 745–812.

7. On Confucianism's transformation during the Hàn and subsequent dynastic periods, see Mark Csikszentmihalyi, "Confucius and the *Analects* in the Hàn," in *Confucius and the Analects: New Essays*, ed. Bryan W. Van Norden (New York: Oxford University Press, 2002), 134–162, and *On Sacred Grounds: Culture, Society, Politics, and the Formation of the Cult of Confucius*, ed. Thomas A. Wilson (Cambridge: Harvard University Asia Center, 2003).

8. On the development of Confucianism in later imperial China, see Carsun Chang, *The Development of Neo-Confucian Thought* (Westport: Greenwood Press, 1957); *The Unfolding of Neo-Confucianism*, ed. Wm. Theodore de Bary (New York: Columbia University Press, 1975); Patricia Buckley Ebrey, *Confucianism and Family Rituals in Imperial China: A Social History of Writing about Rites* (Princeton: Princeton University Press, 1991); Thomas A. Wilson, *Genealogy of the Way: The Construction and Uses of the Confucian Tradition in Late Imperial China* (Stanford: Stanford University Press, 1995); and Rodney L. Taylor, "The Religious Character of the Confucian Tradition," *Philosophy East and West* 48, no. 1 (January 1998): 80–107.

9. For a sense of the diversity and breadth of contemporary Chinese religious revivals, see Ian Johnson, "The Rise of the Tao," *New York Times*, November 5, 2010; Jinghao Zhou, "Religious Practices—Contemporary," in *Berkshire Encyclopedia of China* (Great Barrington, MA: Berkshire Publishing Group, 2009), IV: 1880–1885; and Jiexia Elisa Zhai, "Contrasting Trends of Religious Markets in Contemporary Mainland China and in Taiwan," *Journal of Church and State* 52, no. 1 (2010): 94–111.

10. See Joseph P. L. Jiang, ed., *Confucianism and Modernization: A Symposium* (Taipei: Freedom Council, 1987); Hung-chao Tai, ed., *Confucianism and Economic Development: An Oriental Alternative?* (Washington, DC: The

Washington Institute Press, 1989); Wei-ming Tu et al, eds., *The Confucian World Observed: A Contemporary Discussion of Confucian Humanism in East Asia* (Honolulu: The East-West Center, 1992); Umberto Bresciani, *Reinventing Confucianism/Xiandai xin rujia: The New Confucian Movement* (Taipei: Ricci Institute for Chinese Studies, 2001); Daniel A. Bell, *China's New Confucianism: Politics and Everyday Life in a Changing Society* (Princeton: Princeton University Press, 2008); and John Makeham, *Lost Soul: "Confucianism" in Contemporary Chinese Academic Discourse* (Cambridge, MA: Harvard University Asia Center, 2008).

11. See "A Madman's Diary," trans. Yang Xianyi and Gladys Yang, in *The Columbia Anthology of Modern Chinese Literature*, ed. Joseph S. M. Lau and Howard Goldblatt (New York: Columbia University Press, 1995), 7–15.

PART ONE

Confucianism and Intellectual Life

The Tenacious Persistence of Confucianism in Imperial Japan and Modern China[1]

ROBERT W. FOSTER

In reading the current news regarding China, those familiar with modern East Asian history may be struck by the similarity of the experiences of Japan's rapid development in the Meiji period and of China's since 1978. Comparative history is, at best, suggestive rather than definitive, but by noting similarities and differences within these two places and periods, one sees that Confucianism was one of the key conceptual resources used by various groups in response to change. We might also benefit from such a comparison to anticipate to some degree the evolving trajectory of Chinese leadership in the future and to reveal popular political perceptions and frustrations. Examining one facet of culture in these two countries offers a lens on societies under stress. Times of social-political stress can often be measured and quantified through statistics. Cultural evidence is perhaps more ambiguous, but the symbols that are marshaled to support different responses to stress point to specific concerns and how those concerns shift over time and differ between societies. Many argue that this is the age of globalization and the homogenization of culture. Yet it seems that the threat of homogenization (be it via Western liberalism or mass consumerism) also can revive traditional cultural symbols and infuse them with new meaning.

The problem for both Meiji Japan and post-Mao China was how to catch up with the wealthy and powerful nations of the

world. For the Japanese, the question was whether modernization
entailed Westernization. In other words, did "catching up" mean
exchanging Japanese culture and sociopolitical models for Western
ones? For the Chinese, the issue has been whether modernization
entails globalization. By globalization, I mean the centrality of the
international market and a pragmatic approach to economic growth
that has placed economic growth ahead of social-political ideals. At
the heart of both the Japanese and Chinese experience has been a turn
toward capitalism guided by the state. At the same time, this shift
to a new economic system and worldview has destabilized previous
social structures and cultural codes. Modernization is at all times
painful and disruptive. To accomplish the task, the government and
people need to find some points of common interest. Governments,
to retain their legitimacy, must convince the populace that the new
path is in their best interest, whereas the populace will ponder if the
government is working for their best interest. At moments of social
stress, governments and people use familiar symbols and concepts to
promote what can be opposing positions.[2] As Michael Kimmelman
recently wrote,

> [C]ulture (often unconsciously) identifies crucial ruptures,
> rifts, gaps and shifts in society. It is indispensible for our
> understanding of the mechanics of the world in this respect,
> pointing us toward those things around us that are unstable,
> changing, that shape how we live and how we treat one
> another. If we're alert to it, it helps reveal who we are to
> ourselves, often in ways we didn't realize in places we didn't
> necessarily think to look.[3]

Comparing the variable use of culture helps us understand where
meaningful comparisons can be drawn between Meiji Japan and post-
Mao China but also demonstrates where real differences exist because
of the differing contexts of Japan in the pre–World War I imperialist
system and twenty-first-century China in a post-Soviet world.
       While Confucianism is not the only set of cultural and conceptual
resources at play within Meiji Japan and post-Mao China, its persistent
place in the debates suggests the flexibility of a social-political-ethical
system often deemed to be at odds with rapid change. This view has
been promoted both inside and outside Japan and China. In Japan,
leading Meiji intellectuals such as Fukuzawa Yukichi encouraged
Japanese to say "good-bye Asia" and cast aside traditional culture. In

1885, he noted that "[i]f one observes carefully what is going on in today's world, one knows the futility of trying to prevent the onslaught of Western civilization. Why not float with them in the same ocean of civilization, sail the same waves, and enjoy the fruits and endeavors of civilization."[4] Furthermore, Fukuzawa was particularly critical of Confucians in China and Korea:

> Their love affairs with ancient ways and old customs remain as strong as they were centuries ago. In this new and vibrant theater of civilization when we [Japanese] speak of education they only refer back to Confucianism. As for school education, they can only cite [Mencius's] precepts of humanity, righteousness, decorum and knowledge. While professing their abhorrence to ostentation, in reality they show their ignorance of truth and principles. As for their morality, one only has to observe their unspeakable acts of cruelty and shamelessness. Yet they remain arrogant and show no sign of self-examination.[5]

Chinese dealing with the turmoil of the Republican period did undergo painful self-examination. Lu Xun's classic short story "Diary of a Madman," written in 1918, held that Confucian ideals of virtue and morality led the Chinese to "eat people."[6] However, Lu Xun saw little hope for China's future. This view of Confucianism's conflict with modernity has also been a dominant theme of Western scholarship on China. Max Weber stated that Confucianism was the most antithetical to capitalist development, a view also presented in such classic works as Thomas Metzger's *Escape from Predicament* and Joseph Levenson's *Confucian China and Its Modern Fate*.[7]

However, like any complex worldview, Confucianism can be used in many different ways. There is a set of symbols and ideas that can be marshaled to promote different causes. In Chinese history, there were sometimes deadly disputes, such as the suppression of the Donglin movement in Ming China, in which both sides claimed the validation of Confucian precedent. While an oversimplification, for the purpose of this chapter, I would like to note two distinct uses: one is "ruler's Confucianism"; the other "popular Confucianism." When the goals of government and people converge, the symbols can be used harmoniously to motivate large-scale changes—as has happened at times in Japan and China. When the goals begin to diverge, we see different uses of the symbols to support the interests of the rulers or the people.

Ruler's Confucianism deploys Confucian symbols to promote
social stability, obedience, and faith in authority. I consciously avoid
labeling this "authoritarian Confucianism," because authoritarianism is
loaded with negative connotations, while the ruler's authority is key
to promoting Confucian social harmony. Examples of the resources in
play here include the Confucian ideal of the ruler as "pole star" around
which the various heavenly bodies arrange themselves harmoniously;[8]
and the image of the good ruler's influence as the wind before which
the grass must bend;[9] the notion that everyone has a place in society
and specific duties for that place: "let a ruler be a ruler, a minister a
minister, a father a father, and a son a son."[10] In Meiji Japan, ruler's
Confucianism was at the heart of the "family state" (*kazoku kokka* 家
族国家), with the emperor as father of the nation. In contemporary
China, it has been expressed in Hu Jintao's "harmonious society" (*héxié
shèhuì* 和谐社会). Again, Confucianism is not the *sole* inspiration for
the family state or the harmonious society; the former is also imbued
with Shintō ideas, and the latter is still meant to advance "socialism
with Chinese characteristics." What is important to underscore is the
flexibility of Confucian ideas, which allows them to be incorporated
into projects as different as Japan's Emperor System and China's
socialist development. In times of social stress, people will call on
symbols they believe have persuasive power to promote specific
solutions to the rifts and ruptures of modernization.

In tension with ruler's Confucianism is popular Confucianism,
which likewise stresses social stability but adds in key features such as
benevolent and responsive government, family, and traditions. Popular
Confucianism draws on a different subset of symbols and principles to
promote its goals: government must lead by virtue, rather than by law;[11]
governments need the trust of the people to succeed;[12] righteousness is
more important than profit;[13] Heaven hears as the people hear;[14] and,
if need be, there is the Mencian "right of revolution" against immoral
rulers.[15] Because ruler's Confucianism is at the forefront of political
agendas and state-run media, examples of popular Confucianism are
more diffuse. However, we see elements of popular Confucianism in
the Meiji People's Rights Movement described by Irokawa Daikichi[16]
and in literature such as Sōseki Natsume's *Kokoro*.[17] In Japan,
popular Confucianism was linked to a nativist nostalgia wonderfully
encapsulated in Tanizaki Junichiro's early Shōwa-period work *In Praise
of Shadows*.[18] In post-Mao China, popular Confucianism is evident
both inside the People's Republic of China (PRC) and outside. Wang
Juntao has argued that Confucian ideas influenced pro-democracy

advocates throughout the twentieth century,[19] while more recently a number of titles have been published in China and abroad about Confucianism and globalization.

Both Meiji Japan and post-Mao China were confronted by similar social-political issues: the need to modernize and to adopt capitalism and non-native political ideas while maintaining state control. The goals of the two governments seem to be essentially the same. The Meiji oligarchs called for a "rich country and strong military" (*fukoku kyōhei* 富国強兵), and these goals were strongly paralleled in Deng Xiaoping's "four modernizations" focusing on technological, industrial, agrarian, and military modernization. Both governments desired a strong economy that could support a powerful military, so both liberalized their economies while not liberalizing politics. As a result, for roughly the first twenty years of Meiji Japan and post-Mao China, traditional moral education was rejected in favor of technical education. The goals were to adopt Western mechanisms to compete with the West. Early Meiji extolled "civilization and enlightenment" (*bunmei kaika*). Deng Xiaoping ushered in "reform and openness" (*gǎigé kāifàng*). In both countries, fascination with Western ideas was fashionable.[20] While popular engagement with Western ideas tended to focus on the liberation of the individual from traditional strictures, the governments' engagement was practically minded: learn from the West to resist the West. Both nations wanted to be recognized as equals with the major world powers. This recognition came for Japan with the renegotiation of the unequal treaties in 1894, while many consider the 2008 Beijing Olympics to have been China's "coming out party."

One might argue that the parallel breaks down when comparing Imperial Japan's goal of dominating Asia with the PRC's goal of military security within its own borders. Fukuzawa Yukichi again captured the spirit of his times when he noted, "We are Japanese and we shall some day raise the national power of Japan so that not only shall we control the natives of China and India as the English do today, but we shall possess the power to rebuke the English and to rule Asia ourselves."[21] The goal of China's military development seems to be directed at ending "150 years of humiliation" at the hands of the West. In this formulation of China's recent history, the Chinese people have endured semicolonial status due to the imperialist encroachments of the West and Japan from the Opium War until the handover of Hong Kong in 1997. Now, China would seem to have the strength to resist future territorial indignities. But we must also ask if China's

continued military growth harbors imperial or expansionist goals as
well. Some might argue that the PRC is already trying to maintain an
empire by continuing to hold onto Xinjiang and Tibet while putting
pressure against Taiwanese calls for independence. Furthermore, the
PRC is pressing territorial claims with its new military technology.
In the summer of 2010, a Chinese submarine planted the Chinese
flag in disputed territory on the bottom of the South China Sea.[22]
On the other hand, China's defense spending is still far behind that
of the United States.[23] Even if China is not intent on nineteenth-
century–style imperialism, it is clear that the government is developing
an economic powerhouse. Perhaps in this regard China's post-Mao
"expansionism" can be seen in the economic rather than the military
sphere, in much the same way that Japan's post–World War II leaders
consciously chose economic development as the means of regaining
international power and recognition. As Yoshida Shigeru, the architect
of Japan's initial postwar policies, said, "history provides examples of
winning by diplomacy after losing in war."[24]

However, getting the economic and military markers of success
in Japan and China was not without cost. The rapid industrialization
and development needed to achieve economic power (and military
strength) were socially destabilizing. Cities became the focal point
for economic, political, and cultural development. People were put in
motion, and traditional social structures of village life broke down.
One Meiji writer described "city fever": "Now is the age of cities.
From those who have learning and seek honor to those who want to
make money or to sell their labor—everyone and his brother is setting
out for the cities, as if gripped by a kind of fever."[25] Irokawa Daikichi
argues that the Meiji stress on political centralization and capitalist
economic development destabilized and destroyed local cultures, both
rural and urban. In the countryside, villages were consolidated to make
administration more efficient and so undermined traditional lines of
authority. Young people who caught city fever left their families and
villages, breaking the grip of the traditional extended family, or *ie*
(家). Their movement to the cities in search of opportunities dislodged
traditional urban social and moral structures.[26] As Sōseki's *Kokoro*
so astutely portrayed, movement to the cities is both liberating and
isolating. Though a generation apart, the two focal figures, Sensei and
the narrator, are both migrants from rural areas living in Tokyo. Both
felt an emptiness in their urban lives. As Sensei tells the young narrator
who looks to him for guidance, "loneliness is the price we have to pay

for being born in this modern age, so full of freedom, independence, and our own egotistical selves."[27]

City fever has also gripped rural Chinese. At first, Deng Xiaoping's reforms greatly changed country life, shifting the economic policies from communes to the household responsibility system, which introduced a profit motive for each household and jump-started the rural economy. But as the reforms progressed, emphasis shifted to urban development, and a tremendous rural-urban gap opened.[28] As residency restrictions have loosened, a tremendous migration has taken place from the countryside to the cities. The stories of rural Chinese who have migrated to coastal cities pursuing economic opportunities echo Sōseki's sentiments about modernization and alienation;[29] so, too, do the accounts of Beijing natives coping with the rapid changes within their home city.[30] The prioritizing of economic development has led to moral decline, or the perception of a moral decline, as the profit motive of individual wealth (contributing to national wealth) displaced communitarian values. This initial phase of development drew heavily on Western ideas and models and undoubtedly led to economic success, but at the price of social destabilization. Although economic development was successful—by 1890 in Japan and 2000 in China—there was still the sense that there was more work to do to fully catch up to the West. Fukuzawa Yukichi noted his desire for Japan to gain the strength to "rebuke England" and "rule Asia," while in China, criticism of American "hegemonism" had become widespread. With the goals of "rich nation and strong military" not fully realized, the state continued to promote national unity but turned more toward traditional symbols of Confucianism that discouraged political liberalization. Perhaps the leaders recognized that the West often coupled economic liberalization with political liberalization. The Japanese leaders appealed to the "beautiful customs" of Japan's *kokutai*, or "national polity," and the Chinese Communist Party (CCP) instilled cultural and nationalist pride in China's 5,000 years of history while reminding Chinese of "150 years of humiliation" at the hands of the West.[31]

Meiji Japan's oligarchs worked with the leading capitalists (the *zaibatsu*) to promote Japan's economic development. This fed into rural disaffection. Farmers tried to organize and influence politics, but there was a strong sense that politicians were corrupt and in cahoots with capitalists; both groups were believed to be more concerned with their self-interested goals than with the good of the whole. It was feared that the nation was moving in the wrong direction.

Currently, a major portion of the populace of the PRC is undergoing a similar disenchantment with the link between politicians and capitalists. The government's pragmatic approach is tainted by the clear connections between officials and those most benefiting from the shift to capitalism. Many people recognize that those who have ties to the Party are those who have access to wealth. Corruption cases are constantly in the news, whether embezzlement by government officials, shoddy oversight of building codes in the aftermath of natural disasters, slave labor in Shaanxi coal mines, or nepotism in awarding contracts. As in Meiji Japan, many in today's PRC lament the loss of a clear moral compass. Wang Hui has written that "members of the political elite or their families directly participate in economic activity and have become agents for large corporations and industries. Can we call them representatives of civil society? In China, political and economic elites have been completely conflated, and they participate in international economic activity. The worst scandals in the economic sphere exposed thus far have all involved top-level bureaucrats and their dependents."[32] And this might be, in part, why both the government and some intellectuals have turned to China's traditions for solutions. In 1994, the government's "Guidelines of Implementing Patriotic Education" focused on using "traditional culture" to "strengthen the education of Marxist views of nationalism and religion."[33] Here was a clear attempt to instill the ideals of ruler's Confucianism. However, at the same time, intellectuals engaged in "national learning" (guóxué 国学), a form of popular Confucianism that challenged the corruption, individualism, and egocentrism of China's development-driven consumer culture. National learning sought to find conceptual resources within Chinese tradition for an alternative path of modernization that affirmed traditional moral resources.

This need for a moral compass was not ignored by the ruler's Confucianism of the Meiji oligarchs and is not being overlooked by the CCP. In times of social and moral destabilization, which occur precisely when the government needs national unity to promote its program of development, the state has mobilized traditional as well as nontraditional symbols to motivate the populace. In Japan, this led to the codification of the Confucian-inspired family-state in the 1890 "Imperial Rescript on Education,"[34] which merits quoting in full:

> Our Imperial Ancestors have founded Our Empire on a
> basis broad and everlasting, and have deeply and firmly
> implanted virtue; Our subjects ever united in loyalty and

filial piety have from generation to generation illustrated the beauty thereof. This is the glory of the fundamental character of Our Empire, and herein also lies the source of Our education. Ye, Our subjects, be filial to your parents, affectionate to your brothers and sisters; as husbands and wives be harmonious, as friends true; bear yourselves in modesty and moderation; extend your benevolence to all; pursue learning and cultivate arts, and thereby develop intellectual faculties and perfect moral powers; furthermore, advance public good and promote common interests; always respect the Constitution and observe the laws; should emergency arise, offer yourselves courageously to the State; and thus guard and maintain the prosperity of Our Imperial state; and thus guard and maintain the prosperity of Our Imperial Throne coeval with heaven and earth. So shall ye not only be Our good and faithful subjects, but render illustrious the best traditions of your forefathers.

The way here set forth is indeed the teaching bequeathed by Our Imperial Ancestors, to be observed alike by Their Descendants and the subjects, infallible for all ages and true in all places. It is Our wish to lay it to heart in all reverence, in common with you, Our subjects, that we may all attain to the same virtue.[35]

The Rescript connected these traditional virtues to the "national polity," or *kokutai*, a term redolent with modern nationalist meaning. The ideal of the Rescript, and even for advocates of "civilization and enlightenment" such as Fukuzawa Yukichi, was that education was to promote the well-being of the family-state. Individual growth was instrumental, employed to promote independence from the powers that held unequal treaties with Japan.[36] In many ways, the Rescript was also a response to the internal political agitation for representative government in the 1880s. With the Meiji oligarchs unwilling to relinquish political power, agitation took many forms. Irokawa Daikichi notes that farmers at the beginning of Meiji were not ignorant of Western political ideas. Irokawa even found a number of draft constitutions in village storehouses in rural Japan.[37] Furthermore, local activists promoted the People's Rights movement through organized meetings, debates, and forums in the late 1870s into the 1880s.[38] Against this popular movement, the government issued the "Newspaper and Public Assembly Laws" in 1880, which "forbade

teachers, students, and public officials from belonging to political
associations and attending political meetings."[39] The government
promoted the orderly, harmonious family-state, wherein politicians
dealt with unsavory politics, and harmonious citizens worked to achieve
a "rich nation and strong military." The order of the ruler's vision of the
Confucian state was melded into late nineteenth-century nationalism.
Even when Party politics were allowed and parliamentary government
established in 1890, Carol Gluck argues that parliamentary politics
were portrayed as unsavory and best left to politicians supposedly
working in the best interest of the people. Popular participation was
discouraged, lest the average citizen be tainted by politicking.[40] It
should be no surprise that in Sōseki's *Kokoro*, the conniving uncle who
bilks Sensei out of his inheritance was a businessman and a member
of the prefectural assembly.[41] The parallels to the current Chinese view
of collusion between businessmen and politicians are telling.

In the PRC, there were two related responses to the destabilization
brought about by 1989: increased economic liberalization spurred
on by Deng's "Southern Tour" in 1991, and nationalist education,
rather than continued ideological debate regarding the appropriate
social path. In fact, in the spring of 1992, Deng directed that there
would be no ideological debate for three years to focus efforts on
development.[42] Instead, the government has stepped up nationalist
education in attempts to shore up support for the government after the
Tibetan uprising of 2008, the subsequent international anti-Chinese
protests plaguing the Olympic Torch route, and the constant litany of
corruption charges. As Orville Schell noted in his perceptive piece prior
to the Olympics, nationalist education focuses on the theme of "150
years of humiliation." This humiliation began with the loss of Hong
Kong in the aftermath of the Opium War in 1842, and has extended
into the present. Propaganda or not, the historical memory shaped by
150 years of humiliation has real consequences and cannot be ignored.
Schell argues that the Party has used this theme of Chinese oppressed
by foreign powers as a "goad" to encourage a sense of victimization
that can be turned into motivation to push China's development.[43] This
narrative can lead to fairly violent behavior, as witnessed by the popular
demonstrations attacking the American Embassy in Beijing after the
bombing of the Chinese embassy in Belgrade, Yugoslavia, in May
1999 by North Atlantic Treaty Organization (NATO) coalition forces.

Nationalist education was supposed to be a stabilizing factor.
It may be stabilizing internally, but Liu Kang underlines the
incompatibility of nineteenth-century nationalism—such as inspired

Meiji Japan's ruler's Confucianism—with twenty-first century concerns in the face of globalization driven more by economic than military power.[44] Yet leading into the PRC's sixtieth anniversary, a highly placed official noted that "patriotic education should serve the development and stability of China's reform, and should be included in the process of tackling the global financial crisis, and maintaining the country's steady and relatively fast economic development."[45] Because presently there is no clear corollary to nationalism inspired by anti-Japanese resistance, which Mao adapted to his revolutionary platform, this patriotic education is now linked to a ruler's Confucian idea aimed at inspiring national pride and cooperation: Hu Jintao's "harmonious society." Made public in June 2006, Hu's speech on this concept was clearly connected to the problems deriving from economic growth; however, with continued focus on growth as the primary goal, the social problems are placed in a larger context and treated as necessary growing pains. "Independent thinking of the general public, their newly-developed penchant for independent choices and thus the widening gap of ideas among different social strata will pose further challenges to China's policy makers," Hu said. "Negative and corruptive phenomena and more and more rampant crimes in the society will also jeopardize social stability and harmony."[46] With China's global influence growing through the 1990s and early 2000s, the leadership had to modify its outlook and shift to broader engagement. Yongnian Zheng and Sow Keat Tok argue that the domestic policy of "harmonious society" and its international relations corollary, "harmonious world," are Hu's attempt to have China take "a more proactive role . . . to shape its own destiny, both internally and externally."[47]

The Opening Ceremony of the 2008 Beijing Olympics was certainly symbolic of China's more proactive stance. As the NBC commentators noted, the ceremony was a statement of intent: "China's coming-out party."[48] While Hu connected the harmonious society to "developing socialist democracy," the ceremony's content raised the question of whether Hu's desire to "strengthen ideological and ethical buildup" drew more on Confucianism than on communism.[49] The ceremony opened with 2,008 drummers chanting part of the opening passage from the *Analects*: 有朋自远方来不亦樂乎, which was translated in the stadium projection as "Welcome my friends," rather than the more accurate "Is it not delightful to have friends come from afar?" Other vignettes celebrated China's creative past: dancers painted a landscape with their hands dipped in ink; a dancer in Tang dynasty garb danced on a platform supported on poles carried by dozens of others (here the American commentators noted the symbolism of the individual depending on the support of the multitude); Admiral Zheng He danced with a giant compass aboard his treasure fleet flagship, celebrating an early moment of Chinese maritime exploration in the early fifteenth century; Qing dynasty beauties, inspired by the novel *Dream of the Red Chamber*, danced and played traditional instruments; hundreds of practitioners engaged in a mass tai chi demonstration; and hundreds of "Confucian disciples" read from bamboo scrolls. Yet one of the most striking sequences involved a group of dozens of large cubic blocks creating intricate, flowing images. The blocks mimicked ripples on water, formed the character *hé* 和 for Hu's "harmonious society" and "harmonious world," and deftly re-created the redolently Confucian image of wind blowing over grass. The precise creation of the images and characters was due to those dozens of brilliantly choreographed, human-powered blocks working harmoniously together. Ripples, perhaps political policy, emanated from the center, while the wind was clearly the influence of Party leadership following the line from *Analects* 12.19: "In administering your government, what need is there to kill? Just desire the good yourself and the common people will be good. The virtue of the gentleman is like the wind; the virtue of the small man is like the grass. Let the wind blow over the grass and it is sure to bend."[50] With no reference to Mao, the Opening Ceremony was a classic statement of ruler's Confucianism. The most prominent themes were the need for solidarity and mutual support so all may flourish, the centrality of leadership in ensuring social stability, and the power of Chinese culture to influence the world.[51]

Both the "Imperial Rescript on Education" and the Beijing Opening Ceremony reintroduced an element of cultural pride to ruler's Confucianism. Japanese were to celebrate their nation's "beautiful customs" embodied in the family-state, while Chinese celebrated their 5,000 years of history, underscoring that China was regaining its rightful place among the world's most powerful nations. These successes were portrayed as developing organically from native traditions, rather than deriving from the rejection of tradition and adaptation to Western models.

No doubt in each case there were real gains in national wealth and power. Imperial Japan came to be considered a "Western" power. While previous editions of Henry Wheaton's *Elements of International Law* argued that international law was "limited to the civilized and Christian people in Europe or to those of European origin," the 1904 edition stated that Japan had achieved "full international status."[52] In

August 2010, China surpassed Japan as the world's second-largest national economy. Yet with ruler's Confucianism linking success to traditional culture, Japan and China moved beyond a phase of rapid development as a response to external challenges and into a second phase. The first phase was characterized by openness to new ideas and the denigration of native ideas among rulers and populace. One Meiji writer noted it was the time when "the voices of loyalty and filiality, imperial reverence and patriotism were put away somewhere like bunting after a festival, and like a roast potato vendor at a fire or an ice stand in the dead of winter, no one would have anything to do with them."[53] This seems to parallel the "culture fever" of the initial post-Mao phase in China in the 1980s, when the "New Enlightenment" thinkers championed the ideas of the liberal West as opposed to Marxism as the means to modernization.[54] At first new ideas promoted the same causes the governments desired: rapid modernization and economic development. However, as the social strains of modernization increased and new ideas were applied to critique political leaders, ruler's Confucianism in both Meiji Japan and post-Mao China encouraged nativist pride as a countermeasure. Carol Gluck argues that the "emperor system" ideology of Meiji really did not develop until 1890[55] and that its main goal was to harness the popular political movements of the 1880s through the Constitution and Imperial Rescript on Education.[56] Success in the first phase of development and modernization led to reconsideration of the native ideology, both by the rulers and the populace in the second phase. The rulers sought both to instill national pride to promote solidarity and to create unity of purpose that would bolster rapid development. In Japan, subjects were to follow the political mandates emanating from the Meiji father of the nation. In China, citizens were to harmoniously enact the policies determined by the Party.

This shift from an initial phase that scorned traditional ideas to a second phase that celebrated them fits with the economic and political model suggested by R. P. Peerenboom. In *China Modernizes*, Peerenboom discusses the trajectory of the PRC in relationship to other Asian nations. Although his comparisons are for development after World War II, he offers the following as common stages of development in the East Asian Model: the first "involves the sequencing of economic growth, legal reforms, democratization, and constitutionalism, with different rights being taken seriously at different times in the process"; the second is "a pragmatic approach to reforms, with governments following some aspects of the [Washington

Consensus] and rejecting or modifying others"; in the third, "as the economy grows and wealth is generated, the government invests in human capital and in institutions"; in the fourth, "democratization in the sense of freely contested multiple party elections for the highest level of office is postponed until a relatively high level of wealth is attained"; in the fifth, "constitutionalism begins to emerge during the authoritarian period, including the development of constitutional norms and the strengthening of institutions; social organizations start to proliferate and 'civil society' begins to develop, albeit often a civil society with a different nature and political orientation than in Western liberal democracies"; and finally, in the sixth, greater protection of civil rights occurs after democratization.[57]

While Peerenboom's concerns are clearly political and economic, rather than cultural, governmental focus on political and economic pragmatism in development means the creation of policies that promote the goals of wealth and power over more traditional social values. In his broader comparisons of various indices of nations' development, Peerenboom notes, "the relationship between wealth and human rights performance in Asia and the Middle East is consistently strong except with respect to civil and political rights, suggesting that *there is a culturally based antipathy to liberal values that explains the variance in those regions*."[58] In other words, although the wealthier nations in those regions tend to have better human rights records, their focus is on economic rights rather than political liberalization. Further on, he writes, "Asian states have generally not treated economic and social 'rights' as justiciable. Rather, government policies reflect traditional paternalistic beliefs that rulers are obligated to ensure the material and spiritual well-being of the people. In East Asian countries, this belief derives largely from Confucianism. . . ."[59]

Part of China's promotion of Hu's "harmonious world" via ruler's Confucianism has been a massive program of disseminating Chinese language and culture throughout the world via Confucius Institutes and the Hanban program for placing language teachers in overseas schools. These linked projects are underwritten by the government. China is no longer depending on foreign investment, inviting others to come to China to do business, and adapting to foreign models. Now China is building cultural bridges throughout the world. Former vice chairman of the Standing Committee of the National People's Congress Xu Jialu has been at the forefront of promoting Confucius Institutes, with approximately three hundred now established throughout the world. In an interview, Xu argued that China's contribution to global culture must proceed hand in hand with Chinese people's appreciating their own traditional culture. He said, "Now many countries in the world are [sic] reaching out to China, eager for an introduction of Chinese culture. What we offered was nothing more than Peking opera, stilts, paper-cutting, clay figures, etc. They are different forms of culture, but they are neither the entire culture nor the essence or core of Chinese culture. We cannot contribute Chinese culture to the world until more and more Chinese people develop a cultural consciousness."[60] Confucius Institutes and Hanban programs seem to fit well with the internal educational directive of 1994 to focus on traditional culture.

In what I see as the second phase of development in Imperial Japan and post-Mao China, however, using Confucian symbols to enhance the ruler's authority also validated using Confucian symbols to support the counterclaims of the populace. The rapid development in Meiji Japan disrupted the popular morality that Irokawa Daikichi found centered in the family and the rural village. Clearly anticapitalist, Irokawa made the case that the social changes brought about by Meiji's capitalist advances put an end to village-centered morality, but these efforts also gave rise to the People's Rights Movement. For example, Chiba Takasaburō drafted his *Way of the King* (Ōdō 王道), which drew heavily on the Chinese classics the *Book of Poetry* and the *Book of Documents* to promote checks and balances between ruler and populace. Chiba went so far as to invoke the "right of revolution" should a sovereign fail in his responsibilities to his people.[61] Likewise, Okakura Kakuzo attempted to reclaim the humane arts of Japan—as opposed to the officially promoted samurai spirit—as part of its national character. In his *Book of Tea*, written for a Western audience in 1906, he bemoaned that the West only came to regard Japan as civilized "since she began to commit wholesale slaughter on Manchurian battlefields."[62] Okakura noted that his Teaism "inculcates purity and harmony, the mystery of mutual charity, the romanticism of the social order."[63] While this is undoubtedly a romanticized view of traditional culture, it is striking that Okakura was critiquing precisely what the Meiji leaders strove for: a rich nation and powerful military. Perhaps most famously of all, Sōseki's *Kokoro* described the isolation of individuals who moved to Tokyo and whose antitraditional dispositions led to loneliness and inhumane actions. Sōseki, while not a popular Confucian, recognized that turning away from the social ideals of Confucianism had a high social cost.

Perhaps as a response to similar social upheaval due to the CCP's economic drive, there has been revived popular interest in Confucianism in the PRC. When one combines the government's

stress on cultural pride with the popular perception that corruption
is one of the largest issues confronting Chinese society, it is not
surprising that Confucianism is seen as a valid curative. In 2006–7,
Yu Dan's Reflections on The Analects sold 4.2 million legal copies and
another 6 million pirated copies, according to the *New York Times*.[64]
Professor Yu noted that part of the work's success was due to the
unsettled nature of the times. Some have dismissed Yu Dan's *Reflections*
as too populist, but more scholarly works dealing with the theme of
Confucianism and globalization have appeared in recent years. Many
of these authors note that globalization means the homogenization
of cultures as mass communication and markets predominate. The
PRC's post-Mao drive to join the global economy has not meant
that the PRC's culture has become Westernized any more than Meiji
Japan's did. Avoiding Westernization seems to be the point of resisting
"peaceful evolution" promoted by the United States. But there is a
moral void in the PRC's developmental pragmatism. Some, such as
Wang Hui, have been advocating a reinvigoration of "traditional"
socialist ideas; others, such as the signatories of "Charter 08," have
promoted further liberal reforms in politics for greater popular voice
in government.[65] Confucianism seems to be one of many sets of
conceptual resources being used in the debates about China's social
problems. Some argue that Confucianism was dealt a fatal blow by the
May Fourth Movement, but Wang Juntao—a 1989 activist—argues
that the Confucianism attacked in the May Fourth Movement was
Confucianism supporting the imperial system[66]—what I am calling
ruler's Confucianism. Examining Sun Yatsen, the man revered both in
the PRC and Taiwan as the father of Modern China, Wang writes:

> In 1924, he told Japanese journalists: "Our *three-min*
> principles [nationalism, citizens' rights, welfare of human
> beings] originate from Mencius and are based on [Song
> Neo-Confucian thinker] Cheng Yichuan. . . . Mencius is
> really the ancestor of our democratic ideas. . . . The *three-
> min* principles are a completion of the development of
> those three thousand years of Chinese ideas about how to
> govern and maintain a peaceful world." According to Sun,
> Confucianism also plays the crucial role of building up an
> identity for Chinese citizens in a democratic republic. As
> the main tradition in Chinese history, Confucianism can
> help to provide a common identity that binds citizens in
> a democratic republic.[67]

Sun's concern was identity and unity. In some ways, he stands between ruler's and popular Confucianism because, on the one hand, he was attempting to organize and encourage modernization as a leader using Confucian symbols; on the other hand, he believed that Confucianism was not incompatible with democratization.

Certainly in Meiji Japan, popular Confucianism did not carry the day. There was no return to village morality, nor did a Confucian-liberal amalgam develop. Ruler's Confucianism triumphed in the form of the family-state and emperor-centered ideology (*tennōsei*) that called on imperial subjects to fulfill the values outlined in the "Rescript on Education" to the point of literally sacrificing themselves for the good of the family-state. Ruler's Confucianism was better suited to a top-down society engaged in empire building during a period highly influenced by Social Darwinism. Otto Bismarck urged the Iwakura Mission to hastily develop a sense of popular nationalism to ensure unity and support for the government as it engaged in the modernization process. In Bismarck's view, "although people say that so-called international law safeguards the rights of all countries, the fact is that when large countries pursue their advantage they talk about international law when it suits them, and they use force when it does not."[68] It was assumed that Great Powers would carve up the "uncivilized" portions of the world and rule for their benefit. Therefore, it was imperative that nationalist education produce patriotic people capable of promoting Japan's modernization. Once modernized at home, Japan could then engage in its own empire building, as it did through victories in both the Sino-Japanese War (1894–5) and the Russo-Japanese War (1904–5). These victories gave Japan's imperial government control of Taiwan, dominance in Korea, and greater access to markets in China. Fukuzawa Yukichi's demeaning view of "backward" Chinese and Koreans fits well with Rudyard Kipling's vision of "White Man's Burden": civilization would be brought to benighted corners of the world, benefiting both the civilizer and the civilized, even if the latter did not always appreciate the process.

The twenty-first-century situation for the PRC is different. While there are strong similarities in the development, symbols, and goals of ruler's and popular Confucianism in both Meiji Japan and post-Mao China, China's situation is more complex because of globalization and the development of Chinese areas outside the PRC's authority. Whereas Meiji Japan's leaders and people lived in a world characterized by competing imperial powers and without a politically independent Japanese diaspora, post-Mao China is confronted by globalized markets, consumer culture, and the dominance of liberal political and economic ideals in areas that were formerly Communist and others that are culturally Chinese. After the collapse of the Soviet Union, the former Soviet Republics and Mongolia took the advice of liberal economists and underwent "shock therapy" to open markets, democratize, and—it was hoped—enjoy the same benefits of wealth and stability as the West. It is hard not to see parallels in their actions to Fukuzawa's earlier call for Japanese to "float . . . in the same ocean of civilization" and "enjoy [its] fruits and endeavors." Unfortunately, shock therapy has caused tremendous social, political, and economic hardship in many places.[69] In 2000, responding to the downward spiral of liberalization in Mongolia, George Soros said that "the new market fundamentalism is more dangerous to the world now than Communism."[70]

On the other hand, the pragmatic orientation of China's leadership has engineered remarkable economic development in the post-Mao period. Randy Peerenboom reconsidered the success of an "East Asian Model" for modernization and found that China's policies for promoting growth fit well with the elements that have led to the success of Japan and the "Little Dragons" since 1945. While the president of the World Bank questioned the stress on pure market forces for Mongolia's economy and for making social welfare second,[71] this, according to Peerenboom, was not the case in the PRC because of the influence of Confucian political culture.

Confucian political culture is alive and well in diaspora communities outside China. Ezra Vogel, much more so than Peerenboom, credited Confucian culture as a factor in the rise of other East Asian societies. "These four institutions and cultural practices rooted in the Confucian tradition but adapted to the needs of an industrial society—a meritocratic elite, an entrance exam system, the importance of the group, and the goal of self-improvement—have helped East Asia make the use of their special situational advantages and new worldwide opportunities."[72] What Vogel points to may be "cultural habits" that can be traced back to Confucian roots but are not strongly Confucian today. However, the issue of combining modernization and Confucianism directly and meaningfully gave rise to the "Third Generation" or "Third Epoch" of Confucian scholars in the 1950s.

This group, led by Mou Zongsan, Tang Junyi, and Xu Fuguan, drew on Confucianism's conceptual resources to promote a democratically minded, modern popular Confucianism. Obviously, the ideas were critical of authoritarian government, such as Mao's PRC, but the Third Generation scholars also sought to use Confucian principles to address some of the problems of development and modernization noted above in both Meiji Japan and the post-Mao PRC: alienation, egotism, and social breakdown. For the Third Generation, Confucianism was to be a contributor to global culture, not something merely for East Asians or only Chinese to use to bolster identity.[73] Yiu-ming Fung describes their project as "how to disclose the spiritual source that had been swept away by the antitraditionalists and how to reconstruct Chinese culture such that it might be used to overcome the crisis of meaning and the crisis of culture in facing the challenge of the West."[74] While Fung states that the project is not "theoretically warranted" on philosophical grounds, he recognizes that it "may be practically significant" as a means of grounding modernization in Chinese culture.[75]

If Fung recognizes a social utilitarian value for Confucianism in the modernization process, Tu Weiming's popular Confucianism continues to underscore the social-religious project formulated by Mou Zongsan and others. Tu believes that Confucian values can be universalizable in ways similar to Western Enlightenment values. Moreover, Confucian values can help ameliorate problems generated by the Enlightenment mentality because "the willingness to tolerate inequality, faith in the salvific power of self-interest, and the unbridled affirmation of aggressive egoism have greatly poisoned the good well of progress, reason, and individualism."[76] Alongside Western values of "instrumental rationality, liberty, rights-consciousness, due process of law, privacy, and individualism," Tu places the Confucian values of "sympathy, distributive justice, duty-consciousness, ritual, public-spiritedness, and group orientation."[77] Yet Tu goes even further and argues that "those who are attuned to the Confucian message inevitably discover that Confucian personality ideals (the authentic person, the worthy, or the sage) can be realized more fully in a liberal democratic society than in either a traditional imperial dictatorship or a modern authoritarian regime."[78] To this end, in an earlier piece written shortly after the Tiananmen incident, Tu argues that the dynamic changes in Chinese culture were and would continue to take place outside the PRC. In the post-1949 world, the "periphery of the Sinic world [Taiwan, Hong Kong, and Singapore] was proudly marching to an Asia-Pacific century, [but] the homeland remained mired in perpetual underdevelopment."[79] Tu therefore fused a modernization of Confucianism with the modernized Chinese forces in areas outside of the PRC: "undeniably, the fruitful interaction among a variety of economic, political, social, and cultural forces at work along the periphery will activate the dynamics of cultural China."[80]

Tu Weiming's take on modernization and Confucianism was met ambivalently at best in the PRC. There are clear political implications in Third Epoch Confucianism that are tied to liberal democracy and capitalism. As such, this use of the tradition openly conflicts with the political and social programs of ruler's Confucianism in the PRC, but it also conflicts with the popular Confucianism of the PRC, which has not rejected the "150 years of humiliation" thesis. True, Tu's peripheral China in 1991 was juxtaposed with the PRC before its spectacular economic takeoff following Deng's "Southern Tour." But it is difficult to see how a style of popular Confucianism melded with liberal democratic ideas can support the ruler's Confucianism encapsulated in the "harmonious society" and "socialist democracy" advocated by Hu Jintao. Instead, the Confucian tradition has spawned two very different subsets of symbols. Tu's is perhaps popular Confucianism in its most developed form, while Hu's "harmonious society" clearly seeks to use Confucian symbols to support the rule of the Party. Within the PRC, there is also the issue of whether Chinese interested in Confucianism are also interested in Tu's liberal democratic version. As nationalist education has been ramped up in the PRC, there is an increasing desire to rely on ideas generated from within the PRC. Liu Kang argues that one cannot overlook the powerful rhetoric of revolutionary change that dominated discourse in the PRC during the Maoist period. Revolutionary change from the past is too deeply rooted. The CCP is still supposed to be a revolutionary party.

> Moreover, the current leadership by no means surrenders itself entirely to the capitalist world-system, as shown by the persistence of the slogan, however vacuous and self-contradictory in its content, of "socialism with Chinese characteristics." All this generates profound uneasiness with the Confucian-oriented "official nationalism" both within the Communist Party leadership and in the public sphere. In intellectual circles a topic in vogue in the early 1990s was the so called *guo xue* (national learning), which consciously posed a distance from "official nationalism" as well as from global new Confucianism.[81]

National learning was another response to the issues deriving from pragmatic development policies and the social problems generated thereby. Intellectuals in the PRC decried the loss of humanistic values with the growth of popular consumer culture. As Liu Kang writes, "nothing seems to be capable of supplanting a pleasure-oriented, ego-centered consumer cultural fashion shaped by the global informa-tion circuit and the entertainment industry, which has become a central component of capitalist globalization."[82] In contrast, "the neohumanists speak a universalist language calling for the reawakening of 'humanist spirits' in the face of commodity fetishism, which reifies traditional culture and 'national learning' among other things."[83]

Whether one looks at Tu Weiming's Confucian-liberal synthesis, culturally patriotic but apolitical "national learning," or anticonsumer neohumanism, it is clear that today there are numerous communities around the world interested in Confucian studies and China's development, and there are the means of immediately connecting and communicating. Popular Confucianism has been used to critique social ills from within the PRC, but one must also consider the external critics of the PRC, who are advocating for Confucian-influenced human rights and democracy. In this way, the tension between ruler's Confucianism and popular Confucianism in the contemporary world is more complex than it was for those arguing both sides in Imperial Japan. There was no Japanese diaspora equivalent of Taiwan or Hong Kong to challenge the authority of the Imperial government. Similarly, the international rules of engagement have changed in the postcolonial world. Imperial colonies are no longer easily justified as areas to be civilized by conquerors, and market liberalization dominates. Still, however, Confucianism provides a humanizing voice in the face of dehumanizing economic self-interest. Now Confucianism in both the ruler's and the popular forms is part of globalized discourse on the role of government, the rights and responsibilities of individuals, and the relationship of individual, community, and state.

It is clear that there is no immutable "Confucianism." The tradition, like all great traditions, provides conceptual resources that have adapted to widespread change throughout 2,500 years of Chinese history and 1,500 years of Japanese history. Early Confucianism was characterized by a plurality of schools; it fused with Taoism and Legalism in the Han dynasty; later imperial China saw violent debates of heterodoxy and orthodoxy; shogunal Japan adopted antimilitarist Confucianism to the samurai code of *bushidō*; the Meiji government fused it with Western Enlightenment thought and Shintō to create the emperor-system embodied in the family-state and *kokutai*; Third Wave and New Confucians outside China have argued for its modern relevance; while Hu Jintao seems to be co-opting Confucian symbols for his "harmonious society." In times of social crisis, when national unity was sought by the rulers to promote change and social stability is sought by the populace, it is not surprising that Confucianism still provides persuasive conceptual resources. It will be interesting to see how Confucianism is marshaled, and to what end, both locally and globally in these broader flows of cultural exchange. Perhaps it is telling that Irokawa Daikichi justified his attempt to recapture popular traditions in the Meiji period by writing

> it seems necessary to work out a way of examining the basic, original thinking of the day when emperor thought was still only one of several possibilities if we are to repudiate it from within. Once we have done that, we will be able to overturn that original structure and work toward a genuine spiritual and mental revolution. If we do not use this method, and instead try to reform Japanese consciousness at the popular level with nothing more than the modern individualism that came out of Western civil society, we will end up in the despair and self-righteousness of empty modernism; bitter experience has shown this to us time and again.[84]

It will be interesting to see if there will be a similar reflection on popular consciousness for the PRC and how the tension between ruler's and popular Confucianism, both within and without the PRC, plays out.

Notes

1. I would like to thank Rebecca Bates, who has spent many hours discussing these ideas with me and helped me refine my thinking about the issues presented here, and Roger Ames, who commented on the draft of the paper that is the basis of this chapter, which was presented at the annual meeting of the Association of Asian Studies in 2010.

2. An American analogue would be the divergent use of the terms "freedom," "liberty," "democracy," and "patriotism" in the aftermath of the 9/11 attacks and the subsequent wars in Afghanistan and Iraq.

3. Michael Kimmelman, "Abroad: D.I.Y. Culture," *New York Times*, April 18, 2010.

4. Fukuzawa Yukichi, "Good-bye Asia (Datsu-A)," in David John Lu, *Japan: A Documentary History*, 2 vols. (Armonk, NY: M.E. Sharpe, 1997), II: 351.

5. Ibid., 352.

6. Lu Hsun, *Selected Stories of Lu Hsun*, 1st ed. (New York: Norton, 1977), 10.

7. Thomas A. Metzger, *Escape from Predicament* (New York: Columbia University Press, 1977); Joseph R. Levenson, *Confucian China and Its Modern Fate: A Trilogy* (Berkeley: University of California Press, 1972).

8. *Analects* 2.1.

9. *Analects* 12.19.

10. *Analects* 12.11.

11. *Analects* 2.3.

12. *Analects* 12.7.

13. *Analects* 4.16.

14. *Mencius* 5A5.

15. *Mencius* 1B8.

16. See Daikichi Irokawa, *The Culture of the Meiji Period*, trans. Marius B. Jansen (Princeton: Princeton University Press, 1985).

17. Natsume Soseki, *Kokoro*, trans. Edwin McClellan (Chicago: Regnery Gateway, 1957).

18. Jun'ichirō Tanizaki, *In Praise of Shadows*, ed. Thomas J. Harper and Edward G. Seidenstricker, trans. Edward G. Seidenstricker (Stony Creek, CT: Leete's Island Books, 1977).

19. Wang Juntao, "Confucian Democrats in Chinese History," in *Confucianism for the Modern World*, ed. Daniel Bell and Chae-bong Ham (Cambridge: Cambridge University Press, 2003).

20. See the writings of Fukuzawa Yukichi and Wang Hui, *The End of the Revolution: China and the Limits of Modernity* (London: Verso, 2009), 105.

21. Fukuzawa Yukichi, "Tōyō no seiryaku hatashite ikan," quoted in Kenneth B. Pyle, *Japan Rising: The Resurgence of Japanese Power and Purpose*, 1st ed., A Century Foundation Book (New York: Public Affairs, 2007), 105.

22. Reuters, "China: A Stealth Move to Make an Underwater Claim," *New York Times*, August 27, 2010.

23. According to Piers Brendon, China's share of global arms purchasing is 6.6 percent versus 46.5 percent for the United States. Piers Brendon, "For China, Will Money Bring Power?," *New York Times*, August 22, 2010.

24. Quoted in Pyle, *Japan Rising: The Resurgence of Japanese Power and Purpose*, 227.

25. Quoted in Carol Gluck, *Japan's Modern Myths: Ideology in the Late Meiji Period* (Princeton: Princeton University Press, 1985), 159.

26. Irokawa, *The Culture of the Meiji Period*, 28–35.

27. Sōseki, *Kokoro*, 30.

28. Wang Hui and Theodore Huters, *China's New Order: Society, Politics, and Economy in Transition* (Cambridge: Harvard University Press, 2003), 48, and particularly 198, n. 4.

29. See Peter Hessler's accounts of former students of his who moved from Sichuan to the coastal boom towns of Shenzhen and Wenzhou in Peter Hessler,

Oracle Bones: A Journey through Time in China, 1st Harper Perennial ed. (New York: HarperCollins, 2007).

30. See Michael J. Meyer, *The Last Days of Old Beijing: Life in the Vanishing Backstreets of a City Transformed*, 1st US ed. (New York: Walker & Company, 2008).

31. Orville Schell, "China: Humiliation & the Olympics," *New York Review of Books* 55, no. 13 (2008).

32. Wang and Huters, *China's New Order: Society, Politics, and Economy in Transition*, 177.

33. Liu Kang, *Globalization and Cultural Trends in China* (University of Hawai'i Press, 2004), 32.

34. Gluck argues that Meiji ideology, in the form of *tennōsei*, did not begin until 1890. Gluck, *Japan's Modern Myths: Ideology in the Late Meiji Period*, 17, 21.

35. "The Imperial Rescript on Education" [Official Document]," in Children and Youth in History, Item #136, accessed March 20, 2010, http://chnm.gmu.edu/cyh/primary-sources/136. Annotated by Brian Platt.

36. Patrick Smith, *Japan: A Reinterpretation*, 1st ed. (New York: Pantheon Books, 1997).

37. Irokawa, *The Culture of the Meiji Period*, 44.

38. Ibid., 95ff.

39. Ibid., 98, n. 28.

40. Gluck, *Japan's Modern Myths: Ideology in the Late Meiji Period*, 244–246.

41. Sōseki, *Kokoro*, 132.

42. Liu, *Globalization and Cultural Trends in China*, 31.

43. Schell, "China: Humiliation & the Olympics."

44. Liu, *Globalization and Cultural Trends in China*, 13–14.

45. Liu Yunshan, head of the Publicity Department of the Communist Party of China (CPC) Central Committee. Xinhua, "More Patriotic Education Urged Ahead of National Day," *China Daily*, August 17, 2009.

46. Liu Yunshan, "Building Harmonious Society Crucial for China's Progress: Hu," *People's Daily Online*, June 27, 2006.

47. Yongnian Zheng and Sow Keat Tok, " 'Harmonious Society' and 'Harmonious World': China's Policy Discourse under Hu Jintao," *China Policy Institute Briefing Series*, no. 26 (2007).

48. Dick Ebersol, *Complete Opening Ceremony: The Games of the Xxix Olympiad, Beijing, 2008* ([United States]: Ten Mayflower Productions, 2008), Visual Material.

49. The only possible parallel in the current Communist world would be nationalist "mass games" as practiced in North Korea. For a visual sample of North Korean mass games, see Daniel Gordon and Charles K. Armstrong, *A State of Mind* (Princeton: Films for the Humanities & Sciences, 2006), Visual Material.

50. Confucius, *The Analects*, trans. D. C. Lau (New York: Penguin Books, Ltd., 1979), 115–116.

51. For the images of the Opening Ceremony, see Ebersol, *Complete Opening Ceremony: The Games of the Xxix Olympiad, Beijing, 2008.*

52. Quoted in Pyle, *Japan Rising: The Resurgence of Japanese Power and Purpose*, 115.

53. Quoted in Gluck, *Japan's Modern Myths: Ideology in the Late Meiji Period*, 106.

54. Wang and Huters, *China's New Order: Society, Politics, and Economy in Transition*, 155ff.

55. Gluck, *Japan's Modern Myths: Ideology in the Late Meiji Period*, 17.

56. Ibid., 23.

57. R. P. Peerenboom, *China Modernizes: Threat to the West or Model for the Rest?* (New York: Oxford University Press, 2007), 31–32.

58. Ibid., 60. Emphasis added.

59. Ibid., 69.

60. Anonymous, "Mission to Accomplish: Xu Jialu's Academic Pursuit(Pic)," *Confucius Institute* 2 (2009), http://www.chinese.cn/college/en/article/2009-09/07/content_69613.htm.

61. Irokawa, *The Culture of the Meiji Period*, 116–117.

62. Kakuzo Okakura, *The Book of Tea* (Champaign, IL: NetLibrary, 1906).

63. Op. cit.

64. Sheila Melvin, "Modern Gloss on China's Golden Age," *New York Times*, September 3, 2007.

65. Perry Link, "China's Charter 08," *New York Review of Books* 56, no. 1 (2009).

66. Wang, "Confucian Democrats in Chinese History," 88.

67. Ibid., 78.

68. Pyle, *Japan Rising: The Resurgence of Japanese Power and Purpose*, 84.

69. For a sober discussion of the effects of policies promoted by the World Bank, International Monetary Fund, and Asian Development Bank, see Morris Rossabi, *Modern Mongolia: From Khans to Commissars to Capitalists* (Berkeley: University of California Press, 2005).

70. Ibid., 89.

71. Ibid., 92.

72. Ezra Vogel, *The Four Little Dragons: The Spread of Industrialization in East Asia* (Cambridge: Harvard University Press, 1991), 101.

73. Wang, "Confucian Democrats in Chinese History," 85.

74. Yiu-ming Fung, "Problematizing Contemporary Confucianism in East Asia," in *Teaching Confucianism*, ed. Jeffrey L. Richey, AAR Teaching Religious Studies Series (New York: Oxford University Press, 2008), 166.

75. Ibid., 168.

76. Tu Weiming, *A Confucian Perspective on Human Rights*, Wu Teh Yao Memorial Lectures (Singapore: UniPress, 1996), 11.

77. Tu Weiming, "Implications of the Rise of 'Confucian' East Asia," *Daedalus* 129, no. 1 (2000): 207.

78. Ibid., 212.

79. Tu Weiming, "Cultural China: The Periphery as Center," *Daedalus* 120, no. 2 (1991): 12.

80. Ibid., 28.
81. Liu, *Globalization and Cultural Trends in China*, 33.
82. Ibid., 13.
83. Ibid., 40–41.
84. Irokawa, *The Culture of the Meiji Period*, 14.

2

Scientism and Modern Confucianism

JENNIFER OLDSTONE-MOORE

"During the last thirty years or so there is a name which has acquired an incomparable position of respect in China; no one, whether informed or ignorant, conservative or progressive, dares openly slight or jeer at it. The name is Science."

—Hu Shi[1]

"I should define science simply as the understanding of the correct explanation or principle for anything at all."

—W. W. Howells[2]

"The true power of the West lies not in its political and technological might, but in its power to define."

—Ziauddin Sardar[3]

Introduction

To understand Confucianism in modern China, it is necessary to understand the influence of science on the global imagination in the past century and a half. One must also consider the even more powerful influence of scientism, a network of social and moral concepts validated by the authority of science. Where science may be defined as descriptive, in search of abstracted universal laws derived from a specific method of inquiry, scientism, by contrast, is "the tendency to use the respectability of science in areas having little bearing on science itself . . . that view which places all reality within a natural order and deems all aspects of this order, be they biological, social, physical, or psychological, to be knowable only by the methods of science."[4] Thus Darwin's observations on natural selection were scientific; the application of natural selection to states and civilizations in Social Darwinism is scientistic.

New biological theories that emerged in nineteenth-century Europe played a central role in the development of scientism in both Europe and China. Darwin's *On the Origin of Species* appeared in 1859; after 1865, the germ theory of disease began to gain currency among professionals and then the public. These paradigm-shifting ideas, which promised to enhance significantly the knowledge of nature and human relations, coincided with the acceleration of Chinese modernization and the intensifying critique of Confucianism both inside and outside China. As science became the sine qua non of modernity, scientific principles and scientistic precepts permeated Chinese intellectual life and official policy. Both science and scientism became powerful tools of social policy in the nineteenth and early twentieth centuries as germ theory was widely accepted and related theories of hygiene led Europeans and Americans to establish standards of public health. These quickly became integral to seemingly universal ideas of civilization and modernity. The primacy of science as a measure of modernity continues to be a mark that is considered universal rather than cultural.[5] Consequently, this "universal" mode of measurement has become the benchmark that has condemned or valorized Chinese culture in general and Confucianism in particular.

David Wright has written that the "transmission of Western science into China is one [of] the great transcultural movements of the last two hundred years, and it is still in process today."[6] Modernization, the creation of citizens, and the formation of nations have all included the appropriation of science as a necessary component. Originally identified by Chinese thinkers as "western," science has, over the course of the twentieth century, come to be perceived as a universal truth. It became a presumed rather than debated framework as the Chinese struggled to rethink their culture and identity. Both science and Confucianism have proved to be powerful and malleable in creating twentieth-century national and cultural identities. Using a comparison of both through time, this chapter shows that major governmental initiatives concerning the value and implementation of Confucianism in the twentieth and twenty-first centuries have used the universalist assumptions of science and scientism as a means to both support and demonize Confucianism. This process is visible throughout the last century, from the New Culture Movement through Republican and Maoist China to the present-day People's Republic of China.

Definitions and Structure

It is regularly noted that modern renderings of "Confucianism" have no fixed referent; that Confucianism is widely malleable to fit a wide range of motives, interpretations, and needs.[7] In this chapter, "Confucianism" refers to the tradition as constructed at various moments by reformers, politicians, and government leaders, usually in service to a project or movement they direct. It is routinely stated that the Confucianism adopted by modern governments is a crafted "political Confucianism"; the chapter considers these various constructions of Confucianism as they are given. This construction may not be not a tradition so much as a "tradition," as per Hobsbawm and Ranger's idea of invented traditions.[8] The repeated assessment and reevaluation of Confucianism was contingent on political, cultural, and psychological contexts that reflect a mind-set or psychology in which "the West" functions as more than a geopolitical reality. Scholars on the effects of colonialism have described the means by which the measure of all things is an adopted, absorbed, and eventually unexamined set of paradigms that emerged originally from Europe and North America. In addition to the "West" (*xifang* 西方) to which the Chinese themselves refer, it is this mind-set or psychology that will be denoted as the "West." This idea of "the West" includes ideas of secularism; "development" that assumes social change; "modernity" that presumes "human progress and liberation"; a notion of history that is linear; a presumption of the superiority of science both conceptually and as a mechanism of progress; and rationality that refers to an "allegedly non-partisan, contemporary embodiment of the post-Enlightenment theories of progress."[9]

The malleability of Confucianism has certainly been evident in the last 150 years as Confucianism has been vilified, lauded, and reformulated for nationalistic endeavors. For many, the increasingly visible reappropriation of Confucianism by the People's Republic of China (PRC) government in the last thirty years has been a startling turnaround. After decades of being considered the greatest enemy to the Chinese people by the Communist government, Confucianism is now embraced as an integral part of means by which a harmonious socialist society will be created. The range of positions of cultural leaders in the Republic was no less startling, from the cries of "Destroy the old curiosity shop of Confucius" in the New Culture and May Fourth Movements to Confucianism as the means to *jiu guo* 救國, or save the nation, during the 1930s and 1940s.

The assessments and appropriations of Confucianism in the Republican and Communist eras, while distinctive, have a strikingly similar pattern. At the outset, the cultural and political leaders and reformers, having adopted the scientistic analysis of civilization, designate Confucianism unworthy of a modern nation, an impediment to the progress promised by science, a throwback to an unenlightened time. Later, in the process of creating a Chinese national identity, there is a perceived need to reintegrate cultural forms, which is accomplished by integrating Confucianism into the scientistic framework. Finally, having successfully adapted Confucianism to the new framework, there is new confidence both in their own cultural specificity and in the authentic, progressive, and modern nature of Chinese culture, which can extend Chinese influence in the world, even to the point of making universalistic claims about the potential impact of Confucianism. Naturally, there are multiple voices and opinions at any of these times, and I have been selective, looking for the seemingly formative or dominant voices of key periods. This framework is only the roughest of heuristic devices for this narrative; it shows the malleability of both Confucianism and the equal flexibility of scientism as tools of assessment throughout the twentieth and into the twenty-first century.

Question of Civilization: Science and Imperialism

Although Europeans were engaged in the practice and discussion of science from at least the sixteenth century, it was really the nineteenth century that was "the true age of science."[10] One of the most powerful developments of science—powerful both in terms of the quality of the observation, but also for the impact on public and private lives, domestic and colonial—was framing microbial theory and the connected need for antisepsis. At the same time that imperialist presence and pressure were increasing in China, European scientists made key observations that affected not only human health but also notions of civilization. It was as recently as 1854 that John Snow demonstrated through an epidemiological study that cholera was in fact waterborne, not carried by miasma. In the 1860s, the work of Pasteur and Lister demonstrated the connection between microbes and disease. These observations not only profoundly changed medical care, but also instituted a drive for sweeping public works and governmental oversight and intervention to ensure the health of citizens and the state both at home and, eventually, abroad.[11]

These observations, made at a high point of imperialist penetration of Asia, had a tremendous impact on relations between the West and China, for they were responsible for a profound shift in Europe and North America in what constituted "civilization." One of the most notable aspects of the shift was a growing focus on personal hygiene and health and a parallel emphasis on the state's role to promote and enforce public health measures, including the right to control individuals and their bodies through practices such as inoculation. States also became responsible for providing hygienic infrastructure through initiatives such as purified municipal water systems. The emphasis today on cleanliness and hygiene that is taken for granted, evident in mundane habits of showering, cleaning, deodorizing, and antibacterial efforts, are habits into which we have been trained, and continue to be trained, by government agencies. It is a body culture dominated by public authorities. This new tool for controlling the bodies and habits of individuals and of changing the structures of cities and states, all by using health as the rationale, was a powerful tool first used by Europeans to criticize and reform Asians, then used by Asians to criticize themselves.

The use of science to create healthy bodies was extended beyond public health and hygiene into physical culture, sports culture, and the development of the military to create a healthy nation. This focus on the body was evident in the combined missionary imperialist adventure in the application of muscular Christianity. A movement to combine a body-oriented physical culture with spreading the gospel, muscular Christianity included bodybuilding and strengthening as a part of its practice. Europeans considered their robust health and muscular bodies to be evidence of a biological and national superiority related to the validity of their imperialist ambitions; in 1901, J. G. Cotton Minchin wrote: "If asked what our muscular Christianity has done, we point to the British Empire. Physical vigour is as necessary for the maintenance of the empire as mental vigour."[12] China, by virtue of both the weakness of the state and the slender physique of the scholar, was identified as the "sick man of Asia" on the microcosmic and macrocosmic levels, and missionaries and reformers tried to ameliorate this by encouraging a vigorous physical culture.[13]

Even at this early stage, Confucianism was identified as an important cause of individual and collective Chinese weakness. The reasons for puny and frail bodies of individual Chinese were identified to be due in part to the preference for effete, weak scholars because of the influence of Confucianism. Moreover, the individual bodies contributed to an overarching societal weakness; Social Darwinist theories posited an unviable China in comparison to imperialist states, in part because of the outdated and moribund nature of Confucian teachings and education that interfered with truly valuable and useful knowledge of science and technology. In response, Chinese tried a variety of ways to salvage their culture in the face of foreign criticism and pressure. During the self-strengthening effort from the 1860s, the *tiyong* 體用 configuration of "Chinese thought for essence; Western thought for application" included Confucianism as the core of Chinese culture and civilization, and Confucian resources and symbols could be used as "banners for contemporary political mobilization,"[14] while knowledge of industry and self-defense was garnered.

After the Sino-Japanese War of 1895 and the Boxer Rebellion of 1900, it was clear that self-strengthening had not worked. Many Chinese continued to identify China's shortcomings as a result of a lack of scientific thinking and education. Confucianism, with its emphasis on scholasticism, morality, virtue, and classical texts, was seen as a primary impediment to the spread of science and science education. Moreover, a core group of Chinese students who had studied abroad began to advocate for science as the key to national salvation.[15] These enthusiasts believed that science could "develop the political and spiritual coherence of the nation." Science would be the means to create a peaceful and enlightened government (*zhiping* 治平). Science was the "great *Dao*" 道 of progress that would result in wealth, a strong military, and an abundant harvest and would open the minds of the people (*kai min zhi* 開民智), ending superstition and its attendant dangers, such as the violence manifest in the Boxer Rebellion.[16] The key to modernity was science.

By the twentieth century, the confrontation with modernity and the West had precipitated a situation where Chinese stopped seeing *foreigners* as barbaric and uncivilized and came to see *themselves* through foreign eyes as the ones who were uncouth and uncivilized. They had good reason to embrace the scientistic construction of civilization, as imperialists were bestowing "civilization" while they exerted political and social control and made financial gains through their adventures in China. This new civilization was based on the recent transformation of the imperialists' own civilizations with the acceptance of germ theory and the establishment of organizations that intervened into private lives for the good of public health.[17]

The "gaze" Foucault describes in the creation of the modern clinic in the relationship between patient and practitioner was expanded to powerful states, assessing the health and welfare not only of their own subjects, but also of other cultures and states. Those subjected to intervention then appropriated that gaze and directed it inward. The gaze of imperialists frequently related to observations of habits of hygiene, cleanliness, and personal care, with palpable and material repercussions. In a study of treaty port–era (1860–1902) Tianjin, Ruth Rogaski shows that "hygienic modernity" was in part responsible as the rationale for the post-Boxer occupation of Tianjin.[18] Chinese were deemed unfit to rule themselves because they did not have appropriate hygienic—scientifically hygienic—standards, which became not only the key to modernization but also to national survival. Authority based in scientistic logic or vocabulary became the route to approval for any aspect of the new culture and civilization.

Critique of Confucianism in the New Culture Movement

The triumph of scientistic thinking led in the first instance to the rejection of Confucianism in the New Culture movement, fueled by a new sense of civilization and a coterie of ardent Chinese reformers, many of whom had studied overseas and returned home determined to establish scientific societies and to popularize the scientific worldview. Science was applied to all aspects of life, as is demonstrated by a selection of article titles by Cornell-trained Chinese students, including "Scientific Spirit," "Scientific Method," "Science and Education," "Science and Morality," and "Scientific Philosophy of Life."[19] Confucianism was attacked almost as a corollary, as it was deemed neither scientific nor modern. Reformer Chen Duxiu, who coined the phrase "Mr. Democracy and Mr. Science," called for "science in the realm of ideas." He, like many others, felt that science would remove the polluting corrosion of religions and superstition. His attack on Confucianism in his influential journal *New Youth* bluntly asserted that Confucianism was an outdated relic that could not help and could only harm China's efforts to become modern.[20]

Hu Shi, a pragmatist who had trained at Cornell, appreciated the "respect for facts and evidence" of science. He was prepared to remove all aspects of Chinese culture and adopt Western culture wholesale, saying in 1923 that "Chinese culture should have no particular claims on China's new culture."[21] Hu claimed that even the habits of traditional scholars, such as their traditional gowns, kept them from developing scientific practices.[22] Scientistic, anti-Confucian theories were shared by Chinese and Westerners alike and were mapped onto a linear concept of progress and success. This was accompanied by an assumption that *all* questions could be answered by science and that the certainty of the laboratory could be replicated in all settings. The future seemed to point to a time when science would create a perfect world, something that could not be accomplished by traditional means. A particular emphasis in the writing of Chinese and Western reformers at the time is the importance of public works and health initiatives, and hygienic practices are evident in many writings of the time. The New Culture Movement's confident scientism peaked in the debate over metaphysics in 1923, when Ting Wen-chiang argued the universality of science and its ability to create a rational society, unfazed by Chang Chun-mai, who questioned the applications of scientific epistemology.[23]

Scientism and Confucianism in Nationalist China and the New Life Movement

The rise of Chiang Kai-shek as leader of the Nationalists led to a reassessment of Confucianism and the Chinese tradition, a reassessment effected by this now established scientistic model. The emphasis given to science in the New Culture Movement had had a tremendous impact on the Nationalist government in the 1920s and 1930s, as did the effort to remove any aspect of culture that worked contrary to science. Scientism had become the mediator between tradition and modernity, and there was a wave of efforts to restore traditional Chinese heritage by recasting that heritage as scientific and to use that heritage in nation building. The New Life Movement demonstrates the power of the scientistic worldview in reframing Confucianism and Chinese culture. The express goal of the New Life Movement was to use Confucian principles updated for a modern context to *jiu guo* 救 國, or save the nation, by creating, through scientific means, citizens who would identify with modern China and develop national pride through applying principles of Chinese civilization. The core values chosen were li, yi, lian, and chi 禮義廉恥, or propriety, righteousness, discrimination, and shame.[24]

In stark contrast to leaders of the New Culture Movement, who felt that no aspect of traditional China need be retained as China modernized, Chiang was explicit about the value of a synthesis of old and new in the New Life Movement. Chiang claimed a timelessness and universality to these values as he updated and reinterpreted them. *Li, yi, lian,* and *chi* were deemed ancient wisdom from the past, flexible enough to be interpreted for modern situations and problems. The updated definitions Chiang gave these concepts reflect the scientistic tone of the time, focusing on natural law, regulation, and discipline and combined with a conservative morality and ethics. *Li* was defined as natural law in nature, discipline in social affairs, and laws and regulations for the nation, that is, a "regulated attitude." *Yi* was deemed the proper action that issues from *li*; *lian,* the ability to distinguish between right and wrong, between that which is "regulated attitude and proper action" and that which is not. *Chi* denoted the feeling that comes when one has erred and the disgust one feels for those who have chosen the wrong path.[25]

The abstractions of *li, yi, lian,* and *chi* were made concrete in the Ninety-Six Rules, a list of behaviors divided into two categories, "orderliness" (*zhengqi* 整齊) and "cleanliness" (*qingjie* 清潔). Chiang's reevaluation of Confucian principles shows his particular interest in delineating the way in which Confucian ideas can promote concepts of modern hygiene and thus strong bodies and a strong nation, all inspired by the internalized Western gaze. The list included rules to encourage all Chinese to keep kitchens clean, exterminate mosquitoes, not urinate on the ground, be vaccinated for smallpox, put waste into the garbage, at all times attend to the details of personal hygiene, walk without smoking or pushing through others, keep walls clean, and wear shoes properly. These rules were to be the backbone of a transformed populace, starting with the simple and working toward the more complicated.[26] This list of rules was intended to be accessible by even the most humble and the most hapless and have often been ridiculed as an example of the not-too-subtle cover of fascist control that Chiang hoped to achieve. Whether or not they mesh with contemporaneous fascist practices, the Ninety-Six Rules served to unify scientific hygienic principles and Confucian values.

The Confucianism of the New Life Movement proved to be a political Confucianism that used a top-down paternalism exhibited in many Confucian writings in order to influence, mold, and control the populace and produce strong, healthy bodies. In his inaugural speech for the New Life Movement, Chiang Kai-shek used *Analect* 12:19

and the image of the grass bending to the wind to illustrate the mechanics of the movement. Hygiene and conformity to "international standards" of scientifically healthy living are particularly poignant in the Ninety-Six Rules, which pronounce dicta that could be from ritual manuals such as the *Liji* 禮記 but that have a different meaning. "Don't eat food that is not clean" resonates with the *Liji*'s advice to "avoid rancid food," and "eat in a mannerly fashion" with the *Liji*'s "Take small mouthfuls to guard against belching and hiccoughs." Both advocate choosing food carefully and eating in a mannerly way; both give instructions for civilized eating and assume that self-cultivation includes moral formation by adherence to specific actions. Both place importance on the bending of body and mind to prescribed ways of acting and the creation of social harmony by prescribed actions and shared expectations.

However, where *Liji* commentary suggests that the result of its *li* are self-cultivation and social harmony, the New Life Movement's Ninety-Six Rules end point is strong bodies in a powerful nation.[27] Thus, a New Life Movement publication reads: "[The success of the New Life Movement] would not only mean that it is going to make China a better place to live in, but would also be a contribution to a better understanding between the Chinese people and the nations of the world, inasmuch as it is not advocating any political or religious reform, but simply [is] devoted to the search for a rationalized way of living in this scientific and mechanized age."[28]

In implementation, the New Life Movement functioned as an umbrella organization for a variety of public works and health initiatives.[29] Articles outlined health education, including for children, to ensure heightened public awareness, asserting that the "cleanliness" campaign of the New Life Movement and the cleanliness precepts in the Ninety-Six Rules were really just a means to health and that Chiang's intention was to guide the country to good health through campaigns that could be understood by all.[30] Cleanliness remained a focus through the last years of the movement and was highlighted as an important component of modernization. One article recited a litany of figures from Western history from antiquity to the modern age who either were concerned with cleanliness or made advances in germ theory and sanitation, and offered statistics showing the importance of sanitary practices.[31]

Traditional ideals were scientized and transformed into a kind of muscular Confucianism. Strong bodies were to be cultivated to help resist the Japanese. An article written toward the end of the movement speaks of physical culture as being just as important as it was during the Japanese resistance to ensure that the country could continue on its path of modernization and industrialization.[32] One article claimed that it was specifically because they did not have the necessary daily habits of hygiene and physical culture that the Chinese suffered foreign invasion; because they were neither clean nor orderly, the bodies of Chinese people likewise were neither strong nor healthy (*shenti de bu qiangjian* 身體的不強健): not knowing how to love and protect their own bodies, how could Chinese protect the country?[33]

In another essay, Wang Jingwei makes the case for the cleanliness campaign as the heart of the New Life Movement, linking it to the Chinese propensity of carelessness (*suibian zhuyi* 隨便主義). Connecting with the disgust at Chinese habits and the need for cleanliness, he cites the many ways in which carelessness leads to unclean and unhealthful practices, such as throwing litter on the ground and heedless spitting.[34]

In attempting to create a new synthesis of Confucianism framed by modern paradigms, the leaders of the New Life Movement were in large part observing themselves through the eyes of European, North American, and Japanese critics. In this second stage of combining science and Confucianism, the effort was to reclaim older forms updated for the construction of a modern civilization. In the New Life Movement, Chiang claimed Chinese have forgotten their cultural heritage and repeatedly described the Chinese as lazy, filthy, debauched, *uncivilized*, and repulsive in every way—"barbaric" (*yeman* 野蠻) and "devoid of reason" (*bu heli* 不合理). This lack of civilization, though, is based on the gaze of the West. Chiang often spoke of Western disgust at Chinese habits and of Japanese fortitude and hardened bodies in comparison to the weakling Chinese. Ancient virtues of Confucianism—updated—are the means to remedy this situation. Thus, *li* that address how one should eat are not merely a means to self-cultivation, but also to hygienic self-cultivation.

New Life Movement reformers were self-conscious in distributing literature that described their aims and progress so that foreigners could see their objectives and, doubtless, appreciate their accomplishments in civilizing the Chinese people. The propaganda wing of the New Life Movement printed many pamphlets translated for the benefit of missionaries and English literate audiences overseas; it is clear that one goal of the movement was to gain foreign support by demonstrating adherence to hygiene and universally "rational" mores.

One of the more surprising outcomes of this combination of retrieving tradition while appropriating a "universal" paradigm was to show that science had always been present in Chinese thinking. Chiang claimed that the Great Learning and its "investigation of things" was "not only China's orthodox philosophy but also the forebear of scientific thought, undoubtedly the source of Chinese science, Chinese invention and development of science." Thus, the scientific method was not discovered in modern times, was not a product of foreign countries, and was something for the Chinese to rediscover in their own heritage. Chiang Kai-Shek, in a lecture to the Guomindang at Lu Shan in September 1934, declared,

> I believe that the book, Great Learning, is not only China's orthodox philosophy but also the forebear of scientific thought, undoubtedly the source of Chinese science. If we bind together the Great Learning and the Doctrine of the Mean, we will have the most complete text on the harmony of philosophy and science and the unity of spirit and matter. Thus I call it the "Scientific Nature of the Great Learning and the Doctrine of the Mean."[35]

A year later, he commented again on science and its relationship to Confucianism and Chinese culture:

> Actually what we nowadays call science is none other than what we Chinese in the past have called the learning of ke-chih [investigation of things leads to knowledge]. [As this approach is found in the Great Learning] we can see that China had science two thousand years ago. Since there was science, there must have been the scientific method. Thus the scientific method is not discovered in modern times, much less is it a sole possession of foreign countries. During the age of Confucius this fact is already clear. What Confucius meant by "everything has its source, and everything has its beginning and end; when one knows the order of things, he is indeed close to the Tao" is the best scientific method for any scholarship and every way of handling affairs.[36]

This is a marvelous loop: retrieving tradition becomes "innovation"; "innovation" becomes a way to redefine "tradition."[37]

In the New Life Movement, Chiang and the nationalists avidly applied scientism to Confucian principles to validate Confucianism as an appropriate resource for a modern nation. In other writings, Chiang claimed that Confucianism provides an ameliorating influence on some of the tendencies of Western culture. He asserted that Chinese weakness had come from the volatile mix of Western and Asian ways and the resulting destruction of China's equilibrium under the impact of Western civilization and the destructiveness of the New Culture Movement.[38] Here Chiang used Confucianism as a tool to re-create Chinese culture. The New Life Movement was described as a "tireless effort to build up a new code to replace the ethics of the past, that have been torn to shreds in this mechanical and materialistic age." Even with his critiques, he claimed that there was something essential to be retrieved in "the ethics, religion, and cultural heritage of all peoples, at all times, which touch upon the spiritual development of Man's feelings towards himself, his family, his society, and towards the human race as a whole. It is the point of emphasis that changes from time to time. The principles in all cases have always remained the same."[39] Thus, traditional Chinese culture—or at least its core—is both a corrective to Western flaws as well as universally applicable and beneficial.

Scientism and Chinese Culturism

Reclaiming Confucianism by way of scientism was only one example of rehabilitating traditional culture during the Nationalist Era; interpreting and reappropriating tradition through scientism spread beyond Chiang Kai-shek's New Life Movement. The power of scientism in recasting aspects of Chinese culture, from childrearing to martial arts, shows the way in which scientism became a primary value and means of crafting a modern identity that was also Chinese during the Republican era. The New Life Movement claimed the Confucian tradition as a *national* characteristic; other cultural markers were also elevated to emblems of modern national identity. Rogaski's study of hygienic modernity demonstrates that the word *weisheng* 衛生, which was used in the twentieth century to justify hygienic practices and public health initiatives of the government, including sanctioned government control over individual bodies, shifted dramatically from its earlier meaning of "protecting life" as seen in the *Zhuangzi* and other self-cultivation texts. "Protecting life" had denoted private practices to preserve the body, such as taiji quan, diet, meditation, and herbal remedies, and now revolved around hygiene and biomedical health.[40]

Scientism changed prescriptions for motherhood and child rearing. As with ideas of *weisheng*, motherhood and housekeeping were scientized for the purpose of creating a strong nation, "scientifically" justifying control and influence over women. Simple housekeeping practices such as ventilating rooms were prescribed by the government, ideologically linked to the good and strength of the whole nation and also in part to avoid the critical eye of foreign observers.[41] The attempt to adopt scientistic approaches to Chinese culture also meant scientizing Chinese physical identity through racial constructions of ethnicity. Scientism combined with a scientistically constructed "racial" identity of the "yellow" race, where indigenous Chinese concepts of identity through genealogy and descent were combined with a vocabulary derived from science to create a rationale for Chinese racial, genetic distinctiveness.[42] Scientistic racial theories also contributed to attempts to control reproduction to ensure a healthier race, a part of the eugenics movement led by Pan Guangdang.[43]

Traditional cultural forms underwent a similar transformation. Early modernizers after the Boxer Rebellion had wanted to completely eradicate martial arts as backward and dangerous, but groups rallied to rescue it with the slogan "scientize martial arts, and spread them to the millions."[44] Martial arts were reappropriated and redescribed using biomedical physiology. This changed them from an esoteric training for fighters to a sport with "universal" rules of engagement and sportsmanship. Martial arts were eventually renamed "national arts" (*guo shu* 國術) and "national skills" (*guoji* 國技).[45] Traditional Chinese medicine was delivered from official condemnation when apologists for Chinese medicine self-consciously—and with much criticism— "scientized" the rendering and understanding of its therapies, and it was also renamed "National Medicine" (*guoyao* 國藥).[46]

The People's Republic: Confucianism Complements Scientism

In the PRC, "science" has included the biomedical heritage as well as scientific socialism of Marxist theory. In the early decades of the PRC, Confucianism was considered incompatible and even threatening to scientific socialism. In the Mao era, the Communist Party viewed Confucianism as feudal, backward, and an inhibition to the realization of a socialist society. The suspicion and persecution of those associated with Confucian thought culminated in the "criticize Lin Biao and Confucius" campaign in the early 1970s. This changed dramatically in the liberalization of the 1980s and 1990s following the Cultural

Revolution. The emerging assessment of Confucianism designated it as an important cultural and political resource that could be used to help construct, as Deng Xiaoping instructed, a "socialism with Chinese characteristics." Confucianism became a part of an overarching scientistic approach to culture and nation building subsumed under a larger political project.

There is no question that Confucianism continues to be malleable to serve multiple functions and goals, beginning with the reconsideration of Confucianism in the "culture fever" (*wenhua re* 文化熱) of the 1980s and the "national studies craze" (*guoxue re* 國學熱) of the 1990s. The richness and ferment of these years has led to many different interpretations of its meanings and many studies of facets and ideologies of new Confucian groups.[47] What is clear is that there is another reworking of Chinese "tradition" to engage, and in this case augment, modernization efforts. In these reformulations, "tradition" sometimes indicates diffuse social and political characteristics that are connected with Confucian orientations, and sometimes it refers specifically to Confucianism itself, but in either case Confucian ideas have been constructed and understood by the government to complement rather than contradict a modern, rational scientistic sensibility. Confucianism has been deemed an appropriate working partner with scientific socialism that serves as a "rational" source of ethics, morality, and education that is not counter to science. Unlike Taoism, Buddhism, or the popular tradition, Confucianism can serve as a native resource that conveniently meets, and even antedates, Enlightenment values of tolerance and rationality. In other words, an underlying scientism, by now assimilated as a universal—not Western—paradigm, confirms Confucianism as rational, enlightened, and appropriate to modernity.

The 1980s saw a Confucian revival on the mainland that has grown over the last thirty years and has encompassed the academic and political worlds. The philosophical "New Confucianism" movement dates from the early twentieth century and today includes scholars in the PRC, Taiwan, Hong Kong, and the United States. The liberalization in the PRC after 1979 created a fertile ground for scholars there as the government supported and funded institutes and conferences.[48]

The beginning of liberalization was cautious, seeking primarily to determine which parts of traditional Chinese culture and particularly Confucianism could be recast scientistically. In the first years of reconsidering Confucianism, there was a call to "divide Confucianism into two [good and bad parts]" by using "scientific Marxist philosophy."[49]

Confucianism's stultifying effect on Chinese development was cited, even as the cultural benefits were lauded. This approach to studying Confucianism was a middle ground between the lavish veneration and the virulent attacks on Confucius of the early PRC.

By the mid-1980s, Confucius was being described as a " 'great thinker, educationist, statesman, philosopher, and historian' and was hailed 'the founder of Chinese traditional culture.'"[50] Since that time, PRC government officials have shown increased support for Confucianism, with a growing number of clear and enthusiastic references to the value of Confucianism and its role in modern China. The Academy of Chinese Confucius Research Institution (*zhonghua kongzi yanjiusuo* 中華孔子研究所) was founded in 1985; in 1986 Deng Xiaoping called for "socialism with Chinese characteristics." In that same year, the government identified Confucianism as a key research topic, to be funded as part of the Seventh Five Year Plan.[51]

A continuing theme in these developments has been culturalism, with academics and officials equating [at least a carefully pruned Confucianism] with an essential Chinese identity. The year after the Seventh Five Year Plan was announced, Vice Prime Minister Gu Mu 穀牧 called Confucianism "a crystallization of Chinese national culture,"[52] and scholar Luo Yijun 羅義俊 stated that "it is only due to the establishment of this great Confucian school [i.e., New Confucianism], that the true lifeblood and spirit imbuing the vitality of Chinese culture has remained unsevered and sustained."[53] In the rubric of the Seventh Five Year Plan, Confucius not only was honored as the founder of Chinese traditional thought and culture, but his teachings also were claimed to have universal applications. By 1990, the New Confucianism was described by scholar Fang Keli 方克立 as an attempt to "reconcile the problems which exist between tradition, modernization and westernization."[54] As we see, Confucianism was assessed in the 1980s through scientific socialist critique, but unlike earlier Republican constructions, Confucianism was not interpreted as itself scientific. Rather, it was complementary with scientific socialism.

Confucianism has become an increasingly significant part of the official rhetoric and agenda of the government since 2003. President Hu Jintao and Premier Wen Jiabao have tapped Confucianism as the moral element of development and cultivation in a larger project to develop a "harmonious socialist society" (*shehuizhuyi hexie shehui* 社会主义和谐社会) that is brought about by uniting scientific socialism with the reappropriation of components of traditional culture and wise planning by the party. Hu has promoted his "scientific development

concept" (*kexue fazhan guan* 科学发展观) as the mechanism to create
the harmonious society that "takes the people as the base" (*yiren weiben*
以人为本). The program to use scientific development is key to the
Eleventh Five Year Plan (2006–2010), and various officials in addition
to Hu and Wen have called for the use of Confucianism as a resource for
China and even the world.[55] In connection to this plan, Confucianism's
role is to provide the moral ballast that is China specific, or at least not
Western. Hu has claimed that Scientific Development Theory is based
on, among other things, China's cultural heritage,[56] and the cultural
heritage includes a diversity of figures, some clearly Confucian.

It is a peculiar happenstance that many details of Confucianism's
rehabilitation by the PRC paralleled the earlier projects of Nationalist
China. Hu first spoke of the "Scientific Development" concept in 2003
in perennially underdeveloped and disadvantaged Jiangxi Province,
coincidentally the starting place of the New Life Movement in 1934.
Like the New Life Movement, PRC leaders have spoken of the
importance of including Chinese cultural resources to shape national
identity.[57] In a manner not unlike Chiang's New Life Movement, Hu
promoted in 2006 the goal of a Harmonious Society by introducing
the Eight Honours and Eight Shames (*barong bachi* 八榮八恥), which
combine love of country, selfless service to the people, following science,
honesty, discipline and diligence, simple living, mutual aid as a core
value system for all Chinese, and "moral yardstick to measure the
work, conduct and attitude of Communist Party officials."[58] The "eight
shames" are the antitheses of the "honors," including not harming
the country or people; discarding ignorance; avoiding indolence,
lawlessness, and excess; and not taking advantage or others or being
unethical for the sake for financial gain. The reference to shame and
the content of the moral exhortations are seen by some as a reference
to Confucian values, and Hu's frequent mention of Confucius enhances
this idea. Shame, or *chi*, was also one of the four ethical principles
undergirding the New Life Movement.[59]

Scholars have added their voices to this effort to recruit
Confucianism in building Chinese identity. In a provocative article
from 2007, scholar Gan Yang 甘陽 suggests the formation of a
"Confucian socialist republic" (*rujia shehuizhuyi gongheguo* 儒家社会
主义共和国) that combines the reforms of liberalization that began in
the 1980s, Maoist elements of "freedom and rights," and Confucianism
as expressed in daily habits. Gan's position has been likened to the New
Life Movement (and, like the New Life Movement, criticized roundly),
but his position is consistent with the effort to place Confucianism in

a key role in modernization and progress.[60]

Today, Confucianism is framed as a cultural resource for scientific socialism in a variety of ways. The role, or the legitimacy, of Confucianism within the Scientific Development Concept is both Confucianism's identification as the quintessence of Chinese tradition but also its fruitful partnership with scientism that is facilitated by its areligious rationality. At a speech at Harvard in 2007, Premier Wen Jiabao stated, "From Confucius to Sun Yat-sen, the traditional culture of the Chinese nation consisted of a large number of precious elements, of many positive things concerning the nature of a people and of democracy (*renminxing he minzuxing* 人民性和民族性). It emphasized, for example, love and the sense of humanity (*ren ai* 仁 爱) community (*qunti* 群體), harmony despite different points of view."[61] Another speech by a military official advised classical culture for "leaders and cadres":

> Confucian culture is a cultural resource which we cannot distance ourselves from in the construction of a harmonious socialist society. . . . As cadres and leaders we must contribute to the radiance of the spiritual specificities of Confucian culture by aspiring to the highest moral qualities and behavior. Every Communist Party cadre must contribute to the radiance of the spiritual specificities of Confucian culture by aspiring to the highest moral qualities and behavior.[62]

As the reclamation of Confucianism has proceeded, thinkers in the PRC have imagined distinct roles for culture and science. Traditional culture, especially Confucianism, is to reign in the areas of morality, education, and social cohesion. Science is manifest in the scientific socialism of the Communist Party doctrine. Scientism is present in the background as the validating context for Confucianism as a modern alternative to European cultural forms because it is assessed as rational, particularly in comparison with other Chinese religious resources now deemed as religious or superstitious. However much Confucianism serves as an "invented tradition," it is clear that Confucianism has been adopted to address the need to be modern without westernizing. Confucianism, identified as the pinnacle of tradition Chinese culture, provides the moral and social components of the new China.

One of the striking features that has developed in descriptions and usages of Confucianism since the 1980s has been the government's way of cultivating a transnational identity drawing on "essential" Chinese characteristics—a "myth of shared sacredness" that Allen Chun evoked from the movements in Taiwan in the 1960s in which definitions of "Chineseness [transcend] ethnic identities and political realities."[63] The result has been a *wenhua zhongguo* 文化中国, a cultural China that transcends national borders and connects the PRC to Taiwan, Hong Kong, and Singapore and is a bulwark against Western trends.[64] Past initiatives to preserve Chinese heritage in Taiwan, especially of the Cultural Renaissance Movement of the 1960s and 1970s that was a continuation of the New Life Movement, highlighted Confucianism and recast tradition through the "sinicization of Western science and modern life, custom and behavior."[65] Likewise in Singapore, Lee Kuan Yew has argued what he calls "Asian values," which are shared by Asians in contrast to the West. Lee characterizes these values as "strong family, strong government, and economic prosperity" and established the Institute of East Asian Philosophy and the Confucian Studies program in the classroom to spread these values.[66] Recent statements in the PRC have expanded this cultural China idea even further to a universal culture, claiming that Confucianism has something to offer, "an important part of human morality and culture as a whole . . . [with] a far-reaching impact on the development and progress of the Oriental civilization and the world civilization."[67]

This claim of universal validity for Confucianism is another significant similarity between the efforts of Nationalist and Communist governments in reforming Confucianism. Again, this universal validity was associated with Confucianism's harmonization with science. Some have gone so far as to claim that science itself was Chinese even before it was Western. In the scientific socialism of the PRC, as in the hygienic scientism of the New Life Movement, the claim is made by some that the relation of Confucian tradition to science is seen not only as historically inextricable, but as ultimately independent of Western influence. This is by no means a commonly expressed idea, but the impetus to claim it shows the extent to which the scientistic model is essential to those using it. We saw this with Chiang and the Chen brothers' claim that science has Chinese origins. This same move is made by Wang Dianqing, who claims that the scaffolding of scientific socialism is of Chinese origin.

> Marxism has three origins. The first is classical German philosophy, established by Leibniz. He undertook a great deal of research on Chinese methods of binary arithmetic

and also Song-Ming Principle-centered Learning (lixue) the Second was English classical economics, One of its founders was Adam Smith whose teacher, Francois Quesnay, was one of the leading Physiocrats. As the founder of the Physiocrats, Quesnay was acknowledged to be "Europe's Confucius." The third origin was French utopian socialism, which was given birth in the context of a century of "China fever," the center of which was at the University of Paris. Against this background Engles wrote an essay in which he demonstrated the relationship between utopian socialism and the Liyun (ritual cycles) chapter [Liji].[68]

Conclusion

Both fluid and elusive in their contours, science and Confucianism have been central in formulating the modern China. In various contexts of cultural China, the words "rational" and "scientific" emerge in relation to Confucianism, often in contradistinction to foreign cultural markers such as Christianity or Islam. Lionel Jensen speaks of the "plasticity" of Confucianism and defends "the creative impulses that have sustained centuries of invention in [Confucianism's] name . . ." Surely this is what we are seeing in the various framings and appropriations of Confucianism in the twentieth and twenty-first centuries. But there is an astonishing fluidity in an equally compelling paradigm of science, which is also pressed to define value and appropriate orientations and to trace a trajectory to the future.[63]

In other words, an underlying scientism that has now been assimilated as a universal—not Western—paradigm has rendered constructions of Confucianism as rational, enlightened, and appropriate to modernity. The gaze of the West on an unscientific and therefore unviable China has been appropriated and assimilated. Once assimilated, it has been used to reframe and reclaim tradition to create a culture that is thoroughly Chinese and thoroughly modern.

Notes

1. Quoted in D. W. Y. Kwok, *Scientism in Chinese Thought 1900–1950* (New Haven: Yale University Press, 1965), 11.

2. W. W. Howells, *The Heathens: Primitive Man and His Religions* (Garden City, NY: Doubleday, 1948), 24.

3. Ziauddin Sardar, "Introduction," in Ashis Nandy, *Return from Exile* (Delhi: Oxford University Press, 1998), 19.

4. Kwok, *Scientism in Chinese Thought*, 3, 12. Kwok notes another definition (by R. G. Owen): "scientolatry, the unrestrained worship of science as the bearer of human salvation."

5. Shigeru Nakayama, *Academic and Scientific Traditions in China, Japan and the West*, trans. Jerry Dusenbury (Tokyo: University of Tokyo Press, 1984), 96. It has been suggested that the commitment to science by scientific professionals has spawned the prevalence of scientism, as modern science is exclusive, "denigrating what did not follow its methods" and "standing in judgment on the rest of the academic world, distinguishing between science and non-science and repudiating the latter."

6. David Wright, *Translating Science: The Translation of Western Chemistry into Late Imperial China, 1840–1900* (Leiden: Brill, 2000), 428.

7. Lionel M. Jensen, *Manufacturing Confucianism* (Durham: Duke University Press, 1997), 79.

8. Eric Hobsbawm and Terence Ranger, *The Invention of Tradition* (Cambridge: Cambridge University Press, 1983).

9. Ashis Nandy, *The Savage Freud*, quoted in Ziauddin Sardar, "Introduction," in Nandy, *Return from Exile*, 20; Mayfair Mei-hui Yang, "Introduction," in *Chinese Religiosities Afflictions of Modernity and State Formation* (Berkeley: University of California Press, 2008), 3–6.

10. Roy Porter, "Medical Science," in Roy Porter, ed., *Cambridge History of Medicine* (Cambridge: Cambridge University Press, 2006), 152.

11. Steven Johnson, *The Ghost Map* (New York: Riverhead Books, 2006), 111–136.

12. J. G. Cotton Minchin, *Our Public Schools* (London: Swan Sonnenschein and Co., 1901), 8.

13. Andrew Morris, *The Marrow of the Nation* (Berkeley: University of California Press, 2004). On the "sick man of Asia, see Susan Brownell, *Training the Body for China: Sports in the Moral Order of the People's Republic* (Chicago: University of Chicago Press, 1995), 22. See also David Palmer, *Qigong Fever: Body, Science and Utopia in China* (London: C. Hurst & Co., 2007), 45; and Ruth Rogaski, *Hygienic Modernity Meanings of Health and Disease in Treaty-Port China* (Los Angeles: University of California Press, 2004), 230.

14. Quoted in Michael Nylan, *The Five "Confucian" Classics* (New Haven: Yale University Press, 2001), 308.

15. David Wright, *Translating Science*, 426.

16. Yang Yuhui, *Gezhi zhiping tongyi* [*An Anthology of Opinions Regarding the Use of Science in Pacifying China*], quoted in Wright, *Translating Science*, 427.

17. In a celebratory article in *Science* in 1926, Andrew Balfour listed the various places in the British Empire that had been improved hygienically and looked to a future when these improvements would be global. Andrew

Balfour, "Hygiene as a World Force," *Science* LXIV, no. 1668 (November 12, 1926): 459–466.

18. Rogaski, *Hygienic Modernity*, 49ff.

19. Kwok, Scientism in Chinese Thought, 14–15.

20. Kwok, *Scientism in Chinese Thought*, 63–64.

21. Ralph C. Croizier, *Traditional Medicine in Modern China Science, Nationalism and the Tensions of Cultural Change* (Cambridge: Harvard University Press, 1968), 106.

22. Wright, *Translating Science*, 67.

23. The idea that China lagged because of undeveloped science was even held by those who supported Confucianism, such as Kang Youwei, who criticized the Chinese tradition: "[T]he root of China's weakness is simply this: not knowing how to teach the study of matter. The Chinese civilization, which is thousands of years old, is actually the foremost on earth. But is has placed undue emphasis upon ethics and philosophy, and is extremely deficient in [the study of] matter." Kang Youwei, "Wuzhi jiuguo lun" ["On the Salvation of the Country through the Study of Matter"], cited in Wright, *Translating Science*, 426.

24. These four values came originally from the *Guanzi* 管子 but were appropriated by the Confucian tradition.

25. "Xin shenghuo yundong zhi neirong" 新生活運動之內容 *Geming wenxian* 革命文獻, vol. 68. *Xin shenghuo yundong shiliao* 新生活運動史料. Xiao Jizong 蕭繼宗, ed. (Taibei: Zhonghua yinshua, 1975), 6–7.

26. Hong Ziliang 洪子良, ed., *Xin shenghuo chubu* 新生活初步, Xinshenghuo shushe chuban, n.d.

27. A sampling of applications of hygiene in the Nationalist era includes personal hygiene (*geren weisheng* 個人衛生), public hygiene (*gonggong weisheng* 公公衛生) or "mass hygiene" (*dazhong weisheng* 大眾衛生), social hygiene (*shehui weisheng* 社會衛生), racial hygiene (*zhongzu weisheng* 種族衛生), family hygiene (*jiating weisheng* 家庭衛生) or "household-affairs hygiene" (*jiashi weisheng* 家事衛生), and women's hygiene (*funü weisheng* 婦女衛生). Sarah E. Stevens, "Hygienic Bodies and Public Mothers: The Rhetoric of Reproduction, Fetal Education, and Childhood in Republican China," in Michael Lackner and Natascha Vittinghoff, eds., *Mapping Meanings: The Field of New Learning in Late Qing China* (Leiden: J. Brill, 2004), 659–660.

28. "The New Life Movement" (Nanking, China: The New Life Movement National Headquarters, February 19, 1948), 15.

29. This was not the first time that matters of hygiene became a pivot between modernization and science. In Shanghai, a "*weisheng yundong*" (hygienic movement) and "*saochu yundong*" (cleanliness movement) were launched in 1928. Like the New Life Movement, the leaders—in this case, the mayor of Shanghai—made a show of sweeping the streets. Christian Henriot, *Shanghai 1927–1937: Municipal Power, Locality, and Modernization*, trans. Noel Castelino (Berkeley: University of California Press, 1993), 204–207.

30. Jin Baoshan 金寶善, "Xin shenghuo yu weisheng 新生活與衛生," in *Geming wenxian*, 188–190; Liu Ruiheng 劉瑞恆, "Xin shenghuo yu jiankang 新生活與健康," in Ye Chucang 葉楚傖, ed., *Xin shenghuo congshu* 新生活叢書 (Nanjing: Nanjing zhengzhong shuju kan, 1934–35).

31. Zhou Shang 周尚, "Minzu shengcun yu zhengjie shenghuo 民族生存與整潔生活," *Xinyun daobao* 新運導報 120 (June 1948): 12–13.

32. Liu Ruiheng 劉瑞恆, "Xin shenghuo yu jiankang 新生活與健康," in *Congshu* 叢書; Jin Baoshan 金寶善, "Xin shenghuo yundong yu minzu jiankang 新生活運動與民族健康," in *Xinyun daobao* 新運導報 117 (June 10, 1947): 22–23.

33. Jennifer Oldstone-Moore, "The New Life Movement of Nationalist China: Confucianism, State Authority and Moral Formation" (PhD diss., University of Chicago, 2000), 195. Jiangxi Province had special New Life programs to line physical culture with hygiene. Citizens were divided into groups by age and participated in physical training two hours a week. This was compared with programs in Europe and America, where "the health of all workers is emphasized." Morris, *Marrow of the Nation*, 218ff.

34. Wang Jingwei 汪精衛, "Xin shenghuo de zhenyi 新生活的真意," in *Xin shenghuo yundong xuzhi* 新生活運動須知 (Nanjing, 1935), 62–69.

35. "Kexue de Xueyong" ("The Scientific Nature of the Great Learning and the Doctrine of the Mean"), quoted in Kwok, *Scientism in Chinese Thought*, 185–188. David Wright notes that even in the nineteenth century, there were Chinese who claimed that Western science had really originated in China, and thus it could be studied without betraying Chinese culture. Wright, *Translating Science*, 19.

36. Chiang Kai-shek, "Kexue jingshen yu kexue fangfa" ("Scientific Spirit and Scientific Method"), quoted in Kwok, *Scientism in Chinese Thought*, 186.

37. Chiang was not the only prominent Nationalist to seek science in Chinese antiquity. In 1934, Chiang's close advisor Chen Lifu combined ideas of Wang Yangming with vitalism (wei-sheng-lun), on which he lectured and published for several years. Chen even applied vocabulary and ideas that sounded like Einstein's work. Kwok, *Scientism in Chinese Thought*, 185–188.

38. *The New Life Movement* (Nanking: New Life Movement National Headquarters, 1948), 14. The movement was also posited as a remedy for the "destructiveness" of the New Culture Movement, which centered on demands for Western-style liberalism.

39. *The New Life Movement*, 13.

40. Rogaski, *Hygienic Modernity*, 22; 3–6.

41. Stevens, "Hygienic Bodies and Public Mothers," in Lackner and Vittinghoff, *Mapping Meanings*, 659–683.

42. Frank Dikotter, "Introduction," "Racial Discourse in China: Continuities and Permutations," in Frank Dikotter, ed., *The Construction of Racial Identities in China and Japan* (London: Hurst and Company, 1997).

62   Jennifer Oldstone-Moore

Immediate Woes, Challenge," accessed August 16, 2010, http://English. peopledaily.com.cn; "Chinese Cultural Development Top Priority," accessed September 3, 2010, ChinaCSR.com/.

57. Joseph Fewsmith, "Promoting the Scientific Development Concept," *China Leadership Monitor*, no. 11, accessed September 1, 2010, media.hoover. org/documents.

58. "New Moral Yardstick," accessed March 24/10, http://www.gov.cn/.

59. Kent Ewing, "All Hail Hu Jintao," *Asia Times*, accessed August 28, 2010, http://ww.atimes.com/atimes/; "New Moral Yardstick: "8 Honors, 8 Disgraces," accessed August 25, 2010, http://www.gov.cn/. See also Billioud, "Cultural Tradition," 56. In Billoud's footnote to the Eight Honors and Eight Shames, he notes that "chi" signals a return to traditional moral philosophy. He also notes that the *barong bachi* are often mocked and parodied, as indeed were the dicta of the New Life Movement. See Graham Peck, *Two Kinds of Time* (Boston: Houghton Mifflin, 1967), 95–96.

60. Quoted in Billioud, "Confucianism, 'Cultural Tradition,' and Official Discourse, 62–63; n. 81, 82.

61. Billioud, "Cultural Tradition," 53–54.

62. Xu Zhuxin, "Lingdao ganbu ye yao sue yidian chuantong wenhua," *Xuexi shibao*, quoted in Billioud, "Confucianism, 'Cultural Tradition,' and Official Discourse," 61, n. 75.

63. Alan Chun, "An Oriental Orientalism: The Paradox of Tradition and Modernity in Nationalist Taiwan," *History and Anthropology* 9, no. 1 (1995): 29.

64. Makeham, *Lost Soul*, p. 7.

65. Chun, "Oriental Orientalism," 34–38.

66. R. S. Milne and Diane K. Mauzy, *Singapore: The Legacy of Lee Kuan Yew* (Boulder: Westview Press, 1990), 104; Michael D. Barr, *Lee Kuan Yew* (Richmond, Surrey: Curzon, 2000), 2.

67. "Senior Official Calls for Inheriting, Displaying Confucianism," September 25, 2009, accessed August 25, 2010, http://English.gov.cn/.

68. Makeham, *Lost Soul*, 316.

69. Jensen, *Manufacturing Confucianism*, 281; 28.

PART TWO

Confucianism and the State

3
_____

Selling Confucius

The Negotiated Return of Tradition in Post-Socialist China[1]

Anthony DeBlasi

Introduction

Most commentators on contemporary China have noticed the return of traditional values during the past three decades of economic reform. What had been viewed by outside observers as essentially dead traditions, surviving for political reasons as mere vestiges in Chinese enclaves outside the mainland, have now become central to a cultural debate about China's future. While one might expect that in the environment of greater openness, academics would begin to discuss the value of China's traditional culture,[2] the popularity of these ideas beyond academia and the government is a phenomenon that requires further reflection. The revival of traditional values in the popular culture has significance for both the way ideas are propagated in contemporary Chinese culture and the interests of the literate population. To begin to understand these interrelated issues, this chapter focuses on the presentation of varieties of popular Confucianism in the Chinese media. Specifically, it examines how academic authors—authors who hold academic positions as professors at universities—are presenting Confucian ideas in the popular press. The authors discussed here and the works they have produced thus far indicate that there is a complex interaction under way between academic discourse, state power, popular culture, and the market economy.

The relationship between these forces has left its mark on the actual content of the Confucian revival. When we read the books published as part of this revival, we see the ideas that have survived the selection process of media production. That selection process has two distinct aspects: initial production and satisfaction of demand. First, the very modes of media production condition the content that ultimately appears in the various media, whether the content of television programming or texts on the shelves of China's bookstores. The transformation of the Chinese media landscape as part of China's economic reform policies has altered fundamentally the incentive structures that determine what gets produced and disseminated. Second, the decision-making process within the media is not an abstract exercise. The media serve a fairly concrete role by connecting different segments of the Chinese cultural world. At the very least, it connects the reading public with the circle of authors. However, in the context of the Confucian revival, it does something more; it serves as the communication portal between the academic discourse described by scholars such as John Makeham and the broader Chinese reading public. The latter primarily consists of readers in the People's Republic, but global economic integration, the development of digital communication, and resurgent Chinese emigration have broadened the geographical scope of "Chinese readership" beyond China's political boundaries. In what follows, the ideas communicated in contemporary Confucian publications tell us much about the culture, but they also tell us about economic power and the contours of political authority. Understanding this provides the basis for drawing larger conclusions about the development of popular culture in general and the role of traditional values in it.

Western journalism frequently focuses on the authoritarian aspects of governance in the People's Republic. Given the tradition of an unfettered press and the assumption of its right to investigate and criticize government actions that prevails in Western Europe and North America, it is natural that coverage of the Chinese media, even by nonpartisan think tanks, tends to focus on the very real restraint of expression there. The Council on Foreign Relations, for example, includes on its Web site an extended description of press restrictions in China.[3] An even clearer case is the organization Reporters Without Borders, which ranks China 168 of 175 nations in the world with regard to press freedom.[4] The changes wrought in both the publishing and broadcast media during China's Reform Era, however, suggest that some nuance is necessary when describing state control. A more productive way of interpreting the emergence of cultural content in the Chinese media is as the result of a multifaceted negotiation process.

The government certainly retains the power and will to intervene harshly when it feels it necessary, but two aspects of the current situation mitigate that power. First, the government's own policies have produced a media environment that is vastly more complex and therefore less susceptible to preemptive control. The abandonment of the ideal of a top-down editorial model means that government watchdogs are often in a reactive posture. Often, clear directives to censor content only appear after a media phenomenon has already manifested itself. Second, the government is far from monolithic when it comes to cultural policies.[5] Disagreements among policy makers and differential enforcement can also lead to slippage in the efficiency of government control. The twin reality of the power to intervene with the impracticability of proactive intervention means that what gets produced results from a combination of editorial choices, market demand, and government policy—in short, a tripartite negotiation.[6]

The balancing of editorial, consumer, and government interests is a negotiation that is ultimately about the harmonizing of economic and political imperatives. Beyond that, however, there is another negotiation under way, one that is more precisely a cultural negotiation. It concerns the interaction between elite intellectual discourse and the tastes of the literate, urban public.[7] As is evident in the analysis below, public intellectuals present their ideas in ways that speak to very specific concerns in the culture. The erudite discussion of Confucian thought and its utility in China's future political development is carefully distilled for broader consumption.

We should take note of a third type of negotiation. The integration of China into the global economy has afforded Chinese consumers much greater access to information about world cultures. How accurate their perceptions of those cultures are is not particularly important for our purposes. More important is the existence of three distinct cultural formations in people's minds: world cultures (dominated by the West); the remnant socialist culture, which the older generation still recalls; and the reemerging traditional values. In other words, what traditional values in general, or Confucian values specifically, mean and the role they play in popular culture is emerging from a negotiation (or perhaps competition) among those three cultures. The form of Confucianism that appears in works aimed at a popular audience bears the hallmarks of all three influences. The contours of popular Confucianism then are emerging at the intersection of three distinct axes: (1) government-market, (2) academia-reading public, and (3) China-World.

To examine this multidimensional process of negotiation, this chapter begins with a brief overview of the Chinese media as they have developed under market reform. It then looks at examples of Chinese academics making their work accessible to a larger audience. Most of the works examined below appeared in 2008, providing a convenient chronological control in what is an admittedly fast-developing field. The texts and scholars considered here display very different approaches to the repopularization of Confucian values. From the broadest viewpoint, they reveal which of the author's concerns have found a market (at least in the judgment of the publishing companies) among the reading public. At that level, we can draw some inferences about the interests of that reading public. No doubt drilling down further into the readership would reveal that different segments of the reading public are more drawn to one or other formulation. At the very least, the marketing of the products implies differential targeting of social strata. Academic outreach under the broader label of "National Learning" (*guoxue* 国学), for example, is occurring in a form reminiscent of continuing education at American universities. Recruitment into such courses is generally targeted to what we might call the elite, business executives, and government officials.[8] Although I mention the target audience where appropriate in what follows, I leave the focus on the varieties of Confucianism appearing in the press.

Among the themes that appear in the writings considered here, the most visible is the use of Confucian ideas in pursuing self-improvement or self-actualization. This constitutes what we might call self-help Confucianism. Certainly a focus on the individual benefit that can be derived from the Confucian tradition is the safest theme, for it is neutral with respect to the political context. In that sense, it does not entail any particular political critique. Certainly the texts that see Confucian thought as a guide for life take that as a source of national pride. That sense of pride, however, is not limited to the self-help genre. It also appears in works that utilize the Confucian tradition as part of a cultural nationalism. Although it appears in a much more direct form in these works, it certainly derives from the rarified academic debates concerning the relationship between *ruxue* 儒学 and the essence of Chinese culture.[9] From this cultural nationalism develops a third theme: Confucianism as China's contribution to a global culture. We can see in various ways an assertion that Confucianism is not simply part of the Chinese national character, but has a more global applicability. Confucians can, to quote the *Yijng*, "transform the world."[10] While cultural optimism does inform the integration of Confucian thought into Chinese cultural nationalism, it also reflects a darker side of the contemporary Chinese experience. In this form, Confucianism is presented as a corrective to the social ills that seem to have emerged with the unraveling of the collectivist spirit of the Maoist era. The impulse to return to tradition thus also responds to an insecurity about the fragility of Chinese society that is never far from the surface. It is in this context that books on Confucianism employ a rhetoric that situates Confucianism as contributing to the creation of the "harmonious society" (*hexie shehui* 和谐社会) that is the special project of China's President Hu Jintao 胡锦涛. Of course, some scholars producing for the popular press remain skeptical that Confucianism has anything to contribute even as they articulate the same concerns about the state of Chinese society.

The Cultural Landscape

The broad outlines of China's twentieth-century cultural crisis have been well described by many scholars.[11] Although there have been, and continue to be, points of heated debate about the nature and significance of that crisis, there is broad agreement on several issues. The trauma of the collapse of the Qing imperium and the subsequent descent into warlordism spurred the critique of traditional culture that developed as part of the May Fourth Movement. The establishment of the People's Republic witnessed the substitution, by a combination of popular enthusiasm and political coercion, of Maoist socialism for both traditional culture and other liberal Western alternatives. The cataclysmic events of the 1960s and 1970s created a cynicism about Maoist culture as a source of legitimate values even as political leadership was passing to reformers who sought to establish a more stable base for Chinese economic and social development. The forces unleashed as part of economic reform have made the process of keeping socialism relevant for Chinese culture all the more difficult. The contradiction between socialist collectivism and free market consumer choice have inspired innovative attempts in both official and unofficial circles to craft a culture that could simultaneously support continued development and provide a basis for social solidarity. The return of interest in traditional intellectual sources—texts, philosophers, and values—is part of that innovation.[12]

The return, however, is also conditioned by a changed institutional context. To be sure, China continues to have a state-controlled media. The government owns much of it and controls what is published and broadcast through both regulation and censorship. Nevertheless, economic reform has changed this landscape in two meaningful ways. First, economic development has been accompanied by a dramatic increase in the number of available media outlets. The growth of the print media in particular has occurred by orders of magnitude. Estimates are that by the late 1980s, 7,000 magazines and journals already were being published in China.[13] Book publishing has more than kept pace. The *China Publishing Yearbook* indicates that in 2008, 136,226 new titles were published at the national level.[14] The same increase in the scope of production is clear in broadcast media. Whereas prior to the reform era, there were only a handful of television stations in the country, all controlled by the central authorities, there are now in excess of 1,500, most of which operate in a competitive relationship with the centrally controlled Chinese Central Television (CCTV).[15] Such numbers render the micromanagement of production by the central government authorities impractical. Too many articles, books, television programs, and radio broadcasts are appearing to allow for pre-dissemination review and clearance, even if we presume that there is at all times a single authoritative viewpoint at the national level. The result is a decentralized environment that requires editors and producers to estimate the limits of acceptability. Those charged with the management of media outlets then have a good deal of responsibility for ensuring that their product will pass scrutiny after the fact. The career implications (such as lost positions or delayed promotions) of mistaken judgment induce those in positions of responsibility to exercise caution when dealing with politically sensitive topics. The hazards of wading into sensitive waters naturally affect the nature of what is disseminated.[16] Evidence from Beijing, for example, suggests that media have played a role in shifting public attitudes away from politics and toward popular and consumer culture.[17] Were it simply a matter of scale, the problem would be a relatively simple one. There would be a race to the banal, leaving larger questions of social stability and cultural direction unaddressed. A second change, however, ensures that complicated issues do appear in the media.

That second change in the landscape concerns the economics of production. Market incentives introduced as part of economic reform have forced publishers and broadcasters to pay greater attention to the consumers of their product (i.e., viewers, listeners, and readers).

The government's decision to defray the cost of media production via the market, meaning either through outright sales of the product in the form of serials and books or via advertising revenue, has given consumers a greater role in determining what is actually produced. The stakes for producers are significant. China's advertising industry is now worth at least 10 billion dollars annually.[18] To maintain the flow of revenue into their enterprises, they must deliver consumers. In this context, lifeless political programming represents a weak business model. Furthermore, evidence is emerging that government offices are themselves motivated by the allure of revenue.[19] The implication of this market mechanism is that producers must consider two different constituencies: government watchdogs and the consuming public. Not surprisingly, they tend to avoid overt political topics in favor of those focused more on individual interests. Whether or not the media have fostered the creation of an apolitical public, as Wang Xin contends, it is clear that there is a resonance between what consumers say interests them and what all types of media actually supply.[20] Nevertheless, there is slippage in the system. Many observers have noted episodes when the government's willingness to allow for greater media openness results in what government regulators, ex post facto, see as transgressive media behavior. One might note, for example, Chinese news coverage during the aftermath of the Wenchuan earthquake of 2008, which began unfettered[21] but soon went afoul of state interests as critical stories about school construction standards began to multiply.[22]

As China's experience of reform has unfolded against the backdrop of growing cynicism over socialism and the changed economics of the media, it is clear that two different, and in some ways contradictory, feelings have emerged. On the one hand, the growth of the Chinese economy and its concomitant enhanced global power have instilled a strong sense of national pride in the public at large. That pride is accompanied by a desire for the international community to recognize China's accomplishment and for China to play a larger cultural role in the globalized world. At the same time, post-1970s cynicism has combined with the unraveling of much of the old social safety net to provoke a sense of insecurity. To the subtle alienation of the Maoist regime woven into the music of someone like Cui Jian 崔健, China's rock 'n' roll pioneer, has been added a suspicion that corruption and selfishness have suffused the society. The works of the popular Confucian revival display all of these aspects, from an apolitical interest in personal realization through cultural pride to social anxiety.

Spreading the Word of Self-Help Confucianism: Yu Dan

The first variety of popularized Confucianism is most widely associated with the now world-famous Yu Dan 于丹. Although her work has been viewed as less sophisticated than that of scholars engaged in the serious academic debates about the Confucian revival and New Confucianism, Yu Dan has made the biggest splash of any of the academics who have endeavored to make traditional values accessible and applicable to the lives of the middle class. This is perhaps not too surprising given her academic training and standing as a professor in and chair of Beijing Normal University's Department of Cinema, Television, and Media (*Yingshi chuanmei xi* 影视传媒系). Her series of televised lectures on the *Analects* was a cultural phenomenon and was followed quickly by its publication under the title *Yu Dan* Lunyu *xinde* 于丹《论语》心得 (*Yu Dan's Wisdom from the Analects*).[23] Her celebrity has also led to a growing international presence. Not only has her *Lunyu xinde* been translated into English,[24] but she was also invited to Japan for a speaking tour. The Chinese version of the lecture that she delivered in Japan is included in a work produced by Kong Jian 孔健, an independent researcher with professional ties to Japan: *Lunyu li* 论语力 (*The Power of the Analects*).[25] These two works, the *Lunyu xinde* and the *Lunyu li*, reveal much about how to make Confucius relevant in contemporary China.[26] Daniel Bell has discussed at some length the reasons for her success and offered an evaluation of her *Lunyu xinde*. He points out that it simultaneously responds to contemporary concerns over materialism and offers a politically conservative interpretation of the text.[27] The material she contributed to the *Lunyu li* adds dimensions that I think make much clearer her larger vision. It is certainly not an academically sophisticated argument about the import of the *Analects*, but it does fit well the market that she is addressing.

Her main interest is providing her readers with advice on achieving a happy life. It is clearly not aimed at a restructuring of Chinese governance. It is unlikely that her readers are looking for an interpretation that challenges the contemporary political structure. They are looking for a way, as Bell notes, to make good decisions and lead a happy life. Take this passage from the "Way of Friendship" chapter of the *Lunyu xinde*:

> What kind of friends one has reflects directly the kind of person he or she is. If you want to understand someone,

it is enough simply to examine the person's social circle. From that you can see his value orientation. This is what we often say: "Things group according to their type, and people separate according to group." People often say, "When you're at home, rely on your parents; when you are away, rely on your friends." Friends are, without doubt, extremely important in one's social activities. A friend is like a book: if you go through him, you can open the entire world."[28]

This introduction to the chapter lays out its thrust. At one level, it is seductive because it relies on common wisdom (we might say clichés), but, more importantly, it presents the opportunity to use the remainder of the chapter to explore the practical concern set up in this introduction: How does one choose friends so as to get the most out of one's interactions in the social world? Although Bell is correct that there is no need to see Yu as simply utilitarian, Yu explicates the concrete benefits of each type of friend much more than the original *Analects* passage or its traditional subcommentary.[29] While one suspects that this also addresses her readers' fears that trust has broken down in the society, because Yu devotes most of the chapter to analyzing the *Analects'* three categories of desirable friends: the upright (*zhi* 直), trustworthy (*liang* 良), and knowledgeable (*duowen* 多闻), the practical benefits (as opposed to the moral benefits) naturally rise to the fore. Thus, readers discover that each has its particular benefit for the reader, both psychological and practical. Both Yu and the original *Analects* passage are concerned with the impact of friends on one's character. Yu's formulation has a more immediately functional aspect. Upright friends "can give you courage when you are timid and also can give you resolution at your moments of hesitation." When we have trustworthy friends, on the other hand, "our spirits can obtain purification and refinement."[30] Most striking are the benefits of knowledgeable friends: "Making a connection with a knowledgeable friend is like owning a very thick encyclopedia dictionary: We can always obtain useful reference points from among his experiences."[31]

Her reflections on friendship are an instance of the larger interest in using traditional sources to steer a course through everyday life. Thus, the core of the *Analects'* message is its advice for dealing with trials and tribulations:

In every person's life, it is difficult to avoid regrets and disappointments. We may be powerless to change this reality, but what we can change is the attitude with which we regard these affairs. One of the essences of the *Analects* is that it tells us how we can use a calm attitude to deal with life's regrets and difficulties.[32]

This passage comes from the chapter on "The Way of the Soul" (*xinling zhi dao* 心灵之道). One way of reading this is as an acceptance of the status quo. The point of reading the *Analects* is not to figure out how to change reality; it is to learn how to accept it. Indeed, in each of the chapters we find an emphasis on the development of mental resources for confronting the world as it is. The chapter on ideals, for example, begins by explicitly moving away from the grand vision of Confucian political transformation (i.e., the connection between cultivating the self, regulating the family, ordering the state, and pacifying the world) to the mental foundation of realizing one's personal dreams: "Regardless of whether your dreams (*lixiang* 理想) are great or small, the foundation of realizing all dreams lies in finding the genuine feelings in one's heart."[33] Ultimately, the *Analects* provides advice that will lead to an effective and valuable life. As her final sentence puts it, "This is probably the ultimate meaning provided by the *Analects*: it allows those types of classical spiritual strengths to smoothly come together into an element of effectiveness within the rules of modernity, and it allows every one of us to genuinely establish a life that has efficiency (*xiaolü* 效率) and value (*jiazhi* 价值)."[34]

These passages are clear evidence that Yu's interest is not so much in Confucian theory as in the genre of self-help. Any trip to a Chinese bookstore indicates that the self-help genre is a dominant one in publishing today. Yu's market strength derives from her ability to speak persuasively to readers of this material. It is not her academic research into Confucian theory but her choice of a Confucianized psychology as a way of touching her readers that makes her significant in the popular revival of traditional ideas.

If the *Lunyu xinde* provides the basis for a self-help Confucianism, *Lunyu li* elaborates both rhetoric of the former as well as its relationship to the wider phenomenon of "National Learning." Kong Jian packaged Yu's trip to Japan and the lecture she delivered there by reaffirming its usefulness in everyday life to sell Confucianism to the book's readers. In this case, the effort was aimed at two different national communities because the work consists of Chinese versions of lectures delivered to Japanese audiences in Japan. In the process, both Yu and Kong place the value of the *Analects* in an international context and show that it can be part of a larger cultural conversation.

In his sections, Kong Jian is more explicit about the need to meet the readers where they are if Confucianism is going to be made relevant to their lives. His thoughts on this are particularly evident in his consideration of how to present Confucian ideas to the public. He signals the connection between self-realization and pedagogy by borrowing rhetoric from American self-help writing. In his chapter titled "Confucius' Experience in Teaching: Chicken Soup for the Soul Is Inherited from Here," Kong draws the following conclusion from his discussion of why Confucius answered the same question differently depending on his students' situations and temperaments:

> From Confucius' experience in teaching, we should be inspired to undertake an investigation of the reading, listening, and viewing audiences of magazines, radio stations, television stations, and publishers to understand their situations in order to strengthen the focus of our teaching.[35]

Kong then criticizes large Chinese media outlets for lacking public relations departments devoted to handling audience letters. From such correspondence, it would be possible, he argues, to know what the audience likes, dislikes, and wants to see. Such information could then form the basis of media plans and future production. What is interesting about this argument is the contrast between its aims and the passages from which he draws the conclusion. The *Analects* passages record how Confucius tailored his message to the needs of his students. Kong has taken that student-centered educational approach and turned it into a programming feedback mechanism, the presumption being that this will refine the effectiveness of the Confucian message. Of course, one cannot miss the other aspect of Kong's interpretation, namely that the Master has something to teach media production outlets. Nevertheless, this is not exactly the kind of individualized instruction that the Master practiced. It is teaching tailored to the collective needs of the audience.

Despite Kong's call for more feedback to identify the needs of the audience, Yu Dan focuses on a central characteristic shared by her viewers and readers: they are modern. Their changed historical condition requires an adjustment of the message. In the lecture she delivered in Japan, she does not stray very far from the ideas of the

Lunyu xinde, but she introduces the problem of technological society as their context:

> Everyone one of us modern people live in the twenty-first century and our material conditions are far more developed than over two thousand years ago. Our technology is also extremely advanced, but for many of us our lives are becoming more and more exhausting, more and more confusing. Instead, our souls have no peace or feeling of happiness.[36]

Here we have the same goal of psychological tranquility; however, she develops a more eclectic vision than in her earlier work on the *Analects*. New Confucians are right to view her as advancing a different agenda. In the *Lunyu li*, she explicitly pairs Confucian values with the benefits of a spirituality based on the Daoism of Zhuangzi. Taken together, Yu Dan's work sees the tradition as a whole as providing an antidote to the pressures of modern society. A willingness to present multiple aspects of the tradition for "popular" consumption is certainly not unique (one can point to the array of courses offered in Beijing University's Qianyuan National Learning Classroom),[37] and her reconciliation of the tensions between Confucianism and Daoism is, frankly, not very original. She sees them as complementary, enacting Confucian values when at work and Daoist when on one's own time. Her contribution, however, is that she has formulated this eclecticism so that it can resonate with audiences that are looking to minimize the pressures of the frenetic, modern life.

The changed circumstances give license to tailor Confucian values to the concerns of her readers. When we look at her interpretation of some of Confucius's cardinal virtues, we see reflections of the twenty-first century. Thus, respect (*jing* 敬) secures the goodwill of others; tolerance (*kuan* 宽) earns the love of others; trust (*xin* 信) brings the assistance of others in a competitive environment; insight (*min* 敏) provides the ability to rescue a bad situation; and, finally, beneficence (*hui* 惠) is essential to being a skilled leader. Yu's Confucianism is not fundamentally alienated from the ranks of corporate management. Her easy assumption of the right to adjust the Confucian message extends to the status of the Master himself: she prefers to see Confucius as a "beloved, plain and warm-hearted elder" rather than an unerring sage.[38]

If the *Lunyu xinde* and Yu Dan's contribution to the *Lunyu li* focus largely on the personal benefits that derive from reading the *Analects*, the *Lunyu li* also folds in the larger issues of popular pride and social anxiety. The pride appears in her confident assertions that the Confucian tradition transcends China and constitutes a larger East Asian culture, one that also encompasses Japan.[39] But that culture ultimately derives its power from her sense that Confucian culture is a vital resource for solving contemporary social problems. This is because it is never very far from the surface. Indeed, she explains the current "Confucian fever" (*ruxue re* 儒学热) as deriving from the fact that Confucian culture is part of China's "cultural genes" (*wenhua jiyin* 文化基因).[40] No problem, however, is more obvious than the factiousness of contemporary society. To address that, Yu argues for an explicit connection between the social values of Confucianism and the construction of "harmonious social relations" (*hexie de guanxi*).[41] The obvious echo of the current formulation of the Chinese government's ideological goals is simply another manifestation of the shared recognition that social relations are fraying as economic development continues in the current century.

Confucianism in Comparative Perspective: The Vision of Cai Degui

Yu Dan's tour of Japan naturally triggered reflections on the pan-East Asian value of the Confucian message, but that was not her primary focus. Others have taken up the problem of the relationship between the Confucian tradition and the wider world more systematically. One example is the work of Cai Degui. His approach is laid out in a book of comparative religion with the provocative title *Confucius versus Jesus*.[42] Unlike Yu Dan, who forthrightly acknowledges that she is first and foremost a scholar of media studies and that her interpretations of Confucius's message are not based on rigorous "National Studies" (*guoxue* 国学) training, Cai Degui 蔡德贵 was trained in comparative religion and has served at length in a series of academic institutions devoted to Confucian Studies in the People's Republic. In that capacity, he has participated in some of the academic debates that John Makeham describes.[43] His *Confucius versus Jesus* is a logical expression of his desire to present his scholarship to a larger audience in a more accessible format. But this is not a work aimed at self-realization. Instead of offering advice on how to succeed in life, Cai reassures his readers that the Chinese tradition, and specifically Confucianism, will play a vital role in the development of global society. He thereby shifts the focus from the individual to the culture.[44]

To demonstrate the continued relevance of Confucian tradition, Cai must first explain how it relates to other intellectual and cultural systems. He grounds his interpretation of that relationship in a very particular vision of the nature of Confucian learning. For Cai, the essential nature of the Confucian tradition is that it has constantly developed via intellectual exchange throughout its history:

> Looked at from the viewpoint of cultural exchange (*wenhua jiaoliu* 文化交流), we should even more regard Confucianism (*ru xue* 儒学) as a dynamic intellectual system (*sixiang tixi* 思想体系). Treating the development of Confucianism with an open mind, it continuously absorbed elements from outside intellectual cultures to complete, augment, and develop the thinking of Confucians (*ru jia* 儒家).[45]

Here, Confucianism's ability to respond to its changing circumstances is derived directly from its history of absorbing elements from other traditions. Cai writes the history of Confucianism in terms of a series of transformations, the central feature of which is cultural exchange.

Thus, he argues that there historically have been five forms of Confucianism, each corresponding to a different epoch: (1) exclusive devotion to Confucian techniques (*ru shu duzun xing* 儒术独尊型). This period culminated in the Han dynasty's designation of the Confucian school as the official ideology of the state, but the development to that point was marked by intellectual exchange, be it that resulting from Confucius's and Mencius's travel in the Eastern Zhou or the amalgamation of Confucian thought with correlative cosmology in the Han; (2) Confucian and Daoist mutual augmentation (*ru dao hubu xing* 儒道互补型), which was most marked in the Wei-Jin period, saw the impact of new forms of Daoist practice; (3) Three Teachings Syncretism (*sanjiao he yi xing* 三教合一型), in which Confucianism was influenced by efforts to reconcile it with Buddhist and Daoist ideas, stretched from the Song dynasty to the late Ming; (4) the Confluence of the Four Teachings (*sijiao huitong xing* 四教会通型) occurred from the late Ming into the Qing and witnessed mutual influences of two distinct varieties, a Confucian-Daoist-Buddhist-Christian one and a Confucian-Daoist-Buddhist-Islam one; and (5) Multiple Source Fusion (*duoyuan ronghe xing* 多元融合型) represents the last and ongoing stage in which Confucian scholars of all varieties are in the process of fusing Eastern and Western traditions.[46]

A certain optimism suffuses Cai's presentation. He does not, for example, address the question of whether some essential truths are lost in the process of development. Instead, he presents Confucianism's continuing evolution as one of its strengths and sees that process continuing into the present day. The implication of this is that the teachings still have value:

> However, Confucianism is not fixed and unchanging. Confucianism was able to follow the changes in the ages and continuously change form. Therefore, from the Warring States to the Qing dynasty, there were the Confucian schools of different eras such as the Han Confucians, the Tang Confucians, the Song Confucians, the Ming Confucians, the Qing Confucians and others. Since the modern era, the New Confucians have appeared.[47]

The assertion that Confucianism changes over time is an important one in setting up the next step in his argument. While certainly there is a sense that earlier Confucianism had feudal elements unsuited to the modern era (in this he echoes Yu Dan's interest in a Confucianism suited to contemporary life), Cai's invocation of an evolving tradition emerges as part of his vision of Confucianism as a world tradition that has made contributions to an ever-widening circle of countries beginning with Korea and ultimately reaching the West.[48] He can therefore conclude that Confucianism has a broader historical destiny. To that end, he provides a number of reasons why he believes that Confucian thinkers will inevitably play a leading role in the emerging global society. His third reason is fairly explicit:

> Spiritual elements are even more important than material ones, and Confucian culture (*rujia wenhua* 儒家文化) excels at spiritual culture (*jingshen wenhua* 精神文化). Therefore, the world culture of the future will certainly be the result of the spiritual nurturing of Eastern Confucians. This is truly a logical inevitability.[49]

The argument is perhaps not as ironclad as Cai asserts here, but the passage is good evidence that he is responding to a deeper insecurity in his and his audience's mind, namely that there is a danger that Western tradition, embodied in Christianity, will render the Chinese tradition irrelevant. As a scholar of comparative religion, he defends passionately the idea that the Confucian tradition is fundamental to the future of world culture. In making that defense, he can reassure his readers that pride in China's material accomplishments will be accompanied by a corresponding spiritual influence. In a sense, he projects a reversal of the logic of "spiritual pollution" that has worried Party officials since reform began. In response to their concern that economic development on the Western model would bring Western bourgeois culture into China, Cai suggests that the success of that development is setting the stage for the flow of cultural influence outward from China.

Cai's explanation of why future world culture will necessarily emerge from the interaction and exchange of cultural influences between the major world civilizations appears in his penultimate chapter, "Confucius' Chopsticks and Jesus' Knife and Fork." Cai has crafted his argument around the entertaining metaphor of culinary customs, one that is sure to appeal to the well-developed Chinese penchant for food imagery. In the chapter, Cai associates the major world cultures with specific eating methods: the Chinese with chopsticks, Indian and Arabic culture with fingers, and Western culture with knives and forks. He then maps these eating methods onto particular intellectual characteristics that he associates with them. All are ultimately necessary for the continued stability of the world community:

> China's chopsticks represent a unified Nature [derived] from an integrated mode of thought. What it produces is a developed spirit of human culture. Fingers represent the Indian [Hindu] and Arab Islamic cultures. They are [ones that] personally verify Nature. They can be called the school of personally verifying Nature. What they create is a type of dialectical thought. One result derived from dialectical thought is the special development of the religious spirit. The method of thinking utilized by Westerners, who use knives and forks to eat, is analytical logic. What results from this method of analytical logic is a dissected Nature. Because of this, natural science and the scientific spirit are especially developed. Now today, we should meld the three great cultures into one body—that is use chopsticks, fingers, and knives and forks. Afterwards, having unified them organically, we can thus have hope for this world.[50]

Earlier, he had put the same argument in more familiar Chinese
ideological terms when he asserted that bringing together the scientific
spirit of the West, the religious spirit of India and Arabia, and the
cultural spirit of China would result in a "harmonious society consisting
of a single body with three strands."[51] If we put aside the temptation
to see the reference to the harmonious society ideal as merely a nod
to political power, we see that Cai's formula presents an idealistic
vision in which Confucianism plays the leading role in assuring world
harmony precisely because it is, by its very nature, a tradition that
excels in integration.

In the end, Cai offers his readers a reassuring vision in which
China's particular contribution to world culture will continue to be
central to its survival, thereby validating the culture from which it is
derived. The elegance of his presentation lies in the way the Confucian
contribution to world culture depends on its ability to engage in
meaningful exchange with other traditions—something that, in Cai's
view, its history demonstrates is its fundamental nature. He concludes
his work by citing Tu Wei-ming's belief that Confucianism is already
influencing other world religions, producing such hybrids as Confucian
Christianity and a Confucian Buddhism.[52]

The Iconoclastic Commentary of Li Ling

Finally, we end with an examination of a more skeptical assessment of
Confucianism's role in contemporary China in Li Ling's iconoclastic
look at the *Analects*: his *Stray Dog: My Reading of the Analects*. Not all
academics view their scholarly enterprise as an opportunity to extol the
value of the Confucian tradition. Li Ling offers a different avenue for
addressing the challenges of the modern world. As a scholar, Li has a
reputation for being circumspect in his views on the issues surrounding
the New Confucian movement.[53] His *Stray Dog: My Reading of the
Analects*, however, displays his talent for provocation and iconoclasm,
done in the somewhat unlikely form of an extended commentary and
analysis of the *Analects*.[54] He uses these postures to reject the need for
Confucian values to address social problems.

Yu Dan, Kong Jian, and Cai Degui demonstrate that they
understand many of the concerns of the wider reading public, but Li
Ling touches much more intimately on the cynicism that has brought
about the sense among Chinese intelligentsia that it now confronts a
spiritual void and the potential disintegration of social order. The target

audience is consequently a much more restricted one. It is difficult to see how *Stray Dog* could appeal to the same audience held rapt by Yu Dan's *Lunyu xinde*.

Li acknowledges the alienation at the root of his project from the outset. His preface makes easy reference to subversive pop culture elements to suggest his point of departure. Take, for example, his explanation for why he was uninterested in reading the *Analects* in his youth. As someone born in 1948, he could have used the political imperatives of the Cultural Revolution, notably the movement to criticize Confucius, to explain his disinterest. Instead, he was simply apathetic.[55] He sees himself as an "egg hatched by the Red Flag" (*hongqi xia di dan* 红旗下的蛋), using Cui Jian's 崔健 memorable lyric, and recognizes his own contrarian tendencies:

> In the past, there was another reason that I was not fond of reading the *Analects*: I don't like to listen to others preach. When people get a little older, they believe they have passed through the vast ocean and can then act as moral teachers, but I think being old is not honorable. When I see someone speaking such words and writing whatever life philosophy, my scalp becomes numb.[56]

Instead, Li prefers to go his own way. Yet he does so with a serious purpose. His lighthearted self-deprecation notwithstanding, he lays the groundwork for a direct assault on the foundations of the Confucian revivalist logic.

He recognizes the rhetorical power of invoking Confucius as a moral exemplar and believes that within the current "Confucius Fever" (*Kongzi re* 孔子热) that is sweeping the country, the name of "Confucius" is simply a slogan that rests on a flimsy foundation.[57] Li rejects the grand claims made under that slogan:

> It is a mistake to say that, if one doesn't read the *Analects*, one can't become a person, or that contemporary human hearts are so bad (as in sinking into corruption, manufacturing and selling counterfeit medicine, or selling chemically reddened duck eggs) entirely because they don't read the *Analects* and don't respect Confucius.[58]

Ultimately, then, he is not particularly interested in spreading Confucianism throughout the world. Yet his critique is more

substantive than simple discomfort with the grandiose claims of
Confucian enthusiasts. This also explains his choice of a commentary
on the *Analects* itself as his vehicle. Unlike Yu Dan, Li constructs his
commentary not to identify the contemporary value of the tradition, but
rather to debunk myths about Confucius. Unfortunately, this will make
solutions to personal and social problems much more complicated.

The question of how to understand Confucius and his vision is
central to Li's purpose. His reading of the *Analects* reveals a Confucius
with very particular characteristics. He is a man who was emphatically,
by his own definition, *not* a sage. Li takes seriously Confucius's use of
terminology and his own sense of his role. In the *Analects*, he finds a
work primarily focused on the ideal of holding office to benefit society.
Li notes that all the Sages whom Confucius identifies were rulers
of the past who exercised real political power with intelligence and
thereby ordered the world.[59] Confucius was incapable of either feat:
he held no position of power and did not materially affect conditions
in his own day. In fact, Confucius recognized that there were no sages
in his own day and that his mission had failed. Hence, Li titles his
commentary *Stray Dog* after an episode recorded in the *Shiji* in which
Confucius recognized that his lack of success and his alienation from
the world gave him the appearance of a stray. In this, Li sees a larger
metaphor for the position of intellectuals:

> When Confucius lost hope in his ancestral state, alone he
> uttered the lament about "floating on the ocean and living
> amidst barbarians."[60] But having worked with feudal lords
> everywhere, there wasn't one who took him up on it. At last
> he returned to the land of his birth. In his later years, he
> was brokenhearted year after year. He buried his son and
> lamented the appearance of the *qilin*,[61] while Yan Hui 颜
> 回 died and Zhongyou 仲由 passed away,[62] so that he cried
> his tears dry. He died in his home, but he had no family.
> Regardless of whether his thought was correct or mistaken,
> in his person, I see the fate of intellectuals.

> Any person who cherishes an ideal and who cannot find a
> spiritual home is a stray dog.[63]

In the end, Li has a very clear sense of the limited potential of
intellectuals for productive political action. Advocates for the political

leadership of intellectuals are caught on the horns of a dilemma: the platonic ideal of a philosopher-king does not work in government, but the will of the people does not guarantee that the ruling class will possess intellectual heft.[64]

Li's critique of the Confucian intellectual revival is a more far-reaching one because he sees that the Confucianism that is being channeled into the present is not ultimately the original doctrine. He makes the same observation as Yu Dan and Cai Degui—that modern Confucianism is a changed doctrine, but he is looking at it from a far more pessimistic standpoint. The revival of tradition and Confucianism depends on ideas imported in the modern era, and therefore what seems like tradition is actually a modern creation:

> What is the national essence (*guocui* 国粹)? "National essence" arose because of Westernization. Westernization was pushed from the coast to the interior and from the cities to the villages. Every place that Westernization could not reach and remaining points that were not changed are what we call "national essence." Martial arts and prognostication, Chinese medical practice and Chinese medicine, poor and remote Chinatowns, regional operas that old people like to listen to, and every type of prostration by foolish husbands and wives are even more the national essence among national essences (not all traditions are "national essences"; many are the national dregs).[65]

It is in this light that Li is scornful of attempts to foster a broader modern synthesis of Chinese and Western civilizations. These are ultimately naive because they are based on a series of self-deceptions about Western civilization that overemphasize Western individualism, Western alienation from nature, and Western neglect of the family.[66] Yet Li Ling recognizes that the advocacy of Chinese values in the world is symptomatic of a moral crisis. The fact that people are talking about them suggests that the society lacks them.[67] A simplistic advocacy of an artificially constructed moral and religious system like the Confucian revival will not erase that reality.

So what, then, does Li present as the alternative? Although his is an iconoclastic account based on careful scholarship about the text, *Stray Dog* does have a liberating quality to it. Li speaks well the language of cynicism and recognizes the existential crisis that contemporary Chinese face. Moreover, he suggests that Chinese society has the resources to save itself without the Confucian revival: "Confucius cannot save China, and he cannot save the world. There has never been a ruler who saved the world, and we do not rely on an immortal emperor. If we want to create happiness for humanity, we rely completely on ourselves."[68] Li thus ends on an optimistic note, one that is made possible by his careful textual scholarship debunking much of the revival mythology. No doubt he appeals to a different market segment than Yu, Kong, or Cai, but he shares a similar cultural angst, a concern with the fractiousness of Chinese society and how to correct it.

Conclusion

The idea of negotiation is a useful one for interpreting the popularity of published books dealing with the Confucian tradition. That university professors see this as a worthwhile enterprise argues for the presence of a significant market for such works.[69] Publishers also recognize this or they would not devote scarce resources to the effort. The question is how to translate the potentially dry academic subject of Confucianism to the popular audience. These four authors found that connection, whether it be through the language of self-help, the language of popular cultural self-validation, or the iconoclast's penchant for challenging sacred truths. These texts all imply a readership that has benefited from the remarkable success of economic reform but that harbors lingering doubts about the implications of the changes in society from which they are benefiting.

One other axis of negotiation lurks in the background here. That is the negotiation between market demand and politically sensitive subjects. Whether or not the government of the People's Republic is moving to more explicitly embrace Confucian tradition, discussions of social order and political effectiveness are topics to be approached with caution, market or no market. Publishers want to sell books and authors want to reach readers, but that is not possible if the politics are too far out of sync with the leadership. It is not surprising, then, that at least two of the works discussed here (Yu/Kong and Cai) hitch their Confucian arguments to the ideal of the "harmonious society." That is an ideal that even the politically cynical recognize as a broader popular aspiration. Li Ling's circumspect analysis of the limitations of the intellectual's role in politics is a similar way to blunt his call for everyone to take responsibility for bringing about human happiness.

Notes

1. I would like to acknowledge the insightful comments by Anna M. Shields, Josephine Chiu-Duke, and Huaiyu Chen on an earlier draft of this essay.

2. John Makeham, *Lost Soul: "Confucianism" in Contemporary Chinese Academic Discourse* (Cambridge: Harvard University Asia Center, 2008) provides an excellent overview and analysis of the debates surrounding the emergence of New Confucianism.

3. Preeti Bhattacharji, Carin Zissis, and Corinne Baldwin, "Media Censorship in China," Council on Foreign Relations, accessed September 9, 2010, http://www.cfr.org/publication/11515/media_censorship_in_china.html.

4. Reporters Without Borders, "China," Reporters Without Borders, accessed September 9, 2010, http://en.rsf.org/report-china,57.html.

5. Commentators acknowledge that the government has not been completely consistent and that it recognizes a tension between the utility and the danger of press freedom. See comments by Elizabeth Economy quoted in Bhattacharji et al., "Media Censorship in China."

6. Ying Zhu, *Television in Post-Reform China: Serial Dramas, Confucian Leadership, and the Global Television Market* (London: Routledge, 2008), xvii–xviii discusses this type of negotiation in television production.

7. The audience here is essentially the emergent Chinese middle class, those with the resources needed to consume both culture materials produced and respond to the material incentives with which they are bundled. One estimate is that this middle class consists of approximately 100 million individuals, though to be sure, more than that do come in contact with various media, especially broadcast and Internet media. For the estimate of the size of the middle class and the categories of people included in it, see Xin Wang, "Seeking Channels for Engagement: Media Use and Political Communication by China's Rising Middle Class," *China: An International Journal* 7, no. 1 (March 2009): 31–32 and 39–41. Note that population statistics justify the use of the adjective urban since 100 million constitutes less that 10 percent of the population, but the middle class constitutes 20 to 25 percent of the Beijing population (42). Of course, statistics on China's middle class are a moving target. Janice Hua Xu, "Building a Chinese 'Middle Class': Consumer Education and Identity Construction in Television Land," in *TV China*, ed. Ying Zhu and Chris Berry (Bloomington: Indiana University Press, 2009), 152 cites a report by the Chinese Academy of Social Sciences estimating that the middle class forms 19 percent of the Chinese population. That calculation would yield a middle class numbering approximately 247 million.

8. A good example is Beijing University's "Heavenly National Learning Classroom" (*Qianyuan guoxue jiaoshi* 乾元国学教室). Its Web site advertises courses that cost RMB ¥48000, and the eligibility qualifications include education at or above a bachelor's degree and a career in business or

government: Beijing University, "Qianyuan guoxue jiaoshi," Beijing daxue 北京大学, accessed September 9, 2010, http://www.qianyuangx.com/pkugx.jsp. I am indebted to Huaiyu Chen for pointing this out to me.

9. Makeham, *Lost Soul*, 9–17, esp. 15–17.

10. Ruan Yuan 阮元 et al., *Shisanjing zhushu fu jiaokan ji* 十三经注疏附校勘记 (1935 repr. Beijing: Zhonghua shuju, 1980), 37(3).

11. An accessible account of the intellectual aspects of the transformation from imperium to the threshold of economic reform appears in Jonathan Spence, *The Gate of Heavenly Peace: The Chinese and Their Revolution, 1895–1980* (Harmondsworth: Penguin Books, 1981).

12. In this context, Edward Gu's account of the development of what he terms "cultural space" in the 1980s is of interest: Edward X. Gu, "Cultural Intellectuals and the Politics of the Cultural Public Space in Communist China (1979–1989): A Case Study of Three Intellectual Groups," *Journal of Asian Studies* 58, no. 2 (1999): 389–431.

13. David S. G. Goodman, "Contending the Popular: Party-State and Culture," *positions* 9, no. 1 (2001): 248 (accessed via Project Muse).

14. Zhongguo chuban gongzuozhe xiehui 中国出版工作者协会, ed. *Zhongguo chuban nianjian* 中国出版年鉴 (Beijing: Zhongguo chuban nianjian she, 2008).

15. Xiaoling Zhang, "Seeking Effective Public Space: Chinese Media at the Local Level," *China: An International Journal* 5, no. 1 (March 2007): 55–56.

16. Jonathan Hassid's notion of the "regime of uncertainty" is instructive here. The absence of clear guidelines creates a stronger impulse to self-censorship: Jonathan Hassid, "Controlling the Chinese Media: An Uncertain Business," *Asian Survey* 48, no. 3 (2008): 423–424 (accessed through JSTOR).

17. Wang, "Seeking Channels for Engagement," 55–56.

18. The scale of advertising in the new economy is clearly significant. The actual figure is a little harder to pin down. Gao Zhihong, "What's in a Name? On China's Search for Socialist Advertising," *Advertising and Society Review* 4, no. 3 (2003) (accessed via Project Muse) gives a figure of US$9.6 billion for advertising "turnover" in 2001. Hassid ("Controlling the Chinese Media, 416) cites a figure of $18 billion in advertising revenue for the "Chinese news business" in 2005. In any event, the jump from no advertising before reform to more than $10 billion represents a fundamental change in the business model of the industry.

19. Xiaoling Zhang, "Seeking Effective Public Space," 56 notes the tension between central and local governments over access to political publicity and revenues via local television programming.

20. Wang, "Seeking Channels for Engagement," 52–53.

21. Even the US government praised this aspect of the Chinese government's response: Stephen Kaufman, "China's Government Praised for Easing Media Restrictions," America.gov, May 20, 2008, accessed September

10, 2010, http://www.america.gov/st/freepress-english/2008/May/2008052015
3034esnamfuak0.7039911.html.

22. Qian Gang, "Looking Back on Chinese Media Reporting of School Collapses," China Media Project, Journalism and Media Studies Centre, The University of Hong Kong, posted May 7, 2009, accessed September 10, 2010, http://cmp.hku.hk/2009/05/07/1599/.

23. Yu Dan, *Yu Dan* Lunyu *xinde* 于丹《论语》心得 (Beijing: Zhonghua shuju, 2006).

24. Yu Dan, *Confucius from the Heart: Ancient Wisdom for Today's World*, trans. Esther Tyldesley (New York: Atria Books, 2009).

25. Yu Dan 于丹 and Kong Jian 孔健, *Lunyu li: Yu Dan Lunyu Fusang xing* 论语力：于丹《论语》扶桑行 (*The Power of the Analects: Yu Dan's Analects Trip to Japan*) (Beijing: Xin shijie chubanshe, 2008). The degree of collaboration between Yu and Kong is a problematic question. The two are currently engaged in a legal dispute over whether or not Kong had authorization to publish a number of books resulting from their interaction. See, for example, Zhong Gang 钟刚, "Kongzi houren Kong Jian bei Yu Dan zhikong qinquan, shouci xiangshu shijian shimo" 孔子后人孔健 被于丹指控侵权首次详述事件始末, Sohu.com, June 3, 2010, accessed September 10, 2010, http://yule.sohu.com/20100603/n272542569.shtml; and Beijing Morning News (Beijing chenbao 北京晨报), "Shi qinquan haishi 'shuo hao de' de hezuo? Yu Dan Kong Jian wei li fanlian?" 是侵权还是'说好的'的合作？于丹孔健为利翻脸？ www.chinanews.com.cn, June 3, 2010, accessed September 10, 2010, http://www.chinanews.com.cn/cul/news/2010/06-03/2320320.shtml. Because my interest is mostly in the way the ideas are presented, the ongoing dispute does not fundamentally alter the analysis, though I am careful to distinguish between the two authors when referring to the *Lunyu li*. I am grateful to Josephine Chiu-Duke for calling the dispute to my attention.

26. As is evident below, however, Yu is far from having an exclusive interest in Confucius. She followed up *Lunyu xinde* with a companion set of lectures on Zhuangzi: *Yu Dan* Zhuangzi *xinde* 于丹《庄子》心得 (Beijing: Minzhu fazhi chubanshe, 2007).

27. Daniel Bell, *China's New Confucianism: Politics and Everyday Life in a Changing Society* (Princeton: Princeton University Press, 2008), 163–174.

28. Yu, *Lunyu xinde*, 68. Translations are mine unless otherwise indicated.

29. The original passage is *Analects* 16.4: Ruan, *Shisanjing zhushu*, 2521(3).

30. These two quotes appear on *Lunyu xinde*, 69.

31. Yu, *Lunyu xinde*, 70.

32. Yu, *Lunyu xinde*, 20.

33. Yu, *Lunyu xinde*, 84.

34. Yu, *Lunyu xinde*, 117.

35. Yu Dan and Kong Jian, *Lunyu li*, 149.

36. Yu and Kong, *Lunyu li*, 21.

37. Beijing University, "Qianyuan guoxue jiaoshi," Beijing daxue 北京大学, http://www.qianyuangx.com/pkugx.jsp.

38. Yu and Kong, *Lunyu li*, 223.

39. Yu and Kong, *Lunyu li*, 231. Makeham has noted the thorny philosophical problem with New Confucian efforts to interpret Confucianism as essential to East Asian culture: see Makeham, 92–94.

40. Yu and Kong, *Lunyu li*, 222.

41. Yu and Kong, *Lunyu li*, 25. An explicit reference to the "harmonious society" slogan appears on page 231.

42. Cai Degui 蔡德贵, *Kongzi vs. Jidu* 孔子 vs. 基督 (Beijing: Shijie zhishi chubanshe, 2008).

43. Makeham, *Lost Soul*, 92–93 and 111.

44. The presumed audience for his work is an interesting question. Clearly, by presenting a fairly abstract argument about the history of Confucianism and its role in the world, he is aiming at a more reflective audience than is Yu Dan. The presence in the text of homey examples and the occasional cartoon illustration suggests, however, that he and the publisher still have a popular, nonacademic audience in mind.

45. Cai, *Kongzi vs. Jidu*, 31.

46. The epochs and their characteristics are described at some length in Cai, *Kongzi vs. Jidu*, 31–53.

47. Cai, *Kongzi vs. Jidu*, 45

48. Much of his evidence for the historical and global influence of Confucian thought is presented in his final chapter: *Kongzi vs. Jidu*, 195–251.

49. Cai, *Kongzi vs. Jidu*, 231.

50. Cai, *Kongzi vs. Jidu*, 192.

51. Cai, *Kongzi vs. Jidu*, 191.

52. Cai, *Kongzi vs. Jidu*, 265. This follows from an examination of the emergence of what Cai calls Confucian Christians (*Rujia Jidu tu* 儒家基督徒).

53. Makeham, *Lost Soul*, 217–218. The list of professors engaged in the New Confucian movement who have begun to meet a market hunger for popularizations could easily be expanded. For example, the very active participant in the New Confucian debates, Guo Qiyong, is one of three authors of the following: Fu Peirong 傅佩荣, Guo Qiyong 郭齐勇, and Kong Xianglin 孔祥林, *Kongzi jiu jiang* 孔子九讲 (Beijing: Zhonghua shuju, 2008). This consists of published versions of lectures given by the authors on Shandong Satellite Television. For Guo Qiyong's contributions to the New Confucian debates, see Makeham, *Lost Soul*, 133–138 and passim.

54. Li Ling 李零, *Sangjia gou: wo du Lunyu* 丧家狗: 我读《论语》 (Taiyuan: Shanxi renmin chubanshe, 2008).

55. Li, *Sangjia gou*, preface, 3–4.

56. Li, *Sangjia gou*, preface, 4.

57. Li, *Sangjia gou*, preface, 5.

58. Li, *Sangjia gou*, preface, 4.

59. Li, *Sangjia gou*, 345.

60. A reference to his travels looking for a worthy ruler.

61. This refers to the event that inspired Confucius to stop writing the *Spring and Autumn Annals*. The inauspiciousness of the appearance of the benevolent *qilin* when there was no benevolent ruler on the throne implied the decline of the Way of the Zhou dynasty. See Ruan, *Shisanjing zhushu*, 2172(2).

62. This refers to the deaths of his disciples, especially his favorite, Yan Hui. See *Analects* 11.9.

63. Li, *Sangjia gou*, preface, 2.

64. Li, *Sangjia gou*, 394.

65. Li, *Sangjia gou*, 392.

66. Li, *Sangjia gou*, 390–391.

67. Li, *Sangjia gou*, 391. Note that his views on the Cultural Revolution follow a similar analysis. He takes issue with those who would see the chaos of those years as a result of the loss of morality. Rather, the moral failings exhibited during that event resulted from the loss of order (5).

68. Li, *Sangjia gou*, 394.

69. Of course, we should not discount the importance of financial incentives. Writing for a mass audience undoubtedly provides a lucrative source of income for scholars not ordinarily engaged in the private economy.

4

The Return of the Repressed
The New Left and "Left" Confucianism in Contemporary China

Kenneth J. Hammond

The learning of the *ru*, known as *ruxue* 儒学 or *rujiao* 儒教, and generally referred to as Confucianism in Western writing, has for more than two thousand years been a broad stream of discourse within Chinese culture. Confucian thinkers have been concerned with issues of educational theory and practice, aesthetics and literary values, family ritual and management, and many other themes and topics. But throughout its long history Confucianism has been first and foremost a set of ideas concerned with ethical and political life. Through more than two millennia of imperial history, Confucianism was consistently associated with the power and legitimization of the state and was in many ways a vehicle for the hegemony of social and economic elites. Confucianism also served, at least intermittently, as a challenge to and a check upon the abuse of power and as a means to articulate political subject positions that, while not subverting the class dominance of landed interests, did oppose entrenched groups and policy positions in the name of a vague general good.[1]

The long association of Confucianism with the imperial state meant that as that state became increasingly incapable of meeting the challenges of domestic unrest and the incursions of Western, and later Japanese, imperialism, the traditional teachings of Confucius, Mencius, Xunxi, and their later interpreters came to be seen as implicated in the weakness and humiliation of the country. As more and more Chinese

93

sought ways to respond to the challenges of Western modernity, the rejection and overthrow of the imperial political order became central to that task, and the repudiation of Confucianism as a political doctrine was an integral part of that process.[2]

The twentieth-century revolutions in China were dominated by ideologies of Western origin, whether scientific, democratic, or Marxist. Confucianism was marginalized, preserved as a quaint relic or a vague literary disposition. This marginalization was so successful that when Confucianism was targeted in the later phases of the Cultural Revolution, in the campaign to criticize Lin Biao and Confucius in 1972, the teachings of the Master had to be reissued so that people could understand what it was they were supposed to be criticizing. It seemed for much of the twentieth century that Confucianism, especially as a system of political ethics, had indeed been consigned to the dustbin of history.

However, as the various chapters in this volume show, Confucianism has come back from the dead and resumed a role, or more properly a number of roles, in contemporary Chinese life. It has become clear that although Confucianism had disappeared from public conversation and was no longer the language in which political discussion took place, many aspects of Confucian values had remained alive in ordinary Chinese society and family life. And the abiding textual tradition of China, despite the ravages of war, invasion, and class struggle, has preserved the primary texts and the rich currents of commentary and application that formed the heritage of Confucian civilization. To a great extent, the revival of Confucianism in the late twentieth and early twenty-first centuries has been a mix of official patronage, emphasizing the ideas of harmony and hierarchy that can be used to reinforce the existing political order, and a renewed popular embrace of "traditional family values." But there is also a revival of the Confucian praxis of political ethics, and as in imperial times, this can be counterhegemonic, a mode of opposition and a means of challenging the state and those in power to truly fulfill the terms of the Mandate of Heaven.

Contemporary Chinese political culture, like the Confucian culture of the imperial era, is a complex field of discourse. It can encompass positions that support and conform to established power or it can generate ideas and potentially actions that resist that power and promote alternative visions of how Chinese political society should be organized and managed. The post-socialist era, since the triumph of Deng Xiaoping and the beginning of the period of reform and market-driven development, has been a time of challenge for both public and private life. Rapid economic growth, the social stresses of urbanization, and the widening gap of inequality have all contributed to a sense of malaise, of something absent from the heart of society. The ubiquity of corruption and the widespread abuse of power by government and Party officials and businessmen have fostered a sense of moral vacuum, a vulgar materialism in which the pursuit of wealth and private interest overrides concerns for the common good.

In this new era, what is to be the basis for moral order? The Party/state maintains the official rhetoric of socialism, but the widespread perception of the primacy of money, the worship of material wealth, and the pervasiveness of corruption makes this seem like rank hypocrisy on the part of those who are gleefully enriching themselves at the expense of others. Recent examples like the milk scandal of 2008 highlight the substantive dangers to which this lack of a moral compass gives rise.

The quest for a basis for morality has led many Chinese to turn to religion. Buddhism, Daoism, Christianity, and a variety of local or generic cult activities have reemerged and become widely popular, both among older generations who remember their former place in society and young people encountering them for the first time. Many people engage with more than one such doctrine, and religious and spiritual activities seem to provide many people with solace and ways of coping with the stresses and challenges of life in modern society.

The Party/state has also sought to offer more generic moral guidance, promoting slogans and guidelines for public morality that often articulate "traditional values" without the use of specifically socialist language. These efforts have largely sought to promote social harmony and respect for authority. Like the revival in religious life, these campaigns are essentially directed toward the private sphere, aiming to promote proper behavior in individuals and largely eschewing any kind of political activism. Yet the political has not entirely disappeared as a mode of public life.

In fact, the responses to the problems of society, from corruption and the abuse of power to the spread of cynicism and vulgar materialism, have been many and varied. Public debate, in newspapers and journals, in books, on television, and of course on the Internet, gives a good picture of the dynamics and range of opinion. This is not just a matter of an outpouring of random thoughts. There are discernable clusters of ideas about what the key issues are and what basic approaches should be taken in addressing them. Some of this is based in the social science and philosophical discourse of global, Western modernity–inflected academic and political theory and practice, while others have turned, or returned, to ideas and behaviors rooted in China's own historical culture.

Jin Canrong, of the School of International Studies at Renmin University, related to me a model of political positions within contemporary China. He suggested that if China had a European-style parliamentary system, these might well be five political parties contending for influence. This is not meant to be a comprehensive catalogue of all political life, but it is broadly descriptive of certain significant positions within politically engaged elements in the country. These are general and policy orientations with support both within and outside the Party. I want to lay out the broad outlines of this terrain to situate the specific positions and connections with which I am concerned. My argument is that there is, in the early twenty-first century, an emergent congruence between a "New Left" that seeks to advance a vision of a socialist China that draws on China's traditional political culture and explicitly roots itself in the heritage of political Confucianism, and a "Left" Confucianism that seeks to revive and reanimate Confucianism as a basis for public life and political ethics within a modern socialist state. Let me first present an overview of the field of political culture as suggested by Jin Canrong.

Five main groupings can be discerned. These are not organized factions, but rather loose associations of individuals advocating particular policy orientations. First among these are the Developmental Pragmatists. This is essentially the group that currently dominates the Chinese Communist Party (CCP) and that has provided the leadership over the past three decades, with Hu Jintao and Wen Jiabao as the current representative figures. Developmental Pragmatists seek to build up China as a prosperous nation with sufficient military strength to provide credible defense. They endorse the use of market mechanisms to develop the productive capacity of the Chinese economy to enrich the country. They want China to be open to and actively engaged with the global economy. They recognize that rapid economic growth generates problems, but see these as the price that needs to be paid to achieve the goals of wealth and power that have been sought by Chinese modernizers for more than a century. They see the preservation of the political monopoly of the CCP as critical to their ability to deliver on their promises of increased prosperity. Stability is the key component of their socialist morality.

A second group that has been important in the past but seems to be in serious decline is the Old Leftists. This grouping is largely within the Party and consists of mostly higher-ranking cadres who, while accepting the need for reform and development, want to maintain a stronger role for the central state and Party authorities and mistrust many aspects of the policies of opening to the outside world. This group has fought rearguard actions to combat spiritual pollution and resist the decadent influences of the West, and it retains a certain nostalgia for aspects of the Maoist era.

While the first two groupings are based primarily within the Party, there are also significant political voices that, while having supporters inside the CCP, are largely found in the academic world and intellectual circles. The next perspective I want to note is that of National Studies, or *Guoxue* 国学. For thinkers like Qin Hui 秦晖, the main task at hand is to make China wealthy and powerful and to gain the respect and admiration of other countries. The advocates of National Studies draw on the legacy of statecraft scholarship, 经世, or ordering the world. They are not tied to socialist ideology or economic models and are cautious about learning from the West or being too influenced by Western ideas and practices. They seek to draw on the experiences of Chinese history to find solutions to contemporary problems. They accept the realities of the political hegemony of the Party as a matter of practical necessity but not as a matter of ideological principle.

Another academically based position is what has come to be known as the New Left, 新左派. This group, with major figures such as Wang Hui 汪晖 and Gan Yang 甘阳 as representative figures, emerged from the intellectual turmoil of the 1990s. The term "New Left" was originally applied to them by their opponents, but they have embraced it, rather in the spirit of the New Left in the West in the 1960s, as marking them off from the problematic past of Marxism in China while expressing their ongoing commitment to the ideas and ideals of socialism and communism. I consider the ideas of the New Left in greater detail below.

The last of the five political positions can be characterized as Traditionalists. This is perhaps the least coherent of the groupings and in some ways is simply a catchall for a range of specific orientations that share a basic affinity for the classical spiritual and intellectual beliefs and practices of China's long cultural tradition. The contemporary revivals of Buddhism, Daoism, and Confucianism are all aspects of the Traditionalist orientation, as is a more generic veneration for anything associated with "ancient" ideas, places, or historical figures. Much of this activity is hardly political at all. But there are important political issues and activities that fall within this Traditionalist arena. In this study, while I wish to consider the overall revival of Confucianism today in its political dimensions, I am particularly interested in two figures, Yu Dan 于丹 and Jiang Qing 蒋庆, each of whom I discuss further below.

The first three of the political/intellectual positions suggested by Jin Canrong are not of concern to this study. The Pragmatists are essentially neoliberals with Chinese characteristics. The Old Leftists are a fading phenomenon, maintaining nostalgia for the simplicity and honesty of the Maoist era. Their numbers are dwindling, as they are concentrated among the older members of the leadership. The National Studies perspective is largely academic, with an emphasis on developing China's wealth and power without gesturing to socialist ideology. Even within the Traditionalists I will not be dealing with those who embrace Daoism, Buddhism, or other religious/spiritual paths.

I am, rather, concerned with the ways in which Confucianism has returned as an aspect of contemporary political life, and especially with the counter-hegemonic aspect of New Left and Left Confucian ideas. Political engagement is by no means the mainstream of Confucian discourse in China today. But without considering this aspect of the Confucian revival, we miss an important dimension that links contemporary Confucianism to powerful currents within the long history of Chinese intellectual culture.

As Confucianism has revived over the last twenty or thirty years, there has been a process of broadening and deepening with regard to the diversity of Confucian ideas and practices. Initially, as described by John Makeham in his pioneering work *Lost Soul: "Confucianism" in Contemporary Chinese Academic Discourse*, Confucianism was largely of interest to academics and was discussed largely in philosophical and historiographic terms. Makeham notes that already by the late 1980s, there were scholars such as Fang Keli exploring the links between Marxism and Confucianism, rejecting the view that the two thought paths were entirely antithetical. These explorations had the approval of state and Party authorities, who were themselves endeavoring to develop a new understanding of the role that Confucian thought might play in a rapidly evolving context of social and economic flux.[3]

Some elements within the state and Party became advocates of what has been called "neo-authoritarianism," influenced in part by the policies and practices of Singapore's Lee Kwan Yu. The deployment of Confucian-inflected rhetoric by advocates of this perspective has largely been interpreted as an effort to appropriate the cultural capital still inherent in the Confucian "brand" and use it to advance a statist agenda of top-down reform and economic development, with values such as the much-vaunted "harmonious society" serving to preserve social order while a process of primitive capital accumulation is pursued. As Jeremy T. Paltiel has noted, "The cautious embrace by the regime of the neo-authoritarian 'Confucianism' of Lee Kwan Yu is widely seen as a transparent shield for Beijing's own brand of post-Leninist authoritarianism."[4]

Other state and Party leaders not directly associated with the neo-authoritarian position have also sought to assimilate the image of Confucius and Confucianism to their political agendas. Both Hu Jintao and Wen Jiabao have made multiple public pronouncements invoking the ideas of Confucius as valuable elements from China's historical tradition that should be used to facilitate social harmony and rapid economic development.[5] This is not only a matter of central government leaders seeking to utilize Confucianism for their contemporary objectives. Local governments have also embraced at least the trappings of Confucian tradition, often in association with educational reforms or to exhort young people to study hard and contribute to national development. A typical example was a government-sponsored convocation held in Nanning, capital of the Guangxi Zhuang Autonomous Region, on February 21, 2011, at which 2,600 students read aloud selections from the *Lun Yu* while dressed in purportedly traditional scholar's robes to inaugurate the new academic term.[6]

The place of Confucius and Confucianism within official political life is by no means fully settled. While there have been repeated efforts to appropriate the aura of the Sage for the purposes of the present leadership, not all elements within the state and Party accept this or endorse the efforts to use the Confucian past to promote contemporary activities. The controversy over the placement of a monumental statue of Confucius at the front of the newly renovated Museum of History at the eastern edge of Tian'anmen Square highlighted how contentious the image of Confucius can be. The statue was put in place on January 11, 2011, without major fanfare. It quickly became the subject of heated debate and discussion on the Internet and in other media. On April 22, the statue was moved from the front of the museum to a small courtyard within the grounds, out of direct view from Tian'anmen Square. This was apparently the result of serious disagreements within the national leadership over the appropriateness of displaying such a major tribute to Confucius in such a politically significant setting.[7]

While the state and Party have made various efforts to utilize Confucianism for its own ends and to shape the understanding of Confucian thought and the use of Confucian imagery, alternative engagements with the Confucian heritage have also been unfolding, at least some of which have had an explicitly political dimension. One important example of this has been Jiang Qing, about whom more is said below. John Makeham discussed the development of Jiang Qing's thought and his call for an explicitly "political Confucianism" in the context of the largely academic discourse that was the focus of his book, though Makeham largely dismisses Jiang as a utopian fantasist. For Makeham, Confucianism remained essentially a "lost soul," divorced from the dynamic realities of daily life.

The work of Daniel Bell, a Canadian scholar now based at Qinghua University in Beijing, has sought to bring the political dimensions of contemporary Confucianism into clearer focus. Bell's 2008 book *China's New Confucianism: Politics and Everyday Life in a Changing Society* provides both a critique of the apolitical Confucianism of the popular television figure Yu Dan and a concise exposition of Jiang Qing's call for a new mode of Confucian political advocacy. In the discussion that follows, I draw significantly on Bell's work, while trying to go beyond it in exploring the links between Left Confucianism and New Left thinkers.

I want to focus on some of the figures I have noted above to exemplify the positions I believe have taken shape in the last decade or so. I use Wang Hui and Gan Yang to represent the New Left and Jiang Qing for the Left Confucians. Both groupings are of course much broader and more complex than what I can present here in any detail. I begin with the New Left and then take up the Left Confucians.

The term New Left has, of course, a long history in Western discourse, going back to the late 1950s to designate radical leftists who repudiated the Stalinist Communism of the Soviet Union and who sought to build a radical alternative while continuing to work within a Marxist materialism. A lively intellectual engagement with both theory and practice has been carried on through journals such as the *New Left Review*, *Radical Philosophy*, *Historical Materialism*, and many others. In China, however, the label New Left began to be used in the 1990s to criticize thinkers who were challenging the negative effects of neoliberal economic policies on the economy, society, and environment while continuing to uphold ideals of socialist justice and egalitarianism. At first, writers like Wang Hui sought to distance themselves from this label, but as time passed they came to embrace it as their own. Lively exchanges between Western New Left activists like Perry Anderson, Tariq Ali, and Slavoj Žižek have taken place with increasing regularity.

Wang Hui has been perhaps the most prominent exemplar of the Chinese New Left. He is currently a professor at Beijing University, having taught at Qinghua University for several years. Born in 1959, Wang worked in a factory for two years after graduating from high school before embarking on his academic career. His early work was on Lu Xun, and this has developed into an ongoing exploration of literary and intellectual history. He took part in the 1989 demonstrations in Beijing and spent a year in a reeducation program in Shanxi afterward but did not face any serious charges. In May 1996 he became editor of *Dushu*, a monthly journal of book reviews and essays, which he soon guided to being an important forum for critical writing about social and political issues. He remained as executive editor until July 2007, when he was removed under controversial circumstances. He has continued to be quite active and outspoken, however, and has if anything expanded his interactions with the global radical left.

Wang's writings are not particularly polemical. Indeed, his work is very carefully crafted intellectual history and commentary on contemporary affairs. I want to focus on two recent works in particular, his four-volume 现代中国思想的兴起, *The Rise of Modern Chinese Thought*, published in 2004, and 去政治化的政治, *Depoliticized Politics*, published in 2007. Two books of Wang's writings have also been published in English: *China's New Order* (2003) and *The End of the Revolution* (2009).

Wang's work on the history of modern Chinese thought does not limit itself to the recent past but is a comprehensive survey of Chinese intellectual history, beginning in the Zhou dynasty and sweeping through the ensuing three millennia.[8] His engagement with this history is intended to elucidate the origins of contemporary thought and to provide guidance in dealing with the challenges facing China today. One powerful motif that emerges from Wang's massive exposition is an image of ongoing dialectics between the past and the present and between ideas that have deep roots in Chinese history and the influences of theories and concepts coming into China from the outside world in recent centuries.

Not surprisingly, Confucianism as a political ethical order has a central place in Wang's thought. He explores the more radical and progressive aspects of Confucian thought in the Ming and Qing dynasties while also recognizing the predominance of Confucianism as a conservative force within imperial political culture. His embrace of the potential for radical critique and action within the traditions of Confucianism is important for contemporary China, where it can interact with modern socialism in ways that promote agendas of social justice and equality.

But Wang sees the struggles for progressive social reform in China as deeply threatened by the depoliticization of public life in the present era. The emergence of a new urban middle class in the 1990s within the context of a public political life that was exhausted by the aftermath of the struggles of the Cultural Revolution, the rapid changes of the 1980s, and the turmoil of 1989 has created a society in which many people would prefer a managerial state, one that would protect property interests and provide conditions of stability and security for the pursuit of private ambitions. Wang argues that this depoliticization clears the way for the triumph of a Chinese neoliberalism and calls for the repoliticization of contemporary life. This is not to revive the movements of the 1960s or 1980s, but to create a real movement for justice and equity to confront the problems of the present.

Where are people to seek the basic values that could inform such a movement? The need for some foundation for moral order is clear. The current pragmatism of "crossing the river by stepping on the stones" does not provide any solid ground for ethical life, which creates an environment in which abuses such as the tainted milk scandal of 2008 can flourish. What is needed is a critique from the left, to develop true democracy in China in support of a "socialism of movements for social security, social democracy, and against monopoly capitalism."[9]

Wang Hui posits a need to seek a future that will incorporate the principles of socialist justice and egalitarianism, which resonate with the Confucian commitment to an ethical order grounded in the human relationships of daily life. In hearkening back to the ideas of eighteenth-century thinkers like Zhang Xuecheng and Dai Zhen, Wang, too, seeks once again to, as Zhang Yongle has written, "reinvigorate Confucian thought in a depoliticized intellectual climate."[10]

While Wang Hui invokes the heritage of Confucian intellectual culture to promote a revitalized socialist politics, another figure associated with the New Left, Gan Yang, has made a dramatic and explicit call for integrating Confucian and socialist agendas. Gan is a professor at the University of Hong Kong and a prolific essayist. He is also the editor of a book series, *Culture: China and the World*, published by Sanlian Press in Beijing, which includes works such as Chen Lai's 东亚儒学九论, *Nine Talks on East Asian Confucianism* and Wang

Shaoguang's 民主四讲 *Four Lectures on Democracy*. The first volume in this series is a work by Gan Yang himself titled 通三统, *Uniting Three Traditions*, published in 2007, based on a series of lectures given in 2005. In the book, Gan appropriates terminology used in the *Gongyang* commentarial tradition, referring to the common values embodied in the ancient traditions of the Xia, Shang, and Zhou dynasties. Gan takes this phrase and gives it a radically updated meaning, arguing that what China needs today is a fusion of Maoism, Deng-ism, and Confucianism.

Gan writes,

> I believe that the age of globalization which is underway today also requires a uniting of three traditions, and that this can only come about from within China's historical culture, and that this can give rise to a new strength in China's cultural foundations. The first part of this book will discuss the three traditions shaping contemporary China; the tradition of Confucius, the tradition of Mao Zedong, and the tradition of Deng Xiaoping. The latter part of the book will be concerned with how the integration of these three traditions can be carried forward through China's educational system, particularly at the university level, to bring about a new awakening of China's cultural foundations.[11]

Here, as with Wang Hui, we see a convergence of modern socialism with the heritage of Confucian thought. Gan links the achievements of the Communist Revolution led by Mao Zedong with the subsequent development of the economy under the policies launched by Deng Xiaoping but suggests that without the ethical restraint provided by Confucian teachings, the materialism of the modern world will generate injustice and oppression. Only by including Confucian learning in the education of young people growing up in the material context of twenty-first century China can the gains of the socialist revolution be preserved.

On the one hand, Wang Hui and Gan Yang demonstrate some shared concerns between thinkers associated with the New Left and the political ethics of Confucianism. This is not to suggest that either Wang or Gan would identify themselves as Confucians. They hold clearly distinct positions, both from those who would self-identify as Confucians and from each other. But there are clearly openings for dialogue and communication, and both men seek to develop a modern

Chinese political culture that is strongly inflected by the heritage of *ru* learning.

On the other hand, as noted earlier in this essay and elsewhere in this volume, the Confucian revival in contemporary China has often been a matter of the reinvigoration of intellectual currents not necessarily concerned with active political life. The "New Confucians," such as Li Zehou, Chen Lai, Cheng Zhongying, and others in Taiwan, Hong Kong, or on the Mainland, have done much to restore a lively dynamic to Confucian discourse and debate. In the West, the so-called Boston Confucians centered around Tu Wei-ming have also given Confucian thought a new lease of life. Yet these thinkers have for the most part not dealt with Confucianism as a matter of daily engagement in the social and political life of China today. I want to turn now to two thinkers who have, in very different ways, done just that. One, the television presenter Yu Dan, has promoted a kind of self-help Confucianism that has been widely popular. The other, Jiang Qing, is an advocate of a strongly Confucian practice that is also profoundly concerned with the contemporary and future politics of China.

Yu Dan is a professor at Beijing Normal University, where she also serves as assistant to the dean of the Faculty of Arts and Media and as dead of the Department of Film and Media. She received a master's degree in Chinese classical literature and a PhD in film and television studies, so she brings together elements of both traditional learning and a strong engagement with contemporary media. In 2006 and 2007, Yu gave two series of lectures on Confucianism on the CCTV10 program *Lecture Room* 百家讲坛, which became very popular. Both were subsequently published as paperback books, 《论语》心得 published in English as *Confucius from the heart* and 《论语》感悟 *Insights into the Analects*, which became best-sellers. Copies were stacked up at the checkout counters of grocery and department stores. When Yu Dan held a book signing at the Xidan Book Building in downtown Beijing, long lines formed, and people waited for hours to get her autograph.

Yu Dan's approach to Confucianism takes the original text of the *Lunyu* as her main focus. She includes a full version of the text in simplified characters as an appendix in the published version of her first lecture series. Her presentation of Confucius's thought emphasizes its utility as a means of coping with the stresses of living in the modern world. She discusses how to deal with regret and disappointment at the things that happen to us, how to develop and maintain friendships as a buffer against the harsh realities of social life, and how to deal with the challenges and opportunities that day-to-day encounters with other people bring our way. Yu Dan tells her listeners that they should rely on their inner sensibilities—their hearts—to guide them and to trust in their innate predisposition to do the right thing. She also seeks to alert her audience to the nature of life's journey and to help them awaken to their own potential and to be of benefit to those around them, especially their families, but in a broader social context as well.

Yu Dan's view of Confucius is almost entirely concerned with the question of how the individual should live in society. There is virtually no discussion of larger social structures beyond the level of the family. This is most certainly not a political Confucianism. Its popularity shows that Confucian ideas and arguments are not irrelevant to the quest for moral values and guidance in contemporary China, but for Yu Dan this remains an essentially private realm. In this she appears to be articulating a style of Confucianism that resonates with the kind of depoliticized public culture that Wang Hui denounces. The Confucius presented by Yu Dan is quite a comfortable figure for the emerging middle class in urban China today, and her book sales and television celebrity are a clear indication of her enthusiastic reception by that audience.

Yu Dan's success as a popularizer of Confucianism for the modern middle class seems to be perceived as a threat by some. At least two books have appeared attacking her scholarship and criticizing her understanding of classical thought. It should be noted that Yu Dan has also given a television lecture series on the teaching of Zhuangzi, so she cannot be seen as a partisan of Confucianism, but should be understood as more of an eclectic traditionalist. Her ideas have also been criticized, especially on the Internet, as being too closely aligned to the current promotion of the idea of a "harmonious society" by state and Party authorities.

In an article reproduced on the *Danwei* Web site, He Dong reports on protests against Yu Dan that had appeared in various Internet forums. He notes that many of the contributors were academics who apparently felt that their status as authorities would be undermined by Yu Dan's brand of Confucianism for the masses. Another Web contributor, Zhao Yong, in a separate article also picked up by Danwei, further criticizes academics for fearing the possible erosion of their elite monopoly on Confucian discourse, but then goes on in turn to suggest that Yu Dan herself is too scholarly and that what is needed is for the *Analects* to be presented as "the political document mainstream ideology has been waiting for."[12]

Daniel Bell, too, has argued that Yu Dan's version of Confucianism is essentially an apolitical kind of self-help program. He includes a short appendix on Yu Dan's thought in *China's New Confucianism* under the title "Depoliticizing the *Analects.*" In fact, Bell goes well beyond simply suggesting that Yu Dan minimizes the political aspects of Confucian thought, arguing that "by downplaying the importance of social and political commitment, and by ignoring the critical tradition of Confucianism, Yu Dan deflects attention from the economic and political conditions that actually cause people's misery, as well as the collective solutions needed to bring about substantial improvement to people's lives."[13]

Yu Dan represents an important expansion of the discourse about the Confucian tradition and its relevance to life in contemporary China. Yu Dan reaches out to millions of ordinary Chinese and seeks to make the values and concepts of Confucian teachings meaningful as a way of coping with the challenges of social and personal affairs. This is an important aspect of the Confucian revival in that it makes Confucianism more than a historical relic or a set of texts of concern only to an educated few. As Daniel Bell suggests, Yu Dan's Confucianism is not actually entirely devoid of political implications. But the kind of politics embedded in her views is one of accommodation to the hegemonic power of the economic and political elites that have consolidated themselves over the past thirty years of reform and development. The scholar and educator Jiang Qing embodies a radically different approach to Confucianism for the masses, both more profoundly engaged with the theory and practice of Confucian doctrine and explicitly concerned with the active political application of Confucian ideas.

Jiang Qing was born in Xuzhou, in Jiangsu Province, in 1953. He graduated in 1982 from the Southwest University of Law and Politics and worked as a professor there and at the Shenzhen Institute of Public Administration. In 2001 he retired and moved to Guiyang to open a private academy, the 阳明精舍, invoking the legacy of the Ming Confucian thinker Wang Yangming. Jiang is a practitioner of Confucian ritual and education rather than an academic authority on Confucian thought. He is dedicated to propagating Confucian ideas and values but insists on observing many aspects of traditional pedagogy and ceremony. Locating his school in the southwest of the country, out of the mainstream of academic life and away from the main centers of economic development, Jiang is in some ways emulating the spirit of eremitism within the Confucian heritage. But he is also engaged in forms of active outreach, including publishing books and articles and maintaining a Web site. His most important book is *Political Confucianism,* 政治儒学, published in 2006. This book has been the subject of considerable controversy since its appearance. Daniel Bell has provided a vivid overview of *Political Confucianism* that makes clear the extent of Jiang's commitment to revive Confucianism as an explicit mode of active political engagement.[14] Jiang sets out specific proposals, most notably for a tricameral legislature that would include popularly elected representatives, leaders of functional constituencies, and representatives of the great cultural traditions. He calls for once again making Confucianism the basic value system in China while recognizing the contributions that have been made by the Communist Revolution led by Mao Zedong and the economic development launched by Deng Xiaoping. The similarity of this aspect of Jiang's message to Gan Yang's call for unifying Maoism, Dengism, and Confucianism is obvious.

The seriousness with which Jiang's ideas have been greeted is suggested by the publication in August 2008 of a volume titled 儒家社会与道统复兴:与蒋庆对话, *Confucian Society and the Revival of the Orthodox Way: Conversations with Jiang Qing,* edited by Fan Ruiping. This book brings together scholars from the New Confucianism period from Taiwan, Hong Kong, and the People's Republic and includes an essay by Daniel Bell.[15] The contributors engage with Jiang Qing's thought in a variety of areas, including not only the specifics of his political ideas and proposals, but also his views on education and the relevance of his Confucian ideals for the world beyond China itself. Jiang Qing is seen is this book as perhaps the most important innovator in contemporary Confucianism, and his efforts to go beyond philosophical and academic debate and make his ideas and activities relevant to the current needs and challenges of China are both recognized and welcomed, though certainly not uncritically endorsed.

Jiang is careful to situate his political advocacy within the conceptual order of present-day China, arguing, in accord with the stated position of the state and Party leadership, that the country is now in the primary stage of the building of socialism. What, he asks, will the more realized socialism of China look like? By framing his discussion in this way, Jiang is perhaps insulating himself against possible censorship. He also appears to be indicating that he sees Confucian political ethics as compatible with a socialist society. As I show shortly, he makes this claim explicitly elsewhere.

Jiang views Confucianism as the core of Chinese culture and as essentially political. He is highly critical of the influence of Western thought on modern Chinese intellectual culture, especially in terms of political thought. For Jiang, the Western concepts of democracy have been too simplistically introduced and applied in China. "Freedom" and "democracy" are not concepts that originate in China, but in the specific historical conditions of the development of Western societies and economies. In an article responding to various criticisms of *Political Confucianism* published in a volume titled 孔子与当代中国, *Confucius and Contemporary China*, edited by Chen Lai and Gan Yang, Jiang catalogues and refutes the arguments that have been made against him. He posits several schools of thought (派) that he sees as informing the criticisms raised against him and sets out his reasons for rejecting their views.[16]

He begins with the 自由派, the "freedom" school, and dismisses it as being too simplistically focused on individual autonomy, not recognizing the collectivist, communal quality of traditional Chinese society and culture. Jiang views Confucian values as essential to the life of the individual in Chinese society and sees the "freedom" school as essentially advocating a Western neoliberalism that atomizes social life. He also dismisses the second school, which he calls the 民主派, the "democracy" school, which he criticizes as having an unrealistic view of the nature of power in society and as being out of harmony with China's national conditions 国情. He notes that the criticisms of his ideas in *Political Confucianism* raised by the democracy school say that Jiang opposes democracy and humanistic political culture. But he argues that in fact it is only the Kingly Way of governing 王道政治 that can meet the needs of democracy and the people's interests 民意 in the actually existing conditions of China today. It is clear from his proposals for new legislative forms and from the overall thrust of his arguments that Jiang is not advocating any kind of restoration of a monarchy and that the Kingly Way to which he refers is not an institutional form but a concept of political order that emphasizes the obligation of the state to care for the interests of the people and of the people to overthrow a political leadership that abrogated its reciprocal relationship to society. He goes on to argue that while the Kingly Way developed in the conditions of life in ancient times, the same principles are still the most in harmony with contemporary society. He acknowledges that the struggle between the Kingly Way and Western-style democracy will go on in China for a long time and suggests that in twenty years it will be worth seeing how this has developed. There are startling resonances here with the critique of democracy articulated in recent years by Alain Badiou and Slavoj Žižek. In an article in the *New Left Review*, Žižek summarizes this position by noting that "the ultimate enemy today is not capitalism, empire or exploitation, but democracy. It is the acceptance of 'democratic mechanisms' as the ultimate frame [of political engagement] that prevents a radical transformation of capitalist relations."[17] Jiang Qing's rejection of Western democratic forms as suitable for China is not simply a question of nationalist or culturalist bias, but expresses the same kind of unease with the ways in which democratic structures have historically been routinely utilized to reproduce and maintain hierarchies of inequality and exploitation.

It is not only a matter of Jiang's rejection of Western individualist and democratic rhetoric that marks him as a Left Confucian. When we consider the social and political vision that Jiang propounds, we can perceive specific areas of intersection with the perspective of the New Left. One particular area of shared concern is the matter of public morality. Jiang makes the response to the current vacuum of social ethics an important part of his call for Confucian politics. He writes that Confucianism is "利与克服当今中国的信仰危机与价值虚无状态" [of use in overcoming contemporary China's crisis of morality and absence of values].[18] This must be a matter of overcoming the depoliticization of contemporary life, which Jiang characterizes in the same way that Wang Hui does. Jiang's condemns the New Confucians, noting that "他们所理解的儒学已经成为去政治化的儒学" [Their understanding of Confucianism has already become a depoliticized Confucianism].[19]

Jiang himself acknowledges the resonance of his ideas with those of the New Left. He writes, "似乎新左派在很大程度上默认"政治儒学"的主张" [It seems the New Left for the most part is in tacit agreement with the ideas advocated in *Political* Confucianism][20] and goes on to affirm that "儒学天然就具有社会主义因素" [Confucianism certainly includes socialism as an aspect].[21] He also endorses Gan Yang's call for unifying the traditions of revolutionary socialism and Confucianism, though simplifying the formula from 三统 three traditions to 二统 two traditions. He writes, "甘阳原先提出的"三统"并为"二统", 即主张中国未来的政治发展应该是"儒家+社会主义", 并把"儒家"放在"社会主义"前面 . . ." [Gan Yang's proposed "three traditions" should be changed to "two traditions," to advocate that China's future political development should (be a matter of) Confucianism plus socialism, and should place Confucianism ahead of socialism . . .].[22]

Jiang's and Gan's visions of a confluence between socialism and Confucianism are not entirely consistent with one another, but, along with the parallelism of Jiang's critique of depoliticized Confucianism and Wang Hui's condemnation of the same phenomenon in Chinese society, they suggest that the convergence or intersection between the New Left and Left Confucianism may be a conversation worth listening to.

Conclusion

China faces tremendous challenges in the twenty-first century. The need for rapid economic development to raise the standards of living for hundreds of millions of people is a national priority. But this produces further challenges in terms of environmental stress, social dislocation, and political inclusion and empowerment. In addressing these and a myriad of other issues, Chinese avail themselves of a complex repertoire of cultural and ideological instruments rooted in both indigenous and extraneous sources. Without the Communist Revolution of the twentieth century, the present realities of China would be very different, and it is not surprising that even after the tribulations of mass movements and repeated frustrations, many people still hold to the vision of a just and equitable society articulated in the theories of socialist liberation. Today's China is also strongly shaped by the multi-millennial heritage of "tradition" in all its diversity and complexity, and it is also not surprising that many people look to one or another aspect of the past or reinterpretation of this heritage to address the problems of the present.

My goal in this chapter has been to consider briefly one particular locus within the broad and dynamic field of political discourse and action in contemporary China that has caught my attention in recent years and that I feel may yield particular insights and offer specific opportunities for dealing with China's discontents. The intersection between New Left thinkers and advocates of what I see as a "Left" Confucianism is hardly the mainstream of political debate in China. But it brings together two constituencies that share a concern with collective welfare and social justice and that call for upholding standards of public morality in a time of widespread corruption. Where this will lead and whether these two sets of thinkers will further develop their shared ideals in some form of coordinated theory or practice remains very much to be seen. But China may well be better off if they do.

Notes

1. Peter K. Bol. *Neo-Confucianism in History*. Cambridge: Harvard University Asia Center, 2008.
2. Joseph Levenson, *Confucian China and Its Modern Fate: A Trilogy* (Berkeley: University of California Press, 1972).

3. Makeham, John, *Lost Soul: "Confucianism" in Contemporary Chinese Academic Discourse* (Cambridge: Harvard University Press, 2008), 247–257.

4. Jeremy T. Paltiel, "Confucianism Contested: Human Rights and the Chinese Tradition in Contemporary Chinese Political Discourse," in *Confucianism and Human Rights*, ed. Wm. Theodore deBary and Tu Wei-ming (New York: Columbia University Press, 1998), 288.

5. Bell, Daniel A., *China's New Confucianism: Politics and Everyday Life in a Changing Society* (Princeton: Princeton University Press, 2008), 9.

6. Lu Guangming, "Memorial Ceremony Held at Confucius Temple to Mark New Semester," *People's Daily Online*, February 21, 2011, http://english.peopledaily.com.cn/9000/907082/7294166.html.

7. Bai Xu, Wang Haiying, and Chuai Xianyu, "Statue of Confucius Erected near Tiananmen Square," http://news.xinhuanet.com/english2010/china/2011-01/12/c_13687988.htm.

8. For an in-depth review, see Zhang Yongle, "The Future of the Past: On Wang Hui's *Rise of Modern Chinese Thought*," *New Left Review* 62 (March/April 2010): 47–83.

9. Hui Wang, *The End of the Revolution: China and the Limits of Modernity* (London: Verso, 2009), 22.

10. Zhang 2010: 62.

11. Gan Yang, 通三统 *Uniting Three Traditions* (Beijing: Sanlian Publishing, 2007), 6.

12. Zhao Yong, "Why Are We Always Correcting Yu Dan's Mistakes?," accessed August 2, 2010, www.danwei.org/scholarship_and_education/yu_dan_defender_of_traditional.php.

13. Bell, 174.

14. Bell, 175–191.

15. Fan Ruiping, ed., 儒家社会与道统复兴：与蒋庆对话 *Confucian Society and the Revival of the Daotong: Conversations with Jiang Qing* (Shanghai: Huadong Shifan Daxue, 2008).

16. Jiang Qing, "政治的空子与孔子的政治:回应今年来对政治儒学的批评" "The Confucius of Politics and the Politics of Confucius: Replying to Recent Criticisms of *Political Confucianism*," in 孔子与当代中国 *Confucius and Contemporary China*, ed. Chen Lai and Gan Yang (Beijing: Sanlian Publishing, 2008), 321–327.

17. Žižek, Slavoj. "Economic Emergency," *New Left Notes* 64 (August/September 2010): 88.

18. Jiang, 325.

19. Jiang, 324.

20. Jiang, 325.

21. Jiang, 326.

22. Jiang, 325.

5

Chat Room Confucianism

Online Discourse and Popular Morality in China

JEFFREY L. RICHEY

Jackie Chan: Confucian Critic Or Confucian Catalyst?

In April 2009, the well-known actor and Hong Kong 香港 native Jackie Chan (Chan Kong-sang 陳港生) made some controversial remarks at a forum held in China's smallest province, the southern island of Hainan 海南. Before a gathering that included China's prime minister Wen Jiabao 温家宝, Chan confessed that he was

> not sure if it is good to have freedom or not. . . . I'm really confused now. If you are too free, you are like the way Hong Kong is now. It's very chaotic. Taiwan is also chaotic. . . . I'm gradually beginning to feel that we Chinese need to be controlled. If we are not being controlled, we'll just do what we want.[1]

While Chan's remarks drew applause from his Hainan audience, they sparked protests and outrage in Hong Kong and Taiwan. Both mainland and overseas Chinese rushed to comment on Chan's pronouncement in a variety of Internet venues, producing posts such as the following:

> I agree with Jackie Chan, we all know by heart, it is actually the truth.

> I think among those . . . who [have spoken] against Jackie Chan, 80% are kids under 16. Their brains are still in the

113

process of turning mature, so we don't need to pay too much attention to their comment. As long as they grow up, they will understand what . . . brother Chan mean[s].

If the entire Chinese [population] are like Americans, sell[ing] something like guns, then China will become a hell. Why [can't] the people nowadays . . . figure this out? If 1.3 billion Chinese are as open as Americans, then what will be the consequence? We need to see the big picture; I think Jackie Chan is right.[2]

All three of these posts were made by mainland Chinese (from Guangdong 广东 and Hebei 河北 Provinces and the capital of Beijing 北京, respectively). Their sentiments are revealing insofar as they highlight three characteristics of what might be called contemporary popular Confucianism in China: (a) appeal to intuitive group morality, (b) moral critique of youth, and (c) championing of native norms vis-à-vis Westernization. It is contemporary insofar as it deviates from trends established under both Nationalist and Communist regimes in the twentieth century; it is popular[3] insofar as it emanates from, and thrives within, decentralized, nongovernmental arenas of discourse, such as Internet chat rooms; and it is Confucian insofar as it draws deeply upon "freedom with Confucian characteristics," a native tradition of thinking about individual freedom and social responsibility that is rooted in classical Chinese texts and thinkers such as the *Lunyu* 論語 aka *Analects*, the *Mengzi* 孟子 aka *Mencius*, and Wang Yangming 王阳明. Thus, it is not so much Jackie Chan's remarks as the responses they have evoked from ordinary Chinese, and the trends they reveal, that provide a glimpse into contemporary popular Confucianism in China.

Intuitive Group Morality

The appeal to innate moral sentiments shared by a group is an ancient one within the Confucian tradition. Its classical expression may be found in *Mengzi* 2A6 (ca. fourth century BCE):

All human beings have a heart-mind [*xin* 心], which cannot bear to see the sufferings of others. . . . The feeling of commiseration [*ren* 忍] is the sprout of co-

humanity [*ren* 仁]. . . . Humans have [this] just as they
have their . . . limbs. . . . Since all humans have [this]
in themselves, if they give [it] all their development and
completion . . . [it] will suffice to love and protect all within
the four seas. Let them be denied that development, and
they will not even be able to serve their parents.

On Mengzi's account, not only is an individual able to act compassionately
on the basis of his intuitions and involuntary reactions, *all* human
beings qua human beings are able to do so. We all have these moral
feelings; to have them is to belong to the group; not to have them is
to be excluded from the group, even the species. This is not merely an
antique ideal, however. It continues to influence contemporary popular
Confucianism in China, as can be seen from two recent incidents that
attracted widespread attention in Chinese media.

In the first case, an unemployed twenty-eight-year-old man called
Yang Jia 杨佳 became a hero to many Chinese after he killed six
police officers in Shanghai 上海 on July 1, 2008 (the 87th anniversary
of the founding of the Chinese Communist Party).[4] Yang claimed
that he killed the officers as an act of reprisal against his wrongful
arrest for riding an unlicensed bicycle and subsequent physical abuse
during interrogation by police. In his trial, which took place behind
closed doors, he was defended not by his own lawyer, but by a legal
consultant for the government of the Shanghai district in which the
killings took place. Moreover, throughout his prosecution by the state,
Yang's mother, Wang Jingmei 王静梅, was detained in a psychiatric
hospital run by the Beijing police. After Yang's conviction and execution
on November 26, 2008, Chinese contributors to Internet commentaries
compared him with the traditional moral heroes Lin Chong 林冲 and
Wu Song 武松, characters in the classical novel *Shuihu zhuan* 水滸
傳 (*The Water Margin* aka *Outlaws of the Marsh*) whose names are
bywords for righteous resistance and violent revenge against corrupt
authorities. Remarks, slogans, and poems posted online make clear that
Yang functioned as a latter-day exemplar of both filial piety (*xiao* 孝)
and righteous rebellion (*geming* 革命) for many contemporary Chinese:

Why did so many Chinese laud Yang Jia? Because they
instead of you foreigners can best understand Yang. I'm sure
too many Chinese have been caught in similar situations
like Yang. . . .

This incident was inevitable. I do not agree that Yang
should have attacked the police but looking at the entire
social situation in China, which is incredibly messed up,
people like him are the only ones Chinese can have much
hope in anymore. . . .

Yang Jia is our hero!

Down with communism! Down with corruption! . . .

Very soon, Yang Jia will be sentenced to death.
The reason is the killing of 6 Shanghai police officers.
Although we don't know the truth,
Although we learn to keep silence,
We can't lie to ourselves that we don't know who Yang Jia is.[5]

Not only has Yang been idolized as a paragon who fought corrupt
authority for his mother's and his own sakes, but the above comments
also reveal that he has become a symbol of both shared suffering and
shared moral knowledge within the Chinese in-group: a selfless moral
exemplar who courageously struck a blow for traditional values against
a corrupt regime that has lost its mandate to rule.

Rather unusually for Confucian morality tales, the second case
has a happier conclusion. In May 2009, a twenty-one-year-old waitress
called Deng Yujiao 邓玉娇 in Hubei 湖北 Province spurned the sexual
advances of her local county investment promotion office chief, who
was visiting the entertainment venue where she worked. Allegedly,
when the official was rebuffed, he struck Deng in the head with a
wad of cash and attempted to prevent her from escaping by forcing
her onto a sofa, at which point Deng stabbed the official to death
before calling police to summon medical help and surrender to the
authorities.[6] After a court ruled that Deng had acted in self-defense,
she was acquitted.[7] Subsequently, like Yang Jia, Deng became a popular
moral hero, as is evident from the following online postings by Chinese
commentators:

Deng Yùjiāo, you are good. I admire and support you, and
will learn from you. Best regards. . . .

I would be content if I could marry a girl like this. . . .[8]

As in the case of Yang Jia, Deng Yujiao has become a dual icon of Confucian virtue. On the one hand, public outrage at the official corruption that prompted her act, which has been seen as wholly justified both in the courts and on the streets, reflects the attraction of *gémìng* (righteous rebellion) ideology as a mode of response to the present regime in mainland China. In this sense, the popular comparison of Deng with Yang makes sense. On the other hand, while Yang apparently exemplifies a virtue that is particularly incumbent upon Confucian males (*xiao*, the obligation to nurture and defend one's parents), it would seem that Deng has come to symbolize a particularly female Confucian virtue: the necessity of maintaining one's chastity.[9] In both cases, heroic values familiar from more than two millennia of Chinese cultural history appear to come to life for thousands of contemporary Chinese, having walked straight out of classical texts into newspaper, television, and Internet headlines. Finally, the cases of Yang and Deng show how appeals to innate moral sentiments shared by a group are both identifiable with particular Confucian values and useful as a way to articulate a distinctively Chinese moral message, both within China itself and out to the wider world.

Moral Critique of Youth

In nearly every culture and every era, older people tend to complain about the flaccid moral fiber of their younger counterparts. Contemporary China is no different, but the context of its particular complaints is distinctive. After forty years of authoritarian rule by a regime that extolled the modern and the progressive at the expense of the traditional and the conservative and even went so far (in the late 1960s and early 1970s) as to elevate youth over age, China's generations clashed violently during the student-led protests at Tian'anmen 天安門 Square in 1989. In the wake of these protests and the subsequent repression of student activists by the state, a gap between those who attained adulthood before Tian'anmen and those who did so afterward (the so-called *baling hou* 八零后, "post-1980s generation," who number approximately 200 million) began to emerge. Increased suspicion of youth was not confined to the public pronouncements of the state. As Nick Young has pointed out, "China's government and society reflect each other far more closely than most outsiders believe."[10] Beginning in the mid-1990s, ethnographers reported the negative perception of the Tian'anmen protestors as "unfilial" (*bu xiao* 不孝) among non-elites in China's countryside, where devotion to Confucian values remained stronger than in urban areas.[11] More recently, data from a 2007 survey indicate that those born in the 1970s and earlier overwhelmingly share a view of the "post-1980s generation" that is informed by a Confucian critique of society (which helps explain the depth of feeling aroused by the cases of the twentysomethings Yang Jia and Deng Yujiao), while the youth under critique largely reject their elders' depiction of them. For example, more than 60 percent of older respondents affirmed that younger people "always consider themselves the center of attention . . . never defer to others, but always feel that they're really great . . . [lack strong] concepts of morality, right and wrong, and sense of responsibility . . . [and] always have a high assessment of their own abilities,"[12] whereas fewer than 30 percent of younger respondents share these perceptions of themselves. Moreover, in response to public anxiety about the dramatic increase in Chinese divorce rates (from 7 percent in 1980 to more than 20 percent today), voluntary community associations led by neighborhood elders have sponsored ceremonies for the renewal of marital vows by married couples. At one such ceremony in Beijing in 2004,

> 180 couples renewed their vows in a hotel ballroom among friends and family, with government officials as special guests. What's highly unusually about this ceremony was that the couples declared in front of a "holy portrait of Confucius" that they "will never divorce." . . . This is certainly not a traditional Confucian practice, for the notion of legal divorce did not exist in China until the early twentieth century. . . . [T]his ceremony reflects a societal need in such promotion of marital stability.[13]

Such private or non-state Confucian initiatives and perceptions related to youth may be compared to recent official ventures such as the replacement of required courses in Marxist-Leninist thought with coursework devoted to the Confucian "Four Books" (*sishu* 四書) for some humanities students at China's prestigious Tsinghua University[14] or the Chinese government's sponsorship of a $15 million motion picture biography of Confucius starring another Hong Kong action star, Chow Yun-fat 周潤發.[15] Similarly, in 2007, the principal of Shaoxiandui 少先隊 (Young Pioneers) School in Henan 河南 Province told a reporter: "People think they can find happiness in money. We try to teach the original Confucianism here, and it asks people to discipline themselves and treat others well, so that society can be harmonious."[16] Although the film, starring Chow Yun-fat, was expected to draw a large audience despite its traditionalist content and state sponsorship, evidently the government failed to take into account the simultaneous release of James Cameron's 3-D blockbuster *Avatar.* Chinese audiences stayed away from *Kongzi* 孔子 and went to see *Avatar* in droves, earning it a first-weekend gross of 33 million RMB.[17] But when more than 10 million copies of the Confucian *Analects* are purchased by Chinese consumers within a period of less than two years, as occurred between 2007 and the present, it should be clear that the revival of Confucianism is more than a state effort and also more successful than such efforts alone. Private concerns and public policies have colluded to make it happen.

Freedom with Confucian Characteristics

Thus, celebrities, mainstream media consumers, folk heroes, educators, peasants, and the government itself in China are complicit in resurrecting what once seemed to be a dead tradition. The revival of Confucianism as a popular ideology may be understood as evidence of one major expression of globalization that Vedi R. Hafiz has labeled "neo-third worldism."[18] On Hafiz's account, neo-third worldism is "characterized by indigenism, reactionary populism and strong inclination towards cultural insularism . . . [and] nostalgia for a romanticized, indigenous, pre-capitalist past."[19] In contrast with globalization—"conceptualized as an inevitable leap into friction-free flows of commodities, capital, corporations, communication, and consumers all over the world"[20] that promotes trans-local or Western-identified values as liberating, democratic, and cosmopolitan—neo-third worldism advances regional or nationally identified values as resources for the assertion of non-Western and traditional identities and institutions against Western dominance and exploitation. As Gilbert Rozman has argued, "Any effort to revive Confucianism soon is likely to come from the forces against globalization to reduce integration with the outside."[21] Confucianism's utility as an instrument of Chinese cultural, political, and spiritual resistance against hegemonic Western values may assure its future in formerly anti-Confucian China.

To return to Jackie Chan's comments introduced earlier, how might the resurgence of Confucianism as a popular ideology in contemporary China generate ambivalence and skepticism toward "freedom"? In condemning contemporary Chinese society as permissive, self-indulgent, and corrupt, on the one hand, and in championing values of principle, self-sacrifice, and integrity, on the other, popular Confucian moralism reveals its unique understanding of "freedom," which in turn indicates the extent to which contemporary popular Confucianism in China may function as a vehicle for neo-third worldist resistance to Western-driven globalization. Whereas the English term *freedom* (from the Old English *freo*, "exempt, not in bondage") connotes for most Westerners "freedom from chains, from imprisonment, from enslavement by others,"[22] the Chinese term *ziyou* 自有 ("depending on self, self-possession") "signifies 'a license to be bad' . . . in both Chinese Confucian and communist contexts."[23] Clearly, the word may be used to quite different semantic ends in different linguistic and cultural contexts.

But whether English or Chinese, "freedom" as ethical concept entails (1) a description of self (who am I?), (2) a description of agency (what can I do?), and (3) a prescription of responsibility (what should I do?). In the Confucian tradition, "self" is understood as an entity embedded within a web of relationships that are collective (e.g., family, local community, region, nation, world, cosmos), hierarchical (e.g., seniority by age, sex, class, rank, wisdom), and interdependent (e.g., genealogical, economic, political, ecological, spiritual) in nature. As Wang Yangming (1472–1529 CE) put it:

> The ordinary man . . . lives in accordance with nature; but it is carried out by the sage to a greater extent, and therefore the saying, "An accordance with nature is called the Way [*Dao* 道]," refers to the affairs of the sage. . . . The adult is an all-pervading unity—one substance—with heaven, earth, and [living] things. He views the earth as one family and his country as one man. The youth makes a cleavage between himself and others. . . .[24]

For Confucians, who we are, then, is intrinsically limited in ways that militate against Western notions of "freedom" (that is, a theory that links a particular self-understanding with a description of agency and a prescription of responsibility), but instead give rise to a distinctively Confucian notion of "freedom."[25] According to this notion, freedom consists of individual cultivation and development of innate and intuitive dispositions, tastes, and virtues informed by biology, culture, and the transcendent (*Tian* 天, "Heaven"). For example, according to Mengzi, human appetites and tastes are "natural" (*xing* 性) to the extent that they are within our control and desirable to us, but they also have an element of "fate" (*ming* 命) within them—that is, to the extent that they are beyond our control and coercive to us. Similarly, Confucian virtues such as co-humanity (*ren* 仁) and rightness (*yi* 義) also are both "natural" to us and "fated" for us, insofar as they are both chosen (we need not cultivate our "heart-mind [*xin*], which cannot bear to see the sufferings of others") and contingent (we cannot help being born with such a "heart-mind" and its innate potential for boundless compassion).[26] Like sensory relations, social relations are ordered by "fate" (not-self) and manipulable by "nature" (self), and in this perhaps paradoxical relationship between fate and nature lies Confucian freedom.[27] To be neither a slave to self nor a puppet of others is to harmonize both self and other, the personal and the cosmic, which may be taken as the most profound meaning of the phrase *Tian ren he yi* 天人合一 ("Heaven and humanity forming a harmonious unity").

To be convinced by this notion of "freedom with Confucian characteristics" is to be skeptical of both a Chinese Communist discourse that emphasizes total obedience to the Party as "fate" and a Western liberal discourse that emphasizes total indulgence of the self as "nature." It is no wonder that Jackie Chan expressed his ambivalence about freedom in the way that he did, and less wonder still that the majority of his audience, attracted to and shaped by a resurgent Confucianism, responded in the way that they did. A 2007 survey of 629 history students at thirty-three Chinese universities undertaken by the Chinese Academy of Social Sciences (Zhongguo Shehui Kexueyuan 中国社会科学院) found that more than 70 percent of China's young elites reported "individual struggle" as their belief system, while another 10 percent "did not know." Moreover, more than 60 percent identified with "liberalism" (*zìyóu zhǔyì* 自由主义). However, Kongzi 孔子 (Confucius) was included in lists of the ten greatest thinkers in world history submitted by almost 90 percent of respondents, and while most other thinkers listed were Western (Marx appeared on 82.3 percent of responses), the third most popular was Mengzi.[28] This must be what the Chinese sociologist Sun Liping 孙立平 means when he calls Chinese modernity "fractured" (*duanlie* 断裂).[29] Chinese society today is "fractured" because it is confronted by the issues that "flow from processes of self-actualization in post-traditional contexts."[30] Alternatively, one may view contemporary China as being "in transition," as Robert Moore and James Rizor put it:

> It is as though the Great Proletarian Cultural Revolution that drastically disrupted and shaped the lives of [those born in the 1950s and 1960s] was nothing more than a passing storm. The enduring forces that young Chinese continue to respond to are those rooted in their famously ancient culture, and those recently brought to their shores by the fast-paced and commercially driven popular culture of the West. [31]

It is precisely these issues of "fracture" and "transition" that contemporary popular Confucianism in China seeks to address.

In a recent critique published in his blog, Sūn argues that the problem that afflicts contemporary Chinese society is not "social turmoil" (*shehui dongdang* 社会动荡, for which the antidote is "social stability" *shehui wending* 社会稳定, the goal of most current Chinese government policies), but rather "social decay" (*shehui kuibai* 社会溃败, the opposite of which is "social health," *shehui jiankang* 社会健康).[32] As the response to Chan's comments and other parallel developments show, it is to the intuitive group morality defined by Kongzi, Mengzi, and other Confucian thinkers that contemporary popular Confucianism in China appeals in order to offer a moral critique of youth and champion native norms against both Western challenges and indigenous affronts and thereby to promote "social health": moral order, proper relationships, and mutual trust between a benevolent regime and its dutiful subjects. But what might "social health" mean in contemporary China?

In 2007, Chinese newspapers, television programs, and Web sites were abuzz with news of the Wang 王 brothers, two men in their fifties who walked 65,000 steps (about 40 kilometers or 25 miles per day) to carry their aged mother all over China in a custom-built carriage they dubbed *Gan'en* 感恩 ("Thanksgiving").[33] Traveling in this way, they spent 265 days taking their mother to famous sites in twenty-five provinces that their deceased father had hoped to show her. They repeated their extraordinary performance in 2010, when they covered more than 4,500 kilometers (about 2,796 miles) on foot, hauling their mother's carriage all the way from *Heilongjiang* 黑龙江 Province in the northeast to Fujian 福建 Province in the southeast. When asked why they were engaged in such a difficult and seemingly absurd activity, the brothers replied: "We are not doing this for money or fame. We are just spreading the virtue of filial piety [*xiao*]." Why would two middle-aged men willingly endure such hardship? Why would they

articulate their commitment using traditional Confucian language (not
to mention the traditional Chinese religious practice of pilgrimage)?
And why would they do so now, in the early twenty-first century, when
Confucianism long ago was pronounced dead by China's Communist
regime, not to mention a half-century of progressive-minded reformers
who preceded Mao Zedong's Communist Revolution in 1949?

To many in a fractured nation in transition that perceives its "social
health" as imperiled, Confucianism increasingly looks like a cure. Indeed,
in comments recently made on Chinese national television, Chan both
invoked the metaphor of China as a recovering patient and sounded
a Confucian note in his response to the nation's sixtieth anniversary
festivities in Beijing's Tian'anmen Square on October 1, 2009: "China
has never been better in the last five thousand years. Great unity [*datong*
大同] . . . everything is good. Even Heaven [*Tian* 天] is helping us."[34]

Despite his occasional forays into Confucian rhetoric, Chan may
have functioned less as a Confucian critic and more as a catalyst for
Confucian critique by the masses.

Notes

1. Malcolm Moore, "Jackie Chan Says Chinese people Need to Be
'Controlled,'" *The Telegraph*, April 12, 2009, http://www.telegraph.co.uk/news/
worldnews/asia/china/5182114/Jackie-Chan-says-Chinese-people-need-to-be-
controlled.html.

2. "Reactions To Jackie Chan 'Control' Comment & Translation,"
chinaSMACK, April 28, 2009, http://www.chinasmack.com/more/chinese-reactions-
translation-jackie-chan-controlled-comment/.

3. Although I prefer the term "popular" to "vulgar," the term favored by Tu
Weiming and others, I use it to signify much the same thing denoted by their use of
"vulgar": "the essential constitutive element in China's national culture . . . [which]
played a decisive role in the norms of everyday human interaction" (quoted in John
Makeham, *Lost Soul: "Confucianism" in Contemporary Chinese Academic Discourse*
[Cambridge, MA: Harvard University Asia Center, 2008], 100).

4. Oiwan Lam, "China: Yang Jia Is Dead," *Global Voices Online*, November
26, 2008, http://globalvoicesonline.org/2008/11/26/china-yang-jia-is-dead/.

5. Ibid.

6. "Waitress Stabs Government Official Trying to Rape Her,"
chinaSMACK, May 18, 2009, http://www.chinasmack.com/more/waitress-stabs-
government-official-during-rape-attempt/.

7. Jane Macartney, "Waitress Deng Yujiao Who Stabbed to Death
Communist Official Walks Free," *The Times*, June 17, 2009, http://www.timesonline.
co.uk/tol/news/world/asia/article6513750.ece.

8. "Waitress Stabs Government Official Trying to Rape Her."

9. See Fangqin Du and Susan Mann, "Competing Claims on Womanly Virtue in Late Imperial China," in *Women and Confucian Cultures in Premodern China, Korea, and Japan*, ed. Dorothy Ko, Jahyun Kim Haboush, and Joan R. Piggott (Berkeley: University of California Press, 2003), 219–247.

10. Nick Young, "The Cultural Crusades," *New Internationalist* 423 (June 2009), http://www.newint.org/features/2009/06/01/culture/.

11. Andrew B. Kipnis, "Within and against Peasantness: Backwardness and Filiality in Rural China," *Comparative Studies in Society and History* 37, no. 1 (January 1995): 130, 132.

12. Stanley Rosen, "Contemporary Chinese Youth and the State," *Journal of Asian Studies* 68, no. 2 (May 2009): 363.

13. Anna Xiao Dong Sun, "The Fate of Confucianism as a Religion in Socialist China: Controversies and Paradoxes," *State, Market and Religions in Chinese Societies*, ed. Fenggang Yang and Joseph B. Tamney (Leiden: Brill, 2005), 250, n. 9.

14. Daniel A. Bell, "The Confucian Party," *New York Times*, May 11, 2009, http://www.nytimes.com/2009/05/12/opinion/12iht-edbell.html.

15. Peter Foster, "China Backs £10m Biopic of Confucius," *The Telegraph*, March 16, 2009, http://www.telegraph.co.uk/news/worldnews/asia/china/4999702/China-backs-10m-biopic-of-Confucius.html.

16. Maureen Fan, "Confucius Making a Comeback in Money-Driven Modern China," *Washington Post*, July 24, 2007, http://www.washingtonpost.com/wp-dyn/content/article/2007/07/23/AR2007072301859.html.

17. Elaine Chow, "Avatar Cashing In in China," *The Shanghaiist*, January 11, 2010, http://shanghaiist.com/2010/01/11/avatar_cashing_in_in_china_how_you.php.

18. Vedi R. Hadiz, "The Rise of Neo-Third Worldism? The Indonesian Trajectory and the Consolidation of Illiberal Democracy," *Third World Quarterly* 25, no. 1 (2004): 56.

19. Ibid.

20. T. Luke and G. Tuathail, "Global Flow-mations, Local Fundamentalisms, and Fast Geopolitics," in *Unruly World: Globalization, Governance and Geography*, ed. A. Herod, G. Tuathail, and S. Roberts (London: Routledge, 1998), 76.

21. "Can Confucianism Survive in an Age of Universalism and Globalization?," *Pacific Affairs* 75, no. 1 (Spring 2002): 36.

22. Isaiah Berlin, *Four Essays on Liberty* (London: Oxford University Press, 1969), lvi.

23. Frances H. Foster, "Translating Freedom for Post-1997 Hong Kong," *Washington University Law Quarterly* 76, no. 1 (Spring 1998), 40.

24. *The Philosophy of Wang Yang-Ming*, trans. Frederick Goodrich Henke, 2nd ed. (New York: Paragon Book Reprint Company, 1964), 157–158, 204.

25. It is ironic that antiliberal discourse, such as what I am calling contemporary popular Confucianism, is registered most prominently in online

venues, given the extent to which what Yang Guobin calls "online activism" in China today voices quintessentially liberal, modern, and Western concerns such as individual autonomy and self-realization. See Yang, *The Power of the Internet in China: Citizen Activism Online* (New York: Columbia University Press, 2009), 28–43.

26. See *Mengzi* 7B24.

27. "[Confucianism] neatly balanc[es] two contradictory propositions: that life is fated, and so outside our control, ruled by unseen forces, and that humans construct their own fates" (Michael Nylan, *The Five 'Confucian' Classics* [New Haven: Yale University Press, 2001], 207).

28. Rosen, "Contemporary Chinese Youth and the State," 365–366.

29. Quoted in Yang, 40.

30. Anthony Giddens, *Modernity and Self-Identity: Self and Society in the Late Modern Age* (Stanford: Stanford University Press, 1991), 214.

31. "Confucian and Cool," *Education about Asia* 13, no. 3 (Winter 2008): 37.

32. Sun Liping, "The Biggest Threat to China Is not Social Turmoil but Social Decay," *China Digital Times*, March 2009, http://chinadigitaltimes.net/2009/03/sun-liping-%E5%AD%99%E7%AB%8B%E5%B9%B3-the-biggest-threat-to-china-is-not-social-turmoil-but-social-decay/.

33. "Fueled by Filial Piety," *China Daily*, March 10, 2010, http://www.china.org.cn/china/2010-03/10/content_19573827.htm.

34. Both the terms *dàtóng* and *Tiān* are rich with Confucian resonance, referring to the ideal social order and its transcendent source, respectively. Chan's use of the term "Heaven" evidently was inspired by the cloudless, rainless skies that day in Běijīng—ideal conditions guaranteed by the state's use of cloud-dispersing technologies immediately before the parade was to begin. His remarks on this occasion also excited passions in both mainland and overseas Chinese communities. See http://globalvoicesonline.org/2009/10/08/china-jackie-chans-comment-on-military-parade/.

PART THREE

Confucianism and Popular Culture

6

Like The Air We Breathe

Confucianism and Chinese Youth

Robert L. Moore

In the summer of 2000, I found myself at a punk rock concert in a dark basement bar on the north side of Beijing. The punk scene was new to China's youth culture at that time, though its sudden appearance, complete with five-inch spiked Mohawks, gaudily dyed hair, and rambunctious mosh pits, was predictable. By the beginning of the new millennium, Chinese youth culture had taken off in dozens of new directions as influences from international youth culture movements flooded into the People's Republic. On the surface, it seemed that the young punksters, who were dancing and moshing to the sounds of a local band, the Beijing Punx, had embraced the raucous antisocial attitude first expressed by the likes of England's Sid Vicious and Johnny Rotten in the 1970s. But a closer look at the spiked-haired moshers made it clear that there was a distinctly Chinese sensibility peeking out from beneath the antisocial, punkish veneer. The Chinese moshers were smiling and obviously enjoying themselves as they shoved and bumped against each other, always being careful not to inflict pain. These may have been wild-looking punksters, but they exuded an air of benevolence.

The mixing of Western-inspired surface features with traditional, Confucian-based underlying forms is typical of many aspects of China's millennial youth. The surface features, in fact, can be found in cities all over China. Cosmopolitan centers like Shanghai and Beijing, in particular, include venues inhabited by young people with tattoos, pink hair, and pierced lips—though such extreme displays are usually adopted by only a small minority of Chinese. Popular music, on the other hand, is followed in its many forms by almost all urban youth in China. In fact, some foreign visitors claim that the Beijing music scene has surpassed New York, London, and Los Angeles in both excitement and innovation. Clubs like D-22 in Beijing and Mao Live House in Shanghai feature performances that do, indeed, rival those one might find in major Western cities. And CDs of Chinese punk, hip-hop, reggae, classic rock, jazz, and various other musical styles are available in stores or from pirate vendors on the streets of most of China's cities and towns.

Some of the books read by young Chinese also push the envelope of propriety: in 2000, Wei Hui's *Shanghai Baobei* led the way into the realm of the taboo with its explicit portrayals of sexual encounters and drug use by a free-spirited young Shanghainese woman. Though banned, it became an underground best-seller and, translated into English, reached a significant audience overseas. Still, though outlandish clothing and grooming styles can be found among the more rebellious minority, the great majority of young Chinese continue to comport themselves conservatively, and only a tiny minority would indulge in the casual sex and drug scene portrayed in *Shanghai Baobei*. It may be said that one feature of China's urban youth is their interest in what foreigners and those who imitate foreign ways are doing, even when few are willing to follow the more extreme versions of Western rebelliousness. And when extreme Western accoutrements are taken up, there is often an underlying, distinctly Chinese spirit, one whose roots reach back to the ways of the ancients.

The spirit of the Chinese of the millennial generation is difficult to capture in a few descriptive pages, but there are some patterns that are prominent enough to be worth noting. Among these is the fundamental adherence by the great majority of young Chinese to the basic premises of traditional Chinese culture, which typically is associated with the teachings of Confucianism. In fact, given the new respect that Confucius is enjoying as his image is revitalized and brought front and center by the government of the People's Republic of China (PRC), the Confucian culture that never quite disappeared among the young people of China—despite decades of turbulence and occasional outbursts of anti-Confucian hostility—is being acknowledged for what it is: a cultural complex focused on a cluster of closely associated values attributed to Confucius and his followers. Perhaps the most prominent of these is *xiao*, or filial piety, an attitude that requires deference and obedience toward one's parents.

David Jordan describes filial piety as an inclusive complex incorporating a mental state, a behavioral code, a set of actions, and a system of underlying values.[1] To talk about a complex that comprises values, mental states, codes, and actions is to talk about culture, and it is as a cultural complex that Confucianism can best be understood where millennial Chinese youth are concerned. Confucianism can also, of course, be construed as a formal system of thought in a variety of guises—as a religion, a social philosophy, and so forth—but here I emphasize its role as a traditional way of thinking and behaving that has long shaped understandings of the nature of China's cultural roots, to use a widely repeated metaphor. Those aspects of culture that are thought of as being "traditional" in China have, over the past century, been sometimes reviled but just as often cherished by young Chinese. Today, in the wake of the centennial anniversary of the fall of the Qing imperial government approaches, notions of "Chinese tradition" and "the Chinese way" are gaining prestige as the PRC shows that it has taken its place on the world stage and is here to stay as a major player. In other words, ideas about the sources of China's enduring culture are being incorporated in a contemporary nationalistic discourse that casts the People's Republic as a purveyor of a cultural system that might be viewed as an alternative to the long-dominant Western model.

My discussion of Confucianism among contemporary young Chinese is based mainly on material I have collected from middle school and university students living in urban environments. Consequently, much of what I have to say reflects the perspective of this segment of Chinese society. Rural youth and young urban workers face their own unique situations, and, given my limited experiences with these young people, I can only note in passing some of the features of their lives that seem to set them apart from the educated young people I know best. My data include material I gathered while I was a visiting faculty member at Qingdao University during the 1993–94 academic year, supplemented by further data collected during a series of seven visits to Beijing, Shanghai, and Yunnan Province between 1998 and 2008. I should also note that I lived in Hong Kong for about a year (1974–75) while doing research on culture change in what was then a British crown colony.

Among the university and middle school students I have been interviewing and spending time with over the past two decades, the influence of Confucianism is recognized as a constant and pervasive force. When these young people talk about Confucianism, they typically do not focus on Confucius, Mencius, or other authors of specific philosophical ideas, but are more likely to conjure up general notions of "Chineseness" or of those qualities that give the Han Chinese people their distinctive qualities. Along these lines, I have encountered young Chinese who compared Confucian influence to the "spiritual air" they breathe, to a kind of "cultural gravity" that exerts a steady force on one's behavior and even to "a permanent nicotine patch stuck on the body" whose influence ceaselessly permeates one's very being. For many Chinese in the millennial generation, to be Confucian amounts to being Han Chinese, that is, a member of the dominant ethnic group of China. It is the Han Chinese who developed the Chinese writing system, imperial governance, and the world-famous Chinese cuisine, and it is with them that Confucius and Confucianism are identified. It is this identity to which so many Chinese refer when they describe Confucian influence as something akin to the air they breathe. There are, of course, citizens of the People's Republic who are not Han, including members of such minority groups as the Tibetans, the Uighurs, and others, but it is the Han Chinese who closely identify with Confucius and the cultural complex associated with him. This identity is generally positive, but there are also some young Chinese who express a degree of resentment toward Confucius and the Chinese tradition he symbolizes for them. These young people may be compared to those outspoken young Americans who promote socialistic ideals: they are a minority who recognize the dominant current of their national culture but do not approve of it.

The dubious light in which this minority sees Confucian influence may be a reflection of the fact that China, over the past hundred years, has undergone a series of turbulent changes, many of which entailed attacks on Confucianism and most of which were led by rebellious youth. In the midst of this turmoil, Confucius and Confucianism have sometimes been reviled as emblems of backwardness or unjust exploitation. These are not the dominant themes that characterize the image of Confucius today, but they are felt rather sharply by some young Chinese. In any case, the story of how the young people of contemporary China have sometimes opposed but ultimately come to accept Confucianism, as most now do, requires a brief review.

The justifications for anti-Confucian attacks were rooted in those features of Confucianism that were deemed to clash with modern values. Among these were the strong Confucian biases in favor of males over females and of elders over the young. Another recurring point of contention was the absence in Confucianism of democratic ideals. Sometimes the assaults were cast as opposing feudalism or what was commonly regarded as China's backwardness vis-à-vis Japan and the West. At other times, Confucianism, broadly speaking, or even Confucius the man became specific objects of scorn. As Confucianism makes its comeback today, its modern permutations differ from what it was a century ago largely because of the attacks it has endured since 1911.

I focus in particular on a cluster of Confucian values that have been of particular concern to China's youth over the past century and that continue to shape the thinking of the millennial generation. These include special regard for filial devotion, family unity, respect for elders, the chastity of women, social harmony, education, and the ways of the ancients.

Other Confucian values, including those associated with ancestor veneration and ideas about the benevolent patriarch as the cornerstone of good government, have played a part in youth movements at different times. But the ones listed above have often been linked together and today serve as something of a subtle blueprint underlying contemporary Chinese youth culture as the millennial generation seeks to construct its place in China's rapidly changing social milieu.

Closely entwined with these values are issues pertinent to courtship and marriage. Traditionally, Confucianism put a premium on female modesty, and in practice it was the custom in late imperial China for parents to enforce female chastity by restricting contact between their marriageable daughters and any men who were not family members. In some cases, women were confined to their own residences for much of their youth and allowed to walk the streets only when accompanied by appropriate chaperones. Parents also controlled their children, both female and male, by choosing their spouses for them. The Confucian-based justification for parental control of marriage became a prime target of anti-Confucian hostility among young Chinese in the May Fourth era, which began in 1919. Traditional ideas about female modesty were also modified at this time, but in recent years, as I illustrate below, this particular value has again begun to undergo drastic modification.

Down with Confucius! Youthful Iconoclasm, 1919 to 1978

The student-led street demonstrations in Beijing of May 4, 1919, marked the beginning of a new era in China. Though the May Fourth demonstrations were triggered by anger at the government for its inability to defend China's territorial integrity, the New Culture Movement that subsequently grew from this student uprising had broader implications. The students of 1919 belonged to the first generation of Chinese youth who had been extensively exposed to the technical and liberal arts curricula typical of Western education. They and the young intellectuals who supported them promoted a New Culture Movement that emphasized science and democracy as its principal ideals. The proponents of this movement cast Confucianism as the primary reason for China's backwardness and hence China's vulnerability to domination by the foreign powers. One of the more interesting and influential texts comprising this anti-Confucian critique was Pa Chin's (pinyin: Ba Jin) widely read novel *Family*, which was first published in 1931.[2] This largely autobiographical story was based on the experiences the author faced in his own elite Chengdu family, and it embodies a number of themes that reflect the attitudes of China's youth of the May Fourth era. The story focuses on the generational clash that three young brothers have with their hidebound grandfather, the family patriarch. The most rebellious of the brothers is Chueh-hui (pinyin: Juehui) the central character in the narrative. Confucius and the writings of the sages rank high among the objects of Chueh-hui's contempt, as is evident, for example, when he is described as feeling his flesh creep at the mention of "the works of the sages"[3] or when he hears his young cousins reciting from a text on filial piety.[4] Around him Chueh-hui sees hypocrisy on the part of those elders who call themselves Confucian. Men of the senior generations—his grandfather and uncles—acquire concubines and pursue prostitutes and female impersonators for sexual pleasure, all the while proclaiming their attachment to Confucian virtues. In fact, many of those elders belong to the Confucian Morals Society, an organization whose values Chueh-hui and his youthful cohorts despise. *Family* was one of the most widely read works of Chinese fiction in the twentieth century, its popularity among young Chinese in the 1930s stemming from its promotion of values that were seen as modern, though some of its appeal was no doubt also due to the compelling love stories that lay at its center.

Democracy and individual freedom were also points of contention that inspired the May Fourth generation, and these are given attention in *Family* as well. But most of the conflict between the generations revolves around the youths' demand for their right to marry for love. Pa Chin's novelistic portrayal was accurate in that many well-educated young Chinese did begin to find their own spouses in the 1920s and

1930s, but there were limits to how much filial defiance they were able to muster, and as late as the 1990s it was unusual to find young Chinese, even among university students, who were willing to marry against their parents' adamant opposition.[5] The older generation succeeded in holding onto some degree of Confucian authority, even after the Marriage Law of 1950 gave individuals the legal right to choose their own spouses. The highly fraught intertwining of Confucian-based parental authority and youthful romantic impulses has followed a long and tortuous path throughout the twentieth century. As I argue below, it is not without its effect in China today.

When the Chinese Communist Party (CCP) came to power in 1949, it continued to pursue some of the policies it had long promoted in the liberated areas under its control since the 1930s. Among those were the redistribution of property from the wealthy to the poor and a series of actions aimed at undermining the Confucian-based authority of powerful, property-holding lineages. Furthermore, the ranks of the Communist armies were filled with young men whose experiences and new opportunities promoted attitudes that encouraged them to take a number of matters that were once under the purview of their parents into their own hands. In doing so, the CCP ironically wound up promoting a measure of individualism among its younger followers, partly by encouraging young people to act against traditional norms. Selden describes poor peasant youth as the "most explosive element" in the land redistribution program of the 1930s and 1940s and says that young people "not only supplied the manpower for local guerrilla and paramilitary units but began to assume leadership positions in Communist-sponsored mass organizations, party branches, and local government."[6] About the Communist-led peasant revolution in the 1930s, he writes

> Suddenly [young revolutionaries] were exposed to visions beyond the narrow confines of their isolated villages and the network of family and landlord ties which circumscribed their future. . . . Now education and the revolutionary movement opened extraordinary vistas to the young and vigorous.[7]

In overthrowing the old landlord-dominated property system, young Chinese of that era were seeing themselves as effective agents in a society that had previously relegated them to a relatively passive status embedded in traditional family and community hierarchies.

Furthermore, youth organizations included both males and females, and one consequence of this was the beginning of individual courtships where none had previously been allowed. When young peasants participated in organizations or attended classes sponsored by the CCP, they were thrown together in a way that had been unthinkable for villagers of previous generations because of the long-standing emphasis on female modesty. The revolution created circumstances within which romance could blossom. In 2008, an elderly Party member from a village just north of Beijing described to me how, as a young man, he had fled to the hills along with his neighbors when Nationalist troops temporarily occupied his district. While there, he helped organize the young people of the village into a Party auxiliary, and in doing so he met the woman who would eventually become his wife. According to him, there was quite a lot of romancing going on among the village youth during the days of the Civil War between the CCP and the Nationalists.[8] Yan describes a similar pattern in a Heilongjiang village wherein the CCP in the 1940s organized peasants in ways that undermined the authority of parents and other elders and at the same time presented young people with opportunities to form romantic liaisons. This meant that when the authority of the Party weakened in the reform era, young people, now unconstrained by parental control, found themselves with more freedom than any previous generations had known. The unintended and paradoxical effect of the CCP's attack on Confucian institutions was the engendering of the seeds of individualism among many young Chinese.[9]

The era of the Cultural Revolution (1966–76) was one during which Confucius and the tradition with which he was identified were fiercely and directly assaulted. It entailed acts of violence carried out by young people bent on destroying emblems of tradition and undermining the authority of teachers and other elders. During this turbulent period, university and secondary school students, calling themselves Red Guards and enjoying the support of Chairman Mao, took it upon themselves to discipline those adults whom they regarded as lacking in revolutionary ideals. Though the political activities of the Red Guards can be described as part of a youth movement, behind this movement was Chairman Mao himself, who gave the students a green light when he told the police to refrain from impeding youthful revolutionary activities. During the height of the Cultural Revolution, between 1966 and 1969, when youth and student violence were at a peak, a group of Red Guards went so far as to travel from Beijing to Qufu to destroy the Temple and grave site of Confucius.[10]

The attack on the monuments in Qufu was one moment of the Cultural Revolution in which Confucius himself became a target of hostility. Another occurred during the "Criticize Lin Biao, Criticize Confucius" campaign of the mid-1970s, Lin Biao being a prominent CCP leader who died in a plane crash in 1971. The sudden prominence of Confucius as an object of intense scorn took many observers by surprise and is generally interpreted in terms of the ruthless and byzantine politics of the Cultural Revolution. According to the convoluted logic that put Confucius and Lin Biao in the same category, both of these "villains" had conservative tendencies aimed at restoring the power of previously overthrown classes. This campaign was not really a youth movement, however, though millions of youths did respond to the call to criticize Confucius. The basis for the criticism was so misbegotten that it actually had little to do with Confucius at all, and there is no evidence indicating that this campaign had a lasting effect on the status of Confucianism.

In light of the emphasis that Confucianism places on respect for one's parents, it is perhaps not surprising that the rebellious Chinese students who assaulted prominent elders during the height of the Cultural Revolution were usually reluctant to direct their aggression against their own parents. Adolescent assaults against parents did occasionally occur, however. Chihua Wen describes an incident in which a fourteen-year-old boy used a metal rod to beat his father and other men who had been labeled "cow ghosts and snake spirits."[11] In another incident, an adolescent describes a scene in which he was at home drinking, playing cards, and acting rowdy when his father appeared and, angrily turning over the card table, shouted, "You are an evil, wicked boy who deserves to be taken outside and beaten within an inch of his life. You get out of my house. I will not have this kind of a son."

In response, the boy pulled out a pistol he had taken during a raid on a military post and pointed it at his father's head, shouting, "You get out of here instantly or prepare to die!"

The father, stunned at his son's behavior, did leave the room. As the boy recounted the story to Chihua Wen decades later, he expressed regret over his behavior. Like the fourteen-year-old who beat his father with a metal rod, this adolescent was motivated in his unfilial behavior by the conviction that he was serving the revolution and, more specifically, the wishes of Chairman Mao.

The conflict between parental and state authority is an old one in China, but it is one in which Confucius's teachings advocated greater loyalty to parents. In a famous exchange in *The Analects* (XIII, 18), Confucius declares that "an upright father will screen his son and a son his father" even when to do so amounts to circumventing the law. In fact, the case referred to in this quotation involved a father's stealing a sheep, the question thus posed being: Should the son turn his father in, or is it moral for the son to protect his father despite the theft? The Confucius of *The Analects* has it that even in the case of theft, a son should be loyal to his father and not to the state.

This approach to ethics undermines the authority of the state, and so we can assume that few Chinese rulers appreciated it. Certainly it was anathema to Mao and his circle during the Cultural Revolution. The Chairman specified that young people made the best revolutionaries, and from his point of view, any criticism or attacks they leveled against their "bourgeois" or "feudalistic" parents were all to the good. It is nonetheless astonishing that a culture imbued with respect for elders and particularly teachers could have produced a generation of young people willing to be so recklessly aggressive against those adults who for millennia had represented bastions of moral worthiness. The basis for the violence and verbal assaults of the youth of the Cultural Revolution came from their seemingly limitless devotion to Chairman Mao. The one criterion that could righteously sustain any criticism or political maneuver in that era was the claim that it was undertaken in the name of or with the blessing of the Chairman. The entire Cultural Revolution pivoted on the personage of Mao, whose stature was that of a virtually sacred being and who, like the emperors of old, could be neither criticized nor disparaged. Mao was different from traditional emperors, however, in that he represented China itself rather than the will of Heaven. In this he may be said to have combined the traditional Confucian notion of the all-powerful benevolent leader with the modern idea of nationalism. At any rate, for young people who rebelled against their teachers and other elders, he was the touchstone by which all morality was judged.

The Reform Era and the Rise of China's Millennial Youth

In 1978, just two years after Mao's death, Deng Xiaoping launched economic reforms that would culminate in an era of rapid growth whose effects are still being felt throughout the world today. Within China, one of the consequences of these reforms was the emergence of a generation of students who sought to express defiance toward the central government in ways that had not been seen since the May Fourth era. Tragically for these young rebels, their voices were silenced by the crackdown in Beijing of June 4, 1989. The most compelling social-political current of June 4 proved to be Legalism, a traditional philosophy that opposed Confucianism by claiming that moral example on the part of the benevolent patriarch is not crucial to governance and that systematic control and intimidation are the most effective devices for maintaining peace and prosperity. The state's ruthlessness in suppressing the young demonstrators was a reflection not only of Legalism but also of the harshest aspects of Maoism. This suppression introduced a new era in the PRC, one in which the populace was forced to defer to Beijing's authority on major issues but in which the CCP continued to relax its control over most aspects of citizens' private lives. Implicit in this arrangement was the promise that in exchange for compliance, citizens would be allowed to pursue individual economic interests such that prosperity for all would ensue. The promise of prosperity has become a reality for many urban Chinese, and this has contributed to docile compliance on the part of most. Few, however, continue to accept the moral authority of Marxism, and this has resulted in a moral vacuum.[12]

The loss of a moral center has caused many Chinese today to seek guidance from such long-established world religions as Buddhism, Islam, and Christianity or newly invented ones like Falun Gong. The current revival of Confucianism is also partly due to the longing for a viable moral system. Another factor in this revival is the purposeful promotion of Confucius by the CCP. Daniel Bell notes that both President Hu Jintao and Premier Wen Jiabao recently cited Confucian values, such as harmony, community, and love of humanity, in their public statements.[13] The grave site of Confucius in Qufu, smashed by Red Guards during the Cultural Revolution, has been repaired, and it, along with the nearby Confucius family mansion, has become a major tourist destination for Chinese and foreigners alike. A growing number of books about Confucius can be seen in Chinese bookstores, and in 2010 China produced a film about the life of Confucius starring one of China's (and Hong Kong's) most famous actors, Chow Yun-fat. Television programs on Confucius are also increasingly common.

The Chinese government clearly favors the promotion of Confucianism because a Chinese ethical system, as opposed to those offered by foreign religions, is in line with some of the nationalistic sentiments it seeks to promote. But some influential government figures appear to be genuinely taken with many of the premises of

Confucianism and support them for the benefits they may bring to Chinese society. Official adoption of a pro-Confucian position is the culmination of a series of political, economic, and social changes that have moved China away from the hard-line Maoism of the 1960s and 1970s. By the end of the 1980s, in fact, China had already begun to change significantly, but it was the decade of the 1990s that saw the beginnings of some of the most dramatic social changes that China has experienced in many decades. As is so often the case, it was adolescents and young adults who took the lead in initiating the most important social movements in this era. Indeed, some of the new ideas and behaviors exhibited by China's youth in the 1990s astonished and even perturbed many older Chinese, accustomed as they were to the strictures of Maoism. As young Chinese indulged themselves in previously unimaginable individualistic pursuits, their exuberance was particularly jarring to those in their parents' generation, who, in their own youth, would have been ruthlessly crushed for any individualistic talk or behavior. The new attitude that began to gain traction in the 1990s was largely stimulated by international youth culture. Some aspects of China's globally influenced 1990s youth culture had already sparked a measure of intergenerational conflict in Taiwan.[14] But by the late 1990s, it was mainland China's turn to see what increasing prosperity and contact with the outside world could bring.

One of the symbols of this era of change was the appearance of the Chinese slang term *ku* (酷), based on the English youth culture expression "cool," which suddenly became popular in the mid-1990s. In Mandarin, *ku* has a slight twist differentiating it from the English term in that it is closely associated with individualism.[15] One factor promoting this new individualistic attitude was the relatively relaxed attitude of the state vis-à-vis its citizens' private lives; another was the ever-increasing level of interaction Chinese were having with foreigners. This interaction was facilitated by the hordes of international tourists who began to visit China and by the thousands of Chinese students who studied abroad. Added to this were the importation of American movies and television shows. During the 1993–94, academic year, which I spent on the faculty of Qingdao University, I was struck by my students' hunger for the latest movies and other media from the United States.

Finally, there was an entirely new source of international influence that began to have a major impact on China's youth in the mid-1990s: the Internet. Beginning in the mid-1990s, Internet cafés began to appear in major cities, and today Chinese university and secondary school students are as likely to use chat rooms, e-mail, cell phone texts, and other electronic media as are their Western counterparts. The Internet has been responsible for the development and dissemination of new ideas and attitudes as well as an entirely new kind of youth slang, including the previously noted symbol of youth culture individualism, *ku*. Other features of Internet communication include the use of pinyin-derived Romanized abbreviations, as when "mm" is typed as a substitute for *meimei*, a standard term for little sister, which in contemporary youth slang means "cute girl." Similarly, the character 囧 (*jiong*) is used in Internet slang to mean something like "Oh my God" or "I'm so embarrassed" because of its perceived resemblance to a distressed facial expression.[16]

The flood of media from the United States and other Western countries as well as from Japan and Korea marked the 1990s as an era of rapid change. Anyone spending time in urban China in this decade could have observed a series of Western-influenced fashions making their way through Chinese youth culture: long hair, dyed hair, piercings, spiked hair, and tattoos, to name a few. Yet even as these fashions were adopted by various young Chinese, a more conservative trend continued to be evident, one with which I had already become familiar during my previous stay in Hong Kong in the 1970s. The basis for much of this conservatism was a regard for aspects of Chinese tradition that are commonly referred to as Confucian.

While teaching at Qingdao University in the mid-1990s, I was intrigued by the way in which my students balanced their adoption of Western ways with their regard for traditional Chinese values. In particular, I wondered how this balancing act affected the long-standing Confucian virtue of filial piety (*xiao* 孝). I spent a good deal of time talking with them about this topic and followed up this informal data collection with a questionnaire that I eventually submitted to 231 university students at Qingdao University and three other schools: Tsinghua University, Beijing Aerospace University (both in Beijing), and Luoyang Teachers College (in Henan Province). The questionnaires were in Chinese, and all but a few of the students answered them in Chinese. To compare their responses with those from a non-Confucian background, I distributed 249 similar questionnaires to American students at Rollins College and the University of Central Florida, both of which are in the Orlando, Florida, area. Of these questionnaires, 240 proved usable. I did in fact find that there were significant differences in the responses of the Chinese students concerning their relationships with their parents that distinguished them from their American counterparts.

One item on the questionnaires asked the students to identify the most serious conflicts they had experienced with their parents. As it turned out, both Chinese and American students indicated that their most serious conflicts had occurred between the ages of fourteen and seventeen. But overall, the American adolescents had a much higher rate of conflict than the Chinese. Of the 240 American respondents, 196 reported such cases (82 percent), while only 111 of the 231 (48 percent) Chinese did. There were both similarities and differences in the Chinese and American sources of conflict. The most obvious similarities were in the parents' interest in their offspring performing well in school and not stepping out of line in relations with the opposite sex. However, even these seemingly similar categories concealed some real differences, most of which related to the Confucian traditions that cherish modesty and promote education.

The American responses concerning dating relationships were almost always in the context of females who had boyfriends of whom their parents disapproved, though there were also a few cases of concern over boys having unacceptable girlfriends. The Chinese parents rarely focused their complaints on who the dating partner of their child was, but on the simple fact that the adolescent was seeing a member of the opposite sex at all. Typically, the Chinese parents' criticism over a boyfriend or girlfriend specified concern over the time such a relationship would take away from schoolwork. Furthermore, Chinese parents criticized their male and female offspring equally; they wanted neither sons nor daughters to involve themselves in romantic affairs. This is linked to the Chinese idea that young people need to dedicate long hours to intensive study lest they fall off the educational escalator. This concern, of course, is much more typical of middle-class than of working-class parents.[17] For Chinese parents who want their children to rise in the educational system, there seems to be a sense that the most serious potential distraction is a romantic relationship. By aligning themselves against such relationships, the Chinese parents were linking the traditional value of modesty in romantic or sexual matters with the equally long-established regard for education as the path to social betterment. The parents usually present their argument in the form of "Our children must not be distracted from their studies; therefore, they must not have any time-consuming romantic entanglements." It could be argued, however, that the parents were quite anxious to prevent their children from dangerous romantic or sexual liaisons and that the endless hours of study required of university-bound middle school students were largely a device to promote sexual restraint. In any case, the focus on education, the parental involvement in their adolescents' education, and the insistence by most middle-class Chinese parents that their children avoid romantic relationships work together as a set of coordinated expressions of the Confucian ideals that value parental authority, education, and modesty. Reinforcing these are the heavy emphasis on memorization and the great respect extended to teachers, two features of China's contemporary educational system that have their roots in the Confucian tradition.

Another revealing point to come out of the questionnaire responses pertained to the way disputes were settled in China as opposed to the United States. Somewhat surprisingly, the Chinese were more likely to declare that they scored a "victory" than were the Americans. Many Chinese students used phrases like "I succeeded" (over what university to attend): "At last I win the quarrel" (over a girlfriend); "I decided by myself" (over what university to attend); "My parents had no alternative and had to accept my choice" (over attending a general university rather than a teachers' college); "parents' acquiescence" (over a ten-year-old boy's right to stay out all night).

The Chinese responses also had a larger proportion of parents' victories than did the Americans'. In fact, the image of warfare was altogether more evident in the Chinese descriptions of conflicts than it was among the Americans'. Phrases like "I surrendered" and "I win" were not unusual in the Chinese questionnaire responses, for example. The image of cold war also appeared occasionally. One female student said, regarding a dispute about her not studying diligently enough, that the result was "one and a half years of cold war, then mutual forgiving." A student described herself as being close to a boy she liked at the age of fourteen. Her parents objected strenuously, and the result was "cold war."

The imagery of warfare in the Chinese responses might seem to undermine the oft-made claim that the Chinese way of dealing with conflict favors reconciliation over confrontation. But in fact the imagery of war appears to reflect a different manner of expression more than it does a relatively martial spirit. Chinese students in general are more likely to resort to metaphor and vivid imagery in their portrayal of human relationships, a tendency that reflects a long-standing cultural style. The Chinese students with whom I interacted certainly showed a greater interest in language, literature, and poetry than do typical American students. Some claimed that the essence of being Chinese was largely dependent on using the Chinese written language, and one graduate student told me she thought the thread that held Chinese civilization together through the millennia was Chinese poetry. Furthermore, in China there are collections of traditional sayings that are available for sale in every bookstore. These sayings, many of them from traditional Confucian texts, were often called on by students and other Chinese with whom I conversed to explain a point. A few of them also turned up in my questionnaire responses. In short, the bellicose references in the Chinese responses reflect a cultural preference not for violent conflict, but for vivid imagery. This is further emphasized by the much greater reliance among the Chinese respondents on compromise as the ultimate outcome of disagreements with parents. This preference for compromise was, in fact, the most revealing aspect of the Chinese youths' relationship with their parents.

The American students were far more likely than the Chinese to indicate that a dispute was resolved by time or "changed circumstances." For the Americans, the dispute was not so much settled as allowed to die a slow, natural death as the adolescent grew up or moved out of the house. The American responses indicating that a conflict was resolved not at all or resolved only by changed circumstances are best explained in light of the American tradition of individualism. Instead of a discussion leading to a claim of victory by one side or the other or a compromise, the most common American outcome is one in which neither side gives in to the other.

Another response offered by four of the American students but none of the Chinese was the adolescent's resort to lying. American students said they sometimes ended a dispute by telling their parents that they had, for example, quit smoking when they hadn't. The lying tactic is one that points to a mentality on the part of the Americans that casts them as engaged not in open warfare with their parents, but rather in a kind of guerrilla war, where the parents hold the bulk of the power and where avoidance and deceit are among the most useful tactics. This image of the relatively powerless adolescent and the powerful parent is further underlined by the large number of American adolescents who indicated that their conflicts ended with punishment. None of the Chinese students who had been in conflict with their parents described the conflict as ending with punishment.

The questionnaire data matched what I was hearing in my conversations and interviews with students; all showed that an emphasis on harmony and compromise and the rarity of punishment were accurate reflections of the parent-adolescent relations in urban, middle-class China in the 1990s. Furthermore, they continue to be typical of most such families today. One cautionary point is worth raising here:

Chinese parents in the mid-1990s had few means by which they could punish recalcitrant teenagers. Virtually no family owned a car, so there was no such thing as "grounding" an adolescent, and money was in such short supply in those days that teenagers rarely had anything like an allowance that could have been cut off as a form of punishment. Nonetheless, from the way young Chinese described their negotiations with their parents, I have to conclude that the ideal of harmony within the family was the single most powerful factor distinguishing Chinese from American responses to parent-adolescent conflict.

The Chinese youths described themselves as relying heavily on discussion with a hope of compromise. In the absence of compromise, one side usually succeeds in persuading the other and can then claim "victory." The right to claim victory suggests that the losing side willingly accepts the outcome of the conflict for the sake of the greater entity, that is, the family. Thus, family harmony is maintained in all three of these results: parental victory, adolescent victory, and compromise. These three kinds of outcomes accounted for almost three-quarters of all disputes among the Chinese respondents. For the Americans, the conflicting interests of the individuals mean that a dispute can continue until it dies out through changing circumstances, or it may be hidden by the adolescent through deceit. Such outcomes allow each person to hold onto his or her own position without conceding to the other, a result more acceptable to Americans than to Chinese. The family loses a degree of harmony, but the individuals within it defend their positions to the end.

The Confucian cultural complex encompassing filiality, harmony, education, and modesty continued to dominate much of the thinking and behavior of young Chinese until the late 1990s. Lack of disposable income meant that Chinese university students did not have the means to purchase such things as CDs, computers, stylish clothing, or visits to clubs, but today consumerism has become a major part of their lives. As China's economy grew throughout the 1990s, young urbanites found they had more money to spend than their parents could have dreamed of having during their youth. This capacity to spend for pleasure, along with continuing influence from international youth culture, resulted in some significant changes among young Chinese, particularly in the area of romance and sexuality. Though modesty in romantic and sexual affairs had long been a hallmark of propriety among Chinese middle school and university students, as of the beginning of the new millennium, this value has been significantly undermined, particularly for university students.

It is worth noting here that China has long maintained an understanding of youth in general and students in particular that envisions them as more "pure" (*danchun* 单纯) than their elders or young people who are not in school.[18] One student at Qingdao, for example, told me that his older brother advised him to find a girl who could be his wife while he was at the university, because once they left the campus environment young women lost their purity. This purity is most commonly described as simplicity and straightforwardness, and those who lose it do so by behaving so as to present different sides to different people and by saying things they don't really believe. It is also a reflection of the Confucian ideal that links education to morality. It is widely thought that life outside the university campus obligates people to act in impure ways that can be described as "slick" (*yuanhua*) or "sophisticated" (*shigu*). This loss of purity is correlated in the eyes of both students and former students with a loss of innocence about matters of romance and sexuality. The difference between the rather isolated world of the young university student and the sophisticated environment of the workaday world helped account for the student emphasis on modesty up to the late 1990s.

Until then, most romantic affairs among Chinese university students reflected this ideal of purity, being quite controlled and restrained in comparison to student romances in the United States. They were slow paced in their development and restrictive in that, for any given student, the number of romantic partners with whom one could be involved without damage to one's reputation was limited. Also, the amount of information that students typically revealed to their classmates concerning their romantic affairs was limited. Often, a romantic relationship would develop gradually over a period of weeks before anyone, even at times the best friends of the parties concerned, would be allowed to know about it.[19]

A typically slow-paced affair that culminated in marriage was described by a student at a university in Chengdu in the early 1990s who reported that he started things off, or at least made them overt, when he asked his classmate if she would be interested in "being his friend." This occurred after a period of several weeks during which he had helped her with her computer programming assignments. In fact, he posed the question to her—and she responded positively—while they were working together at a computer terminal. Like most pre-millennial generation students, he would not have dared to ask her "to be his friend" or even to go out on a date after, say, only a week or two of studying together.

Most pre-millennial students would reveal their affection for each other carefully and hesitantly. And only after some time had passed would a couple indulge in the physicality implied in the vernacular phrase getting "close and hot" (*qinre*)—what American youth might call "making out" or "hooking up." Student romances up to the end of the 1990s, then, can be described as conservative, both in terms of the caution with which love was handled and in the idealization of virginity, particularly female virginity. Though the official authorities encouraged these ideals and behaviors, it was the Confucian tradition that really underpins their endurance. When pre-millennial Chinese students explained their conservatism to me, they typically did so with reference to Chinese tradition (*chuantong*) and often pointed to the lingering influence of Confucius himself.[20]

But the "Confucian tradition" that students in the 1980s and 1990s referenced was actually a modified version of Confucianism, one transformed by the effects of the May Fourth Movement. A number of well-known expressions in the Confucian tradition specify the worthiness of ancient mores, as in the Analects, for example, where Confucius says, "I have been faithful to and loved the Ancients" (VII:1). This veneration of antiquity lives on among Chinese today. Both young and old often argue that China's very age makes it special and that its deep cultural roots are more durable than those of younger nations. In fact, the idealization of ancient tradition is itself conceptually linked to Confucianism, a philosophical tradition that has dominated China for more than two thousand years. The Chinese valorization of ancient cultural roots can be compared to the way in which Americans glorify "freedom." In each case, the followers of a particular cultural tradition are making the most of what they believe their own nation's history most convincingly embodies.

Given the positive value that Chinese usually place on the wisdom of the ancients, the concept of "tradition" tends to conjure images of a cultural system whose hoary roots reach back thousands of years into the past and whose antiquity confers legitimacy. But when pre-millennial university students explained that they were restrained in their sexual behavior because of the pull of Chinese tradition, they were not saying they felt compelled to act the way their Han dynasty forebears did. The tradition they called forth was that of the 1920s, the tradition established by the students of the May Fourth Movement. Though their romantic and sexual behavior was shaped by the standards of the 1920s, students who explained their conservatism did so in terms of the powerfully resonant concept of

Chinese tradition, with its implication of legitimacy through antiquity. In this way, they were able to see themselves as linked to their cultural roots even while they behaved with a degree of freedom unknown before the twentieth century.

In any case, the pattern of male-female relationships established after the 1919 May Fourth movement among urban students began to change in the late 1990s, particularly at elite Beijing and Shanghai universities where international influences continued to be particularly strong. Soon campuses in cities all over China were accepting a more liberal approach to student romantic affairs, an approach similar in many ways to that found on Western university campuses. Most Chinese university students today are guided by this more cosmopolitan romantic pattern, one that is different from the fairly conservative post–May Fourth model and that has partially abandoned the ideal of the chaste female. One indication of the prevalence of this model is the widespread use among university students of the little hotels (*xiao luguan*) that are often found near campuses for lovers' rendezvous. Observers of the contemporary dating scene in China have noted the more open attitude toward premarital sexuality among millennial Chinese.[21]

While the "sexual modesty" leg of the Confucian pattern outlined above is now undergoing change among university students, secondary school students appear to be continuing a relatively conservative pattern in male-female relations. Secondary school students in China who plan to attend a university do not have the freedom that American high schoolers do, mainly because of the time-consuming nature of the study that entrance into a university requires. Furthermore, secondary students, much more so than university students, are likely to be living at home and subject to restrictions imposed by their parents as well as parental encouragement to focus on their studies.[22]

Notwithstanding the ongoing erosion of the modesty factor in the culture of China's contemporary youth, it can be said that Confucius and Confucianism still loom large. Perhaps the most pervasive and enduring Confucian values are the emphases on family and harmony. Where the family is concerned, young urban Chinese of the millennial generation are just as conscious of their connections and obligations to their families as their parents were. This is evident in the close attention, sometimes amounting to out-and-out supervision, that parents bring to bear when their offspring apply to different universities. Most Chinese university students, for example, choose their majors and sometimes their schools on the basis of their parents' advice or even orders. The degree of parental involvement in education and career choice would be considered unacceptably intrusive by American students.[23] Of course, as my survey data indicate, even in the 1990s, some Chinese students argued with their parents, but students raising objections to their parents on this issue were a small minority. Most students were willing to defer to what they considered to be the superior wisdom of their parents on issues relating to their education.

One of the most profound differences between American and Chinese adolescents—one that contributes to the interest in family harmony on the part of the latter—is the degree of obligation the young Chinese feel toward their parents. A common theme, heard not only in China but in Confucian-influenced societies everywhere, is the sense of obligation that is felt on the part of young people toward their parents. For middle-class Chinese who have managed to make it into a university, this sense of obligation is particularly acute. It is not unusual for Chinese in the millennial generation to have heard stories from their parents of extreme privation suffered in the 1950s or 1960s and for them also to be keenly aware of sacrifices the parents may have made to improve their children's life chances. The reality of such suffering and self-sacrifice, combined with the Confucian emphasis on filial devotion, makes for a very powerful psychological motivator, one that is rarely matched in American families, where individualism and self-reliance are the dominant themes.

The ideal of filial devotion is deeply entrenched in the thinking of young Chinese, but it is also promoted by the state. Daniel Bell has noted, for example, that Chinese law obligates adult children to take care of their elderly parents. Also, it is interesting to note that "the crime rate spikes just before Chinese New Year, when filial sons and daughters are supposed to bring gifts to their parents."[24]

This point draws attention to the issue of class differences in Confucian values. Many of the filial New Year's thieves and robbers referred to by Bell are no doubt members of the working class rather than students. In fact, there is evidence that working-class parents, though they may not expect their adolescent offspring to study night and day, nevertheless build enduring bonds with them in a way that reflects their adherence to Confucian familism.[25] Working-class adolescents are not as dedicated to the Confucian idealization of education as are their middle-class peers. In fact, they often taunt their more studious classmates with the epithet *shudaizi*, or "book fool." The implication is that being too studious deprives one of the capacity to learn about life, and, in fact, in the area of male-female relations, the hard-studying students are less practiced than their working-class counterparts. But though the Confucian respect for education may be rather thin among young proletarians, there are some values that seem to span all social classes, particularly familism and harmony.

The value of harmony, which continues to be prized by young Chinese, is connected to the concept of face, which differs from the Western concept of reputation partly by virtue of the degree of sensitivity to negative affect that the former entails. Sometimes saving another's face requires the overlooking of an obvious truth in the interest of maintaining harmony. A more direct approach to social relations, one that says, "the truth must be told and damn the consequences," goes against this ideal and in the process threatens the ideal of harmonious relations. The Confucian value that promotes harmony at the cost of stifling individualistic assertiveness seems to transcend all social classes in contemporary China. Of course, promoting harmony can impinge on one's freedom, but according to most young Chinese, individual freedom does not trump social harmony. Rather, most of them appear to believe it to be preferable to maintain a balance between these two ideals. In their view, Americans have too much freedom. Some Americans may find such an attitude difficult to grasp given the high valuation put on the ideal of freedom in US culture, but from the Chinese point of view America's high crime rate and widespread violence are indications that people need to be more effectively restrained. Freedom, in their eyes, has led Americans directly into a disharmonious maelstrom. The United States would be better off, they imply, if its citizens would only surrender enough of their individualistic freedoms to allow a benevolent Confucian harmony to prevail.

The influence that Confucius has had, and continues to have, on Chinese society is remarkable. Confucianism has reemerged as a pervasive force in Chinese culture despite the series of assaults it has endured over the past century. The most intense of these assaults occurred during the Maoist years, yet it is Maoism, not Confucianism, that has lost much of its grip on Chinese society. The modifications that Confucianism experienced during the height of the Maoist era included a weakening of the authority of males and elders as well as the undermining of landlords and property-based lineages. In general, the preeminence of the family suffered some setbacks under Maoist campaigns. Today, it is the influence of international youth culture, with its materialism, individualistic ethos, and romantic and erotic themes, that is putting new kinds of pressures on the Confucian tradition. Now that the state has chosen to relinquish its hold on the private lives of China's citizens, new opportunities have appeared that allow for individuals to act more independently than they could have in either the Confucian-dominated distant past or the more recent Maoist years.

But despite this increase in individualistic tendencies, it can still be said that young Chinese never became the relatively autonomous agents who so many young Americans aspire to be. One telling indication of the underlying Confucian current that continues to flow in China is the rule according to which younger siblings are prohibited from addressing their older siblings by name, but are expected to address them with honorific terms of address, such as "Older Brother" or "Second Older Sister." Of course, today most urban millennial youth don't have older siblings, given China's one-child policy, but some do, and for those who do, this deeply rooted feature of traditional culture continues to hold sway—as it does in other Confucian-influenced societies such as Japan and South Korea. Clearly there are limits to the degree of individualism that young Chinese are inclined to indulge in, given the deeply rooted Confucian principles that shape their culture. Another aspect of social interaction that continues to affect the behavior of young Chinese is the tradition of humbling oneself verbally. For example, it is customary for a host to apologize for one's inadequate hospitality to a guest, even though what he or she is offering is actually quite generous. The standard phrase "*xiao yisi*" (小意思 no big deal) is typically uttered when a genuinely expensive gift is given. When serving an elaborate meal that required particular effort on the host's part, the host is likely to say "*jiachang bianfan*" (家常便饭 everyday meal), as though the food being offered is quite modest and not in any way special. These verbal rituals reflect a Confucian emphasis on humility that, again, is not restricted to China but also is found in other Confucian societies.

Along these lines, it can be said that young Chinese assume a relatively humble demeanor in many of their daily interactions. In class, Chinese students are far less likely than their American counterparts to ask questions or challenge statements made by a teacher or professor. In interacting with their dorm mates, students often bend over backward to avoid confrontations in situations where most American students would be likely to openly express annoyance or demand modifications in behavior. One example illustrating this tendency was described to me by a Qingdao University student who was particularly close to me. He lived in a dormitory room with five classmates, one of whom was unusually selfish and uncooperative. For example, each roommate in his dorm room was supposed to take a turn going to the water-boiling vat downstairs from the dorm room to fill up thermoses with boiled water for the entire room to share. The selfish student (who happened to belong to an influential family in Qingdao) never bothered to take his turn, even when reminded to do so by his roommates. Eventually the five students who were willing to fetch water gave up reminding him and simply filled in for him, taking turns to do so. Though they complained to each other about his selfishness, they simply endured it, working around it by taking up the slack themselves. The likelihood of American students simply doing their roommates' chores to maintain group harmony would, in my opinion, be quite low.

Conclusion

The values of harmony, familism, regard for ancient traditions, and respect for education form a coherent whole that most young Chinese view as characterizing their culture and that they attribute to Confucian teachings. There are some aspects of Confucianism that have lost much of their appeal—the stark bias in favor of males and the insistence on premarital chastity, for example. But still, when young Chinese talk about their culture, they typically end up talking about Confucius. For them, Confucius serves as a symbol of traditional Chinese culture whose influence is like "the air we breathe" or the steady pull of "cultural gravity." The sage is viewed as a crucial historical figure, one who, more than any other individual, helped shape Chinese culture. In the past, this resulted in his being at times attacked and reviled, but contemporary discourse does much more to laud than to condemn him. Though some students indicated to me that they view aspects of Confucianism as inappropriate for modern Chinese to follow, the overall attitude is much more positive than negative.

Confucianism is seen as not only having shaped the Chinese tradition, but also having helped preserve it through some 25 millennia. As one student wrote to me in an e-mail, "without him, Chinese culture could not be continued for [such a] long time (more than three thousand years)." This comment reveals a positive regard for Confucius that is thoroughly entwined with the sense of Chineseness and, along the way, includes an approving reference to China's antiquity. Confucius, despite whatever drawbacks his philosophy may present to Chinese of the millennial generation, is above all both ancient and undeniably crucial in the role he has played in making China what it is. For this he is admired, at least by the majority. Less flattering views, of course, are held by some.

It may be said that the Confucian influence that pervades the lives and thoughts of young Chinese is not exactly being revived, but rather is being allowed to surface in full force where at different times in the past, out of necessity, it may have been put on a back burner. The government's promotion of Confucius can be seen as linking up to the deeply rooted cultural premises on which so much behavior of young Chinese has never ceased to be based. It is as though the powers that be have reopened a Confucian temple with great fanfare, and in response, the populace has begun to fetch their old copies of *Mencius* and *The Analects* out of their storeroom cabinets, dusted them off, and placed them prominently once more on the table in the main hall of the household. They had never been forgotten; they had merely been left out of everyday conversation in response to political and social movements aimed against them. Seen in this light, Confucianism for young people is not so much being revived as re-legitimated as a recognized source of so much that is Chinese.

There is an element of national pride linked to the admiration that many millennials have for Confucius and their ready acceptance of his current revival. As the People's Republic of China grows in prosperity and international influence, young Chinese are increasingly drawn to nationalistic sentiments. If China is a great nation (and who would deny that it is?), then some of this greatness must be attributed to the man with whom being Chinese is so closely identified. The prestige of Confucianism and the prominence of Confucius the man are both likely to increase in the coming decades. As the turmoil of the Maoist era recedes from memory, it is not unthinkable that the Great Helmsman's portrait that now overlooks Tiananmen Square may eventually be replaced by an electronic screen that portrays different celebratory images on different days. Should that happen, it's a good bet that one of the images gracing that screen will be a portrait of the Great Sage.

Notes

1. David Jordan, "Filial Piety in Taiwanese Popular Thought," in *Confucianism and the Family*, ed. Walter H. Slote and George A. De Vos (Albany: State University of New York Press, 1998), 271.

2. Pa Chin, *Family*, 2nd ed. (Prospect Heights, IL: Waveland Press, 1964).

3. Ibid., 147.

4. Ibid., 218.

5. Robert L. Moore, "Love and Limerence with Chinese Characteristics: Student Romance in the PRC," in *Romantic Love and Sexual Behavior: Perspectives from the Social Sciences*, ed. Victor C. DeMunck (Westport, CT: Praeger, 1998), 72–94.

6. Mark Selden, *The Yenan Way in Revolutionary China* (Cambridge: Harvard University Press, 1971), 88.

7. Ibid., 91.

8. Robert L. Moore, "Romantic Love in 1950s Rural China: Repressed, Suppressed or Simply Not There?" (paper presented at the Annual Convention of the Society for Anthropological Sciences, New Orleans, Louisiana, February 22, 2008).

9. Yunxiang Yan, *Private Life under Socialism: Love, Intimacy, and Family Change in a Chinese Village, 1949–1999* (Stanford: Stanford University Press, 2003).

10. Deborah A Sommer, "Destroying Confucius: Iconoclasm in the Confucian Temple," in *On Sacred Grounds: Culture, Society, Politics, and the Formation of the Cult of Confucius*, ed. Thomas A. Wilson (Cambridge: Harvard East Asian Monographs, 2002), 95–133.

11. Chihua Wen, *The Red Mirror: Children of China's Cultural Revolution* (Boulder: Westview Press, 1995), 15.

12. Xin Liu, *In One's Own Shadow: An Ethnographic Account of the Condition of Post-Reform Rural China* (Berkeley: University of California Press, 2000); Daniel A. Bell, *China's New Confucianism: Politics and Everyday Life in a Changing Society* (Princeton: Princeton University Press, 2008).

13. Bell, *China's New Confucianism*, 9.

14. Thomas A. Shaw, " 'We Like to Have Fun': Leisure and the Discovery of the Self in Taiwan's 'New' Middle Class," *Modern China* 20, no. 4 (1994): 416–445.

15. Robert L. Moore, "Generation Ku: Individualism and China's Millennial Youth," *Ethnology* 64 (2005): 357–376.

16. Robert L. Moore, Eric Bindler, and David Pandich, "Language with Attitude: American Slang and Chinese Liyu, *Journal of Sociolinguistics* 14 (2010): 524–538.

17. Robert Moore and James Rizor, "Confucian and Cool, *Education About Asia* 13, no. 3 (Winter 2008): 30–37.

18. William Jankowiak, *Sex, Death and Hierarchy in a Chinese City: An Anthropological Account* (New York: Columbia University Press, 1993).

19. Moore, "Love and Limerence with Chinese Characteristics."

20. Robert L. Moore, "Confucian Gravity: The Effect of Perceived Tradition on Talk of Love and Sex among Chinese University Students" (paper presented at the Annual Convention of the American Anthropological Association, Washington, DC, November 28, 2001).

21. James Farrer, *Opening Up: Youth Sex Culture and Market Reform in Shanghai* (Chicago: University of Chicago Press, 2002).

22. Vanessa Fong, *Only Hope: Coming of Age under China's One-Child Policy* (Stanford: Stanford University Press, 2004).

23. Francine Deutsch, "How Parents Influence the Life Plans of Graduating Chinese University Students," *Journal of Comparative Family Studies* 35, no. 3 (2004): 379–393.

24. Bell, *China's New Confucianism*, 11.

25. Moore and Rizor, "Confucian and Cool."

7

The Sage's New Clothes

Popular Images of Confucius in Contemporary China

JULIA K. MURRAY

A mere thirty-five years after the Cultural Revolution, which targeted Confucius as an arch-villain of the feudal past, positive images of the ancient sage now seem to be everywhere in China. Many have been created with governmental support and reflect the striking reversal of its judgment on Confucius's role in Chinese history. Instead of a "reactionary element working for restoration all his life" (*yisheng gao fupi de fandong fenzi* 一生搞復辟的反動分子), as he was branded in the Cultural Revolution, the formulaic phrase identifying him nowadays is "China's great thinker, educator, and statesman" (*Zhongguo de weida de sixiang jia, jiaoyu jia, zhengzhi jia* 中國的偉大的思想家，教育家，政治家).[1] Confucius has become the symbol of Chinese civilization and the theorist of the harmonious society (*hexie shehui* 和諧社會).

Along with his political rehabilitation, visual representations of Confucius have proliferated in a variety of media. From monumental public statues to paintings, movies, and animated cartoons, his images serve new purposes and address a much wider audience than ever before. In ways that would have been unimaginable even half a century ago, Confucius has become part of contemporary popular culture. This chapter explores several of these new representations and the responses they have evoked. To provide perspective, some comparisons are made with images of Confucius that circulated in the late imperial period and with depictions that emerged in the twentieth century under the Republic and the People's Republic.

The Revival of Qufu

For more than twenty-five years, Confucius has steadily been gaining visibility in contemporary Chinese culture. This process has frequently been assisted by the China Confucius Foundation (Zhongguo Kongzi jijinhui 中國孔子基金會), which was founded by the Chinese government in 1984. Shandong provincial authorities have also initiated or supported efforts to bring attention to Confucius, whose hometown has long been identified with Qufu 曲阜, in southwestern Shandong, an area also inhabited by thousands of people claiming descent from the ancient sage. Seeking ways of exploiting Confucius to benefit the province and foster its economic development, the government has allocated considerable funding to restore sites associated with Confucius and his descendants. In addition to promoting cultural tourism, official subsidies have enabled publishers based in the provincial capital, Ji' nan 濟南, to issue innumerable books and reprints of texts dealing with Confucius or Confucianism.[2]

One of the first signs of a Confucian revival was the restoration of the temple of Confucius (Kongmiao 孔廟) in Qufu, which had achieved nearly palatial grandeur under the generous patronage of the Qing dynasty. After major renovations to repair extensive damage inflicted during the Cultural Revolution, the temple reopened to the public and was designated a national-level cultural protection site in 1982.[3] In the main hall, a new larger-than-lifesized sculpture was completed in 1984 to replace the Qing icon destroyed by the Red Guards in 1966 (Fig. 7.1). Confucius is dressed as an emperor and seated on a throne, visually embodying the posthumous titles and honors conferred on him by successive dynasties, which elevated him far above any status he had attained in life.[4] Also restored to their places in the main hall were the attendant figures of the Four Correlates (si pei 四配): Confucius's disciples Yan Hui 顏回, Zengzi 曾子, Zi Si 子思, and his later follower Mengzi 孟子.

To boost the temple's appeal as a tourist destination, exhibitions on the life of Confucius have frequently been mounted in adjacent buildings. In addition to refurbishing the Hall of the Sage's Traces (Shengjidian 聖蹟殿), the building at the north end of the main axis, with a 112-scene pictorial biography incised on stone tablets in 1592, the China Confucius Foundation and Qufu cultural authorities commissioned two other sets of pictorial stones for permanent display in the area identified as Confucius's former house (Kongzi gu zhai). One set reproduced the *Pictures of the Sage and Worthies* (*Shengxian*

Figure 7.1. Altar of Confucius with sculptural icon (restored in 1984), Dachengdian, Kongmiao, Qufu, Shandong. Author's photo.

tu 聖賢圖), a series of portraits of Confucius and seventy-two disciples. Originally incised on stone tablets for the Southern Song imperial university in Hangzhou in 1156, the images have long been widely known through the circulation of rubbings.[5] The other was a completely new version of the life of Confucius, titled *Pictures of the Deeds of Confucius* (*Kongzi shiji tu* 孔子事蹟圖), designed by the Shandong artist Shi Ke 石可 (b. 1924) and completed in 1989 (Fig. 7.2).[6] Carved from slabs of polished black limestone in a deliberately archaic style of bas-relief, which is vaguely reminiscent of southwestern Shandong's Han-dynasty pictorial art, the thirty-one compositions also incorporate techniques from socialist realism, such as showing Confucius as by far the largest figure in most scenes. The pictures and the explanatory texts below present him as a model of studious, diligent, and correct behavior, intended as an inspiration to the contemporary visitor. Supplementing these installations are temporary exhibits in other buildings, often based on or inspired by the extensive collection of paintings and woodblock prints formerly belonging to the Kong Duke for Perpetuating the Sage (*Yansheng gong* 衍聖公), the hereditary office held by the senior male descendant of Confucius in successive generations since 1055.[7]

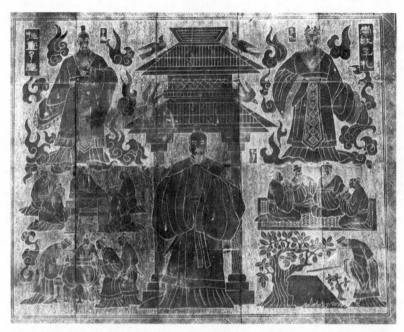

Figure 7.2. Shi Ke 石可, Confucius Pays Homage to Ji Zha, from *Kongzi shiji tu* 孔子事蹟圖 (*Scenes from the Life of Confucius*), 1989, incised stone tablet, Qufu, Shandong. Author's photo.

The Qufu temple has been promoted as one of the "Three Kong" (San Kong 三孔), along with the refurbished cemetery where Confucius and many descendants are buried, called the Kong Forest (Konglin 孔林), and the palatial establishment of the Kong dukes, known as the Kong Mansion (Kongfu 孔府).[8] A steady stream of souvenir books, DVDs, postcards, rubbings, slide sets, playing cards, stamps, bookmarks, and so forth have helped to popularize the San Kong for secular tourism (Fig. 7.3). In 1987, a state-owned brewery in Qufu even adopted the name for a new beer, San Kong Pijiu 三孔啤酒, both exploiting and extending the San Kong brand's cachet.[9] Despite or maybe because of the increasing commercialization, the San Kong were officially designated a UNESCO World Heritage Site in 1994.

In recent years, the Qufu Kongmiao has seen increasing numbers of visitors openly displaying veneration or praying to Confucius in

Figure 7.3. Miscellaneous souvenirs of the San Kong 三孔, Qufu, Shandong (playing cards, enameled metal bookmarks, postcards). Author's photo.

addition to engaging in ordinary sightseeing and snapshot taking. To accommodate this new behavior, which resembles the practices of devotees at Buddhist and Daoist temples, the courtyard in front of the main hall has been provided with facilities where people can perform obeisance, buy and burn incense, purchase and hang votive placards, and donate money to the Merit Box (*Gongde xiang* 功德箱) (Fig. 7.4). People visiting the grave of Confucius in the Konglin also are encouraged to make their prostrations and donations (Fig. 7.5). Perhaps these accommodations allowing visitors to worship were hastened by the success of the Shrine of Confucius, the Sages, and Worthies (Kongzi Shengxian ci 孔子聖賢祠), a nearby facility that is not on the official Qufu tourist itinerary or marked on maps (Fig. 7.6).[10] Located down a side street not far from the Kongmiao, it is a cavernous structure decorated with low-relief mural paintings and room after room of large and gaudily painted statues depicting Confucius and his disciples and later interpreters. For at least ten years, the shrine has served people who approach the figures as popular gods, burning incense before them and praying to them for blessings of all kinds.

In 1986 the Qufu government began sponsoring an annual cultural festival to celebrate the birthday of Confucius, which is

Figure 7.4. Offerings, merit box, and incense burning in front of the Dachengdian, Kongmiao, Qufu, Shandong. Author's photo.

Figure 7.5. Confucius's grave with merit box, Konglin, Qufu, Shandong. Author's photo.

Figure 7.6 . Kongzi Shengxian ci 孔子聖賢祠 (Shrine of Confucius, the Sages and Worthies), Qufu, Shandong. Author's photo.

observed on September 28 (as in Taiwan).[11] The most colorful event of the festival is a ceremony performed in front of the main hall of the temple. Initially, it was a touristic performance primarily of dance, and the doors of the hall were closed to avoid any suggestion that homage was being offered to the image of Confucius inside.[12] In the 1990s, with the tacit encouragement of the central government, the ritual began being modeled increasingly on the liturgy of a late-imperial sacrifice. Moreover, the doors of the main hall began being left open, and descendants of Confucius were allowed to pay homage. By 2005, with permission from central government authorities, the performance was led by a descendant, and more care was taken to re-create traditional costumes and ritual equipment accurately from documentary sources.[13] Attended by high officials and representatives of international organizations, among others, the event was broadcast live on China Central Television (CCTV). In 2008, a spring ceremony was added as a smaller-scale version of the September celebration, reviving an older tradition of semiannual sacrifices offered to Confucius in both spring and autumn. The same year, the revival of the traditional Qingming 清明 grave-sweeping observance led to a separate spring ceremony being instituted at Confucius's grave.[14] Limited to proven descendants, the ritual has attracting increasing attendance from members overseas as well as from other parts of China. A few days before the birthday celebration in 2009, some 1200 descendants also participated in a special ceremony at the Qufu temple to present the new eighty-volume updated genealogy to Confucius, sacrificing three large animals on the altar in front of his statue.[15]

Rebuilding Other Temples of Confucius

Led by the Qufu Kongmiao, in the late 1980s and 1990s many other Chinese cities and towns started renovating their own temples of Confucius, usually called either Kongmiao or Temple of Culture (Wenmiao 文廟) or occasionally Temple of the Master (Fuzi miao 夫子廟). In the late imperial era, these temples stood next to the government school in the administrative centers of provinces, prefectures, and counties, as well as in the two capitals. The main ritual hall of an official temple was an austere, aniconic environment, without the sculptural icons and palace-style decor that distinguished the Qufu temple.[16] Confucius and the other men who were enshrined, including his disciples and later interpreters of his teachings, were represented not by figural images but only by inscribed tablets.[17] The interior space was ornamented only with signboards and placards of calligraphy, often reproducing large-character transcriptions of phrases from the Confucian classics brushed by Qing emperors. After the civil service examination system ended in the early twentieth century, many of these buildings were converted to schools, offices, or museums, and some were badly damaged or even destroyed completely during the Cultural Revolution.

The restoration or rebuilding of temples of Confucius nationwide has frequently introduced representational imagery where there was none before. Initially, the main reason for adding it was to make them more attractive to tourists and thus generate revenue from admissions and souvenirs. Particularly for visitors accustomed to the colorful paintings and sculptural figures of deities in renovated Buddhist and Daoist temples, an aniconic interior not only would be uninteresting but also would seem incomplete. Only elderly scholars steeped in the tenets of late-imperial Confucianism were likely to appreciate the solemnity of a Confucian temple authentically restored to a pre-1949 configuration. However, the presence of anthropomorphic images has encouraged visitors to respond by treating the figures as representing gods who can assist them with personal concerns.

The largest of the official temples is the Kongmiao in Beijing, which is probably the best known of all Confucian temples because of its location in China's capital. Because this was the temple to which the emperor himself might come to sacrifice in person, the size and splendor of its main hall are second only to Qufu's.[18] Both buildings have a double roof of imperial-yellow glazed tiles and stand nine bays wide on a large, high platform, approached by a ramp decorated with an imperial dragon. The interiors are festooned with imperial regalia, such as coffered ceilings containing dragon roundels, calligraphic signboards and placards, and embroidered hangings. However, instead of figural icons, the Beijing Kongmiao in Qing times had only inscribed tablets to represent Confucius, the Four Correlates, and the Twelve Savants (*shi'er zhe* 十二哲).[19] Until the early 2000s, moreover, the temple housed the Capital Museum (Shoudu Bowuguan 首都博物館) and displayed archaeological and historical exhibits. Now it has been restored to a ritual configuration, and the main hall again just has inscribed tablets on the altars, with replicas of sacrificial utensils and offerings placed on tables in front of them, along with cushions to allow the visitor to perform prostrations. However, life-sized clay statues of Confucius's disciples have been added just outside the hall, with a fence on which supplicants can hang votive placards (Fig. 7.7). The poses and attributes of these figures are copied from rubbings of the Hangzhou *Pictures of Sages and Worthies*, which have been translated from small, two-dimensional pictures to large and lifelike sculptures in the round.

Unlike the Beijing Kongmiao, most other renovated temples of Confucius exhibit paintings or statues of the ancient sage and his disciples inside the main hall itself, and sometimes there are other kinds of imagery as well. For example, Suzhou's Wenmiao has a large and colorful painting of a standing Confucius over the altar, and the walls are inset with stone tablets that reproduce rubbings of old sets of pictures and texts. The east side of the building displays pictorial stones, including a thirty-scene version of the life of Confucius (titled *Kongzi Shengji zhi tu* 孔子聖蹟之圖), a twenty-scene pictorial

Figure 7.7. Lifesize clay figures of Confucius's disciples and railing hung with votive placards, Kongmiao, Beijing. Author's photo.

biography of Mencius (*Mengzi shengji tu* 孟子聖蹟圖), and a copy of the Hangzhou portraits of Confucius and seventy-two disciples.[20] On the north and west sides, some 124 tablets reproduce the texts of the Confucian classics in clerical-script calligraphy, including a colophon by the renowned Jiangnan scholar-official and classicist Ruan Yuan 阮元 (1764–1849).[21] In front of the altar, unusual musical instruments used in a traditional sacrifice are individually displayed with labels, flanked by racks of bells and V-shaped stone chimes and a large bell and drum.

The main hall of the Fuzi miao in Nanjing features an extremely large painting of a standing Confucius based on the same iconography as the image in the Suzhou Wenmiao, as well as a spirit tablet inscribed with his post-1530 title "Ultimate Sage and First Teacher, Master Kong" (*Zhisheng xianshi Kongzi* 至聖先師孔子) (Fig. 7.8).[22] In front of the altar are a table holding an incongruous array of sacrificial vessels and modern bronze bust of Confucius and a stand with three compartments containing clay heads representing a pig, ox, and sheep. Competing for attention is a large and colorful installation of thirty-six narrative scenes from the life of Confucius. Created with colored-stone inlays on large hardwood panels behind glass, the pictures cover the

Figure 7.8. Altar of Confucius with painted portrait by Wang Hongxi 王宏喜 (1991), Dachengdian, Fuzi miao, Nanjing.

walls and several interior partitions inside the building.[23] Below each illustration is a textual explanation, written in slightly archaic script, on narrow tablets that evoke the bamboo and wooden slips used for ancient documents. The seal-script title, *Pictures of the Sage's Traces* (*Shengji zhi tu* 聖蹟之圖), exactly copies the calligraphy and wording on the headstone of the 112-scene illustrated biography of Confucius installed in the Shengjidian at the Qufu Kongmiao.[24]

Shanghai enshrines just a gilded sculptural icon depicting Confucius as a seated figure in an ornate niche, with little other decoration of the interior than calligraphy placards.[25] The comparatively austere treatment may reflect a deliberate effort to re-create the historical environment of the government school and temple.[26]

However, just outside the main hall is a monumental bronze statue of Confucius as a standing figure accompanied by incense burners and racks of votive placards for visitors who wish to worship (Fig. 7.9). In recent years, attendance at the temple has surged around the time of university entrance examinations as anxious students and their parents seek Confucius's aid for a successful result.[27]

Monumental statues of Confucius

The large bronze statue of Confucius outside the main hall of the Shanghai Wenmiao was donated by a Hong Kong industrialist to mark the 2,540th birthday of Confucius in 1989.[28] During the 1990s, monumental sculptures of Confucius as a standing figure started appearing with some frequency at restored temples of Confucius. Sited on the central axis, usually just outside the main hall or its gate, this kind of representation was a new addition to the material culture of the Confucian temple. Initially standing in isolation, the large outdoor statues of Confucius served mostly as backdrops for tourist snapshots and group photos. In recent years, however, donation boxes

Figure 7.9. Bronze statue of Confucius by Xu Baoqing 徐寶慶 (1989), racks of votive placards, and incense burning outside the Dachengdian, Wenmiao, Shanghai. Author's photo.

and basins for burning incense have often been added, accommodating or encouraging visitors' prayers and donations. (Temples usually do not allow incense to be burned inside the main hall because of the fire hazard to wooden buildings.) The addition of picket fences and racks as well has made it possible for supplicants to hang votive plaques and prayer tablets around Confucius's image (Fig. 7.10).

In the past decade, monumental statues of Confucius have also been proliferating on the premises of libraries, schools, and museums. In these kinds of environments, unlike temples, the statue is not necessarily placed in a prominent spot, and the visitor may miss it altogether. Furthermore, these settings seem less conducive for making

Figure 7.10. Bronze statue of Confucius donated by Tang Enjia 湯恩 (1997), with incised picture on the stone base, Guozijian, Beijing. Author's photo.

supplications to Confucius than when his figure is placed on the central approach to a ritual hall. Nonetheless, the presence of his image affirms the roles of such institutions in preserving and transmitting China's cultural heritage. At the Shanghai Library, the statue stands next to a walkway in the yard behind the building, as part of a tableau with bushes clipped to form the characters "Pursue Knowledge" (*qiu zhi* 求 知) (Fig. 7.11).[29] The ensemble seems meant to be viewed from inside the building through the large glass wall of the upper level, as a visitor on the ground would have difficulty "reading" the bushes.

Most of the monumental images are made of cast bronze, although some are carved from stone (Fig. 7.12). Often well over life sized, the figures tower over the viewer and typically stand on high, rectangular pedestals. The base usually is inscribed with a title, date, and the identification of the donor. Sometimes there is additional explanatory text or even an inscribed pictorial scene that complements the sculptural representation (e.g., Fig. 7.10). Confucius invariably stands holding both hands before his chest, fingers pointing up and clutching the hilt of a slender sword under his left arm. His voluminous robes typically have patterned borders, and a decorated panel hangs from his belt almost to the upturned tips of his shoes. Always depicted

Figure 7.11. Statue of Confucius donated by Tang Enjia 湯恩佳 and topiary bushes behind the Shanghai Library. Author's photo.

Figure 7.12. Stone statue of Confucius, carved and donated by Yang Qingqin 楊清欽 (1993), outside the Dachengmen, Kongmiao, Beijing. Author's photo.

as an elderly man with a full beard and bushy eyebrows, Confucius wears the cloth cap of a scholar rather than an official's headgear.

Although there is considerable consistency among the monumental images, they vary somewhat in expression and physical details, such as the angle of the arms, prominence of cheekbones, and degree of gauntness. The 1989 statue at the Shanghai Wenmiao, created by the nationally renowned sculptor Xu Baoqing 徐寶慶 (b. 1926), displays an unusually lifelike facial expression and well-modeled hands making a naturalistic gesture. Confucius seems about to speak, with slightly raised eyebrows and dimpling around his high, rounded cheeks and parted lips. By comparison, the white marble statue outside the gate of the Beijing Kongmiao is more schematic, with outsized hands and face that give Confucius a slightly manic expression

(Fig. 7.10). Carved and donated by Yang Qingqin 楊清欽 (1932–2002) of Taizhong, Taiwan, the figure was erected in 1993, when the Capital Museum still occupied the site. It is explicitly titled "Portrait of First Teacher Confucius Practicing the Teaching" (*Xianshi Kongzi xingjiao xiang* 先師孔子行教像), linking it in name to the rubbing of a Qufu stele that the Taiwan Ministry of Education endorsed in 1974 as the most accurate representation of Confucius (Fig. 7.13).[30]

Figure 7.13. Portrait of Confucius, traditionally attributed to Wu Daozi 吳道子 (ca. 689-after 755), rubbing of an incised stone tablet in the Kongmiao, Qufu, Shandong. Photo from Edouard Chavannes, *Mission Archéologique dans la Chine Septentrionale* (Paris, Leroux, 1909), pl. CCCC, no. 874.

The erection of monumental images of Confucius is a practice that seems clearly influenced by Western conventions of public statuary as a medium for commemorating great men of the past.[31] Nonetheless, the iconographic details come primarily from traditional Chinese depictions of Confucius as an elderly teacher, which can be traced back in two-dimensional media at least to the Song dynasty, if not earlier.[32] Portrayals of his standing figure circulated widely in the late imperial period as paintings, prints, and rubbings from incised stone tablets. Some bore notations identifying the artist as Wu Daozi 吳道子 (ca. 689–after 755), a renowned Tang master of figure painting, and Confucius in the role of practicing the teaching (xingjiao 行教).[33] One of this group is the rubbing from Qufu (e.g, Fig. 7.13), which was validated in 1974 by the Taiwan authorities, the most significant of whom was Kong Decheng 孔德成 (1920–2008). Invested as the duke of the 77th generation in his infancy, Kong Decheng had grown up in Qufu,[34] and his endorsement of this portrayal as most familiar to him was persuasive. Soon afterward, Taiwan began presenting large bronze statues based on the Xingjiao rubbing to cultural sites worldwide, in part as an answer to the "Criticize Confucius, Criticize Lin Biao" (Pi Lin Pi Kong 批林批孔) movement then in full swing in mainland China.[35] The Xingjiao image also was subsequently endorsed by Confucian Academy of Hong Kong (Kongjiao xueyuan 孔教學院), an institution advocating the establishment of Confucianism as a full-fledged religion.[36]

A number of bronze statues erected on the mainland in the later 1980s and 1990s (e.g., Fig. 7.10) actually resemble the Xingjiao portrayal much more closely than does the stone sculpture in the Beijing Kongmiao (e.g., Fig. 7.12). Most of them are titled simply "Portrait of Confucius Practicing the Teaching" (Kongzi xingjiao xiang 孔子行教像), typically in large characters on the high pedestal, incised and sometimes gilded.[37] Many were donated by Tang Enjia 湯恩佳, the activist head of the Confucian Academy of Hong Kong since 1992, whose sponsorship of the monumental figures is a form of proselytizing.[38] A noteworthy feature of the inscriptions on the statues is that the date is expressed in the "Confucian calendar" (Kong li 孔曆), meaning number of years since the birth of Confucius. The date on the statue in figure 10, for example, is Kong li 2548, corresponding to 1997. Analogous to the Western calendar's use of the birth of Jesus as its starting point, this counting practice began with Kang Youwei 康有為 (1858–1927), a prominent late Qing proponent of Confucianism as national religion.[39] The Hong Kong Confucian Academy was founded in 1930 by one of Kang's disciples, Chen Huanzhang 陳煥章 (1881–1933), who earlier had organized the Confucius Religion

Association (Kongjiao hui 孔教會) in Shanghai in 1912 to oppose the new Republic's de-Confucianization policies.[40]

In the past decade, the China Confucius Foundation has also entered the arena to assert authority over visual representations of Confucius. In 1999, to mark his 2,550th birthday, the Foundation sponsored the design and production of a limited edition of one thousand statuettes made of twenty-four-carat gold and just under a foot in height (Fig. 7.14). While based on the by-then dominant *Xingjiao* image, the new statuettes were explicitly intended to improve on it. In its promotional literature, the foundation highlighted the changes made to Confucius's clothing, which had been updated with

Figure 7.14 Gold statuette of Confucius, designed for the China Confucius Foundation by Qian Shaowu 錢紹武 (1999). Photo from the China Confucius Foundation publicity pamphlet.

recent archaeological finds dating from his lifetime. Thus, the new image had to be more authentic than any portrait by Wu Daozi that depicted Confucius in Tang garb. Although the statuettes are similar to the large *Xingjiao* figures in some respects, Confucius no longer appears to be talking, and his hands are clasped horizontally instead of pointing upward. More significantly, his sword has been removed. However, the foundation's effort to combine veneration and commerce did not prove entirely successful, as the statuettes did not sell well. Since 2005, they have been repurposed as part of the UNESCO "Confucius Literacy Prize," two of which are awarded annually to individuals and groups working to increase literacy in countries throughout the world.[41] In addition to a monetary grant, winners receive a gold statuette.

In 2006, the China Confucius Foundation called explicitly for a new "standard portrait" (*biaozhun xiang* 標準像) of Confucius, on the grounds that existing images were too varied, even among those made within a single factory, to sell as tourist souvenirs in Qufu.[42] A standard image would help to avoid confusion, which was particularly important as Confucius Institutes (Kongzi xueyuan 孔子學院) were being established worldwide. After research and consultation with scholars, artists, and descendants of Confucius, the foundation selected the Qufu *Xingjiao* rubbing (e.g., Fig. 7.13) as the basis for the new image, the same as in 1974 Taiwan. Confucius was to be represented between the ages of sixty and seventy, with a facial expression that was simultaneously "genial yet strict, imposing and yet not intimidating, courteous and yet at ease" (*wen er li, wei er bu meng, gong er an* 溫而厲, 威而不猛, 恭而安).[43] Following modifications to a full-scale bronze prototype cast in June 2006, the final version was unveiled in Qufu on September 23, just in time for birthday celebrations (Fig. 7.15).[44] To mark the 2,557th anniversary of Confucius's birth, the statue was made 2.557 meters high. Not surprisingly, it is very similar to the *Xingjiao* sculptures, again including a sword, although the face is considerably broader and wears a heavy-lidded expression of gentle resignation. Since 2006, the China Confucius Foundation has sponsored several installations of the full-sized statue as well as the production of smaller versions to promote it as the standard image of Confucius. If anything, however, portrayals have only become even more diverse.

Retelling the Life of Confucius

Statues of Confucius may be the most conspicuous sign of his return to official favor, and their incorporation into rituals of supplication

Figure 7.15. Bronze statue of Confucius (the "Standard Portrait"), designed for the China Confucius Foundation by Hu Xijia 胡希佳 (2006), Qufu, Shandong. Author's photo.

a sign of popular acceptance. Along with the proliferation of static images, however, dynamic narrative representations of his life in a variety of media have also gained a place in contemporary Chinese visual culture. Compared with the relatively minor variations seen in the iconic portrayals, the various versions of his life display a much greater range of approach and emphasis. Their sponsors' contemporary concerns influence the choice of events depicted and how they are portrayed, as was also true of versions created in the late-imperial era.[45]

Pictorial biographies

Serial illustrations of the life of Confucius, often called *Pictures of the Sage's Traces* (*Shengji tu* 聖蹟圖) or some close variant, first appeared in the mid-fifteenth century and developed thereafter in the media of painting, woodblock printing, and incised stone.[46] An initial compilation of about thirty annotated pictures, based on his late second-century BCE biography in the *Shiji* 史記,[47] portrayed Confucius as a merely human exemplar of high moral character and epitomized his career as an itinerant statesman-adviser and teacher-scholar. As the genre of his pictorial biography evolved and expanded, however, numerous events with supernatural elements and demonstrations of his superhuman ability were added. The most grandiosely hagiographical version, created in 1592, is displayed on incised stone tablets in the Shengjidian at the Qufu temple, as mentioned above. Compilers and sponsors of the various *Shengji tu* typically claimed that the pictures embodied important social values and would inspire the viewer to greater moral cultivation. Versions published in the late Qing and Republic have prefaces that also reaffirmed traditional Confucian values as the core of Chinese identity, as against those associated with the West and modernity. A lithographic edition published by the Nation Society of Beiping (Beiping minshe 北平民社) in 1934 was reissued in Taiwan several times after the Republican government's relocation there, particularly during the "Cultural Renaissance" (*wenhua fuxing* 文化復興) period of 1967 to 1977.[48]

In the late 1980s, various versions of the *Shengji tu* started appearing in mainland publications. Early volumes in the ambitious series *Kongzi wenhua daquan* 孔子文化大全 (Complete Works of Confucius Culture) included a 1988 reprint of the 1934 Beiping minshe edition, as well as the first publication of an untitled Ming album of thirty-six colorful paintings.[49] The album, a treasured possession of the Kongfu in Qufu, has subsequently been exhibited all over the world and republished numerous times.[50] At the Qufu temple itself, a new set of prints made from Qing woodblocks that reproduced the Shengjidian's incised stone tablets was installed as a didactic exhibit in the Pavilion of the Constellation of Learning (Kuiwen'ge 奎文閣), another major building on the main axis.[51] Various old editions of the pictorial biography in collections elsewhere in China have also been reprinted in recent years, sometimes introduced with comments to the effect that pictures will help the popular audience become familiar with Confucius.[52]

Animated cartoons

Recognizing that its efforts to standardize Confucius's image and spread an authorized version of his teachings had reached only a portion of the potential audience, the China Confucius Foundation initiated the Confucius Large-Scale Animation (*Donghua dapian Kongzi* 动画 大片 《孔子》) project early in 2007. Although its primary viewers would initially be Chinese children, the animated cartoons were also intended to be shown abroad as "one of the most effective ways to popularize the essence of Chinese culture to the overseas audience."[53] Developed by Shenzhen Phoenix Star Television Media Company (Shenzhen Fenghuang xing yingshi yunmei youxian gongsi 深圳鳳 凰星影視伝媒有限公司) together with Shandong Radio, Film and Television Bureau (Shandong sheng guangbo dianying dianshi ju 山東 省廣播電影電視局), the series of 104 animé-style cartoons took three years and some 50 million RMB of government funding to produce.[54] Titled simply *Confucius* (*Kongzi*), the series is organized into four seasons consisting of twenty-six episodes each. The first episode was broadcast by CCTV as one of many events marking the celebration of September 28, 2009, as the 2,560th birthday of Confucius. Picture books, CDs, and DVDs were also released simultaneously.

Aimed at young people and consciously using the popular animé style to appeal to them, the *Kongzi* cartoon series is outstanding in technical quality. Each episode is about twelve minutes long and centers on an event in the life of Confucius, loosely based on traditional biographies of the sage. Skipping over the supernatural events that some sources associate with his conception and birth,[55] the first episode, titled "The Orchid" ("Lanhua" 蘭花), introduces him as a big-eyed young boy living in poverty with his widowed mother, to whom he is devoted.[56] As in traditional pictorial biographies, the boy displays an un-childlike interest in temple rituals and implements (Fig. 7.16). Here, however, he is given an invented sidekick, Manfu 曼甫, and suffers bullying by Yang Hu 陽虎, known from texts as his nemesis later in his life. A beautiful dream sequence introduces Big Sister Orchid (Lanhua jiejie 蘭花姐姐), a fairy godmother–like figure who reappears throughout the series. In her initial appearance, she comforts the distressed boy and gives him direction, telling him to study. The episode ends after he wakes up and runs to the top of Mount Ni (Nishan 尼 山), where he yells, "I want to study!" (*wo yao du shu* 我要讀書) as a flock of white birds rises over the awe-inspiring panorama.

Figure 7.16. The child Confucius plays at performing rituals, from *Kong-zi*, animated cartoon series, Episode 1 ("Lanhua" 蘭花 [The Orchid]), Part 1. Screenshot from CCTV.com (http://space.tv.cctv.com/video/VIDE1254189206723884).

Using a succession of images to represent Confucius at various stages of his life, the series follows him from childhood through old age.[57] Unlike earlier pictorial biographies, which pass quickly to his young adulthood, ten episodes feature him as a young boy, presumably to establish his appeal to the target audience. Every episode has one or more narrative threads that link it to traditional texts, but they are interspersed with hefty doses of contemporary juvenile popular culture. Homilies on doing the right thing and lessons on Chinese ancient history and myth are leavened with slapstick humor, dramatic suspense, and noisy combat. As Confucius ages in the later episodes, increasingly large roles are taken up with subplots involving minor figures and talking animals, most prominently a bumbling piglet named Pixiu 皮休, who frequently turns to Lanhua jiejie for advice after Confucius has outgrown her (Fig. 7.17). In some of the episodes after Confucius has become an adult, he hardly appears at all. When he does, he speaks

Figure 7.17 Pixiu 皮休, Lanhua jiejie 蘭花姐姐, and Confucius, from *Kongzi*, animated cartoon series, Episode 43 ("Huiyan" 慧眼 [Mental Discernment]). Screenshot from CCTV.com (http://space.tv.cctv.com/video/VIDE1266979112057881).

very slowly and gravely in a resonant baritone, unlike other characters, whose speech is more natural and sometimes jarringly contemporary. It remains to be seen whether the series will fulfill its sponsors' goals of bringing Confucius to life as a viable hero for Chinese children today and inculcating desirable social and cultural values, as well as promoting worldwide appreciation of Confucian thought and Chinese culture.[58]

Film

Late January 2010 saw the opening of *Kongzi*, a major motion picture on the life of Confucius, with a record 2,500 prints issued for simultaneous release (Fig. 7.18).[59] Following Confucius from age fifty until his death at age seventy-three, the movie's storyline is loosely based on his *Shiji* biography and incidents from the *Analects* (*Lunyu* 論語). Featuring the middle-aged Hong Kong action star Chow Yun-fat

Figure 7.18. Poster advertising the film "Kongzi" directed by Hu Mei 胡玫 (2010). Screenshot from zvod.net 中影网 (zvod.net/news/201001/83.html).

周潤發 (b. 1955) in the title role, it was meant to be a commercial blockbuster and received 150 million RMB of government funding (about $22 million). The film was directed by Hu Mei 胡玫 (b. 1958), a 1982 female graduate of the Beijing Film Academy. The cinematography was by Peter Pau 鮑德熹 (b. 1951), winner of the 2000 Academy Award for *Crouching Tiger, Hidden Dragon*, and popular singer Faye Wong 王菲 (b. 1969) performed the theme song.

To reach the desired popular audience of ordinary adults, who either know little about Confucius or were brought up to vilify him, the film presents him as a man of vigor and action as well as ideas. He performs rituals, practices archery, and offers statesmanly advice, even presiding over a contentious summit meeting between his home state of Lu and neighboring rival Qi. Large-scale battle scenes between rival powers are depicted with casts of thousands and dramatic, digitally enhanced effects, reminiscent of the John Woo epic *Red Cliff*. The fellowship of disciples and their sometimes arduous travels among the ancient feudal states in search of a ruler who would employ Confucius all are given their due. Most controversial is the film's portrayal of a romantic relationship between Confucius and the notoriously seductive Nanzi 南子, wife of Duke Ling of Wei 衛靈公, played by the well-known actress Zhou Xun 周迅 (b. 1976). Traditional sources agree that Confucius had an audience with her but attribute it to his desire to enhance his job prospects in the state of Wei. In any case, his disciples disapproved, and he defended his motives with unusual vehemence. However, the film fleshes out, so to speak, what might have been going on.

Despite including elements that some commentators considered tasteless or inappropriate in a portrayal of Confucius, the film gained the endorsement of prominent descendants. At its Beijing premiere, Kong Demao 孔德懋 (b. 1917), 77th-generation descendant and sister of the late Kong Decheng, presented an inscription in her own calligraphy to Chow Yun-fat, which read "Forever Confucius" (*Yongyuan de Kongzi* 永遠的孔子), to which Chow responded by performing a kowtow.[60] To celebrate the nationwide opening on January 22, the film's cast and crew went to Qufu and held a veneration ceremony in the Qufu temple, which included kowtows to the sculptural icon of Confucius.[61] Kong Dewei 孔德威, a descendant who directed the 2009 genealogy project, pronounced the movie to be evidence that Confucianism was playing a significant role in present-day China.[62] However, the film did not meet with a great deal of popular enthusiasm among Chinese moviegoers, some of whom resented that it replaced James Cameron's wildly popular *Avatar* on many two-dimensional screens at the government's behest.[63]

By apparent coincidence, an old movie that covers the same period of Confucius's life has been recently recovered and shown in Hong Kong, generating considerable excitement (Fig. 7.19).[64] In April 2009, the Hong Kong Film Archive screened a partially restored print of *Kong Fuzi* 孔夫子, a long-lost black-and-white film made in 1940 by Shanghai director Fei Mu 費穆 (1906–51), which was shown throughout China in 1940–41 and briefly rereleased in 1948. A more complete version was included in the April 2010 Hong Kong International Film Festival after the Italian lab L'Immagine Ritrovata (The Rediscovered Image) in Bologna devoted eight years of painstaking work to restoring the nitrate negatives.

Figure 7.19 Cover of booklet for the film "Kong Fuzi" directed by Fei Mu
費穆 (1940).

Filmed in Shanghai under arduous wartime conditions following
the Japanese invasion, Fei Mu's *Kong Fuzi* is melancholy in tone, and
its stately pace could hardly be more different from that of the 2010
blockbuster. The producers invested some $160,000, a large sum in 1940,
in hopes of demonstrating that Chinese cinema was capable of more
than the maudlin costume dramas popular at the time, perhaps even
the equal of foreign film. Poetic, often painterly images alternate with
scenes of chaos and warfare, and the formal beauty of the mise-en-scène
and cinematography is breathtaking. An austere and somber Confucius,
played by Tang Huaiqiu 唐槐秋 (1898–1954) moves deliberately and
speaks solemnly, often turning his back on the viewer to gaze at the
landscape. Over and over, the film shows how powerless he is and how
irrelevant his ideal of government through benevolence and ritual in
an age of constant warfare and aggression. Despite repeated failure and

disappointment, Confucius never abandons his quixotic quest to create a moral order, and his steadfast commitment to virtue arouses the viewer's feelings of sorrowful respect and admiration. Near the end, an interlude of ceremonial dance shows the performers trying to create a formation reading "All-under-heaven in great peace" (*Tianxia taiping* 天下太平), but they repeatedly fail to form the last character, suggesting a bleak outlook. But the disciples' pledge to continue spreading Confucius's teachings gives him comfort as he dies, and the film concludes with the age-old hymn "Confucius, Confucius, Great is Confucius" (*Kongzi, Kongzi, da zai Kongzi* 孔子孔子大哉孔子).[65]

Conclusion

The emergence of diverse and widely circulated visual depictions of Confucius is a phenomenon stimulated by the contemporary revival of Confucianism in China. Prior to the twentieth century, ordinary people were not likely to encounter representations of Confucius. Public places did not display images of him, nor were portrayals likely to be seen outside the circles of educated men. Although the teachings of Confucius were among the core values of Chinese social morality, Confucius himself did not have a popular following, nor did he inspire a popular cult of people praying to him for good fortune. China's dynastic regimes espoused ideals of governance associated with Confucius and performed regular sacrifices to him in official temples. The educated elite venerated him as a role model of learning and morality but not as a figure from whom to seek private benefit.

A broader circulation of images of Confucius was initially prompted by various efforts to promote him as China's counterpart to great figures in Western civilization. The late Qing movement to establish him as the founder of a religion of "Confucianism" encouraged people to incorporate him into popular cultic practices, and votive prints (*nianhua* 年畫) depicted him as a god whom ordinary people could worship.[66] Under the Republic, Confucius occasionally appeared on banknotes and stamps as an important historical figure identified with the Chinese nation.[67] The People's Republic has also used his image on stamps at various times, and there is speculation that he will eventually appear on a new 500 RMB note.[68]

While stamps and currency disseminated his image more widely than ever before, the proliferation of government-sponsored representations of Confucius in recent years is even greater in magnitude and different in character. Along with efforts to standardize his depiction and associate him with a core Chinese identity, entertainment media are being used to impart desirable social values and cultivate a respectful, patriotic citizenry. For the first time, Confucius is being promoted to a mass audience through film, and to children through animated cartoons, in lavish productions underwritten by the government. Moreover, his image is also being wielded internationally to symbolize China and Chinese civilization, such as in the establishment of Confucian Institutes and the award of UNESCO Confucius Literacy prizes.

Despite official backing for some representations of Confucius, they do not always achieve their intended purposes, and popular reactions may differ from the expected ones. People who believe in the ideas and values associated with Confucius have questioned whether any visual portrayal is desirable, especially because none can be true to life. The China Confucius Foundation's effort to create a standard portrait in 2006 drew criticism not only about specific details of the depiction but also about the motives behind this attempt to impose uniformity.[69] Suspicions that it was a step toward turning Confucius into a commercial brand seemed reasonable, given how much his image has been exploited to make money for Qufu. Even more recently, the use of Confucius's image on lottery tickets sold in Qufu (Fig. 7.20) prompted

Figure 7.20. Confucius lottery tickets, Qufu (2010). Screenshot from *Xinhua English* (http://english.sina.com/china/2010/0201/302715.html).

objections from people who felt that he should not be associated so directly with money, often quoting his famous saying that profit is the concern of small-minded men.[70]

Those who accept Confucius as the symbol of China's heritage and as a source of national pride criticize the overuse of his portrayal for opportunistic or commercial purposes. On the other hand, the presence of images of Confucius at restored temples has led many people to treat him as a god with the power to influence educational success, seeking his aid in passing examinations and with other practical concerns. It may well be true, as various parties asserted during the controversy over the standard portrait that it does not matter whether an image really resembles Confucius or not, as long as it is recognizable.[71] People will relate to Confucius as they wish.

Notes

1. For examples of each characterization, see *Kong Lao'er* 孔老二 (Shanghai: Shanghai Renmin chubanshe, 1974), 116; and Kuang Yaming 匡亞明, *Qiusuo ji* 求索集 (Beijing: Renmin chubanshe, 1995), 64, 112, and 112, respectively.

2. A prime example is *Kongzi wenhua daquan* 孔子文化大全 (*Complete Works of Confucius Culture*), an extensive series of reprints often of rare editions, published by Shandong Friendship Press (Shandong Youyi shushe) between 1988 and 1994.

3. UNESCO, "A Regular Report on the Implementation of the Convention Concerning the Protection of World Cultural and Natural Heritage," Part II, "Preservation Status of the Specific World Heritage: Confucius Temple, Confucius Forest and Confucius Mansion in Qufu," ed. You Shaoping and Wang Qingcheng for the Qufu City Cultural Relics Administration Committee (UNESCO, 2002), 12, Sec. 5.a, accessed September 1, 2010, http://whc.unesco.org/archive/periodicreporting/apa/cycle01/section2/704.pdf. For a profusely illustrated and high-quality analysis of the architecture, see *Qufu Kongmiao jianzhu* 曲阜孔廟建築, comp. Nanjing Institute of Engineering, Department of Architecture 南京工學院建築系, and Qufu Cultural Relics Administrative Committee 曲阜文物管理委員會 (Beijing: Zhongguo jianzhu gongye chubanshe, 1987).

4. For a detailed discussion and reproduction of sculptural icons of Confucius in the Qufu temple, see my " 'Idols' in the Temple: Icons and the Cult of Confucius," *Journal of Asian Studies* 68, no. 2 (May 2009): 371–411.

5. For the Southern Song tablets, see my "The Hangzhou *Portraits of Confucius and 72 Disciples (Shengxian tu)*: Art in the Service of Politics," *Art Bulletin* 74, no. 1 (March 1992): 7–18. The Qufu replicas were completed in 1991.

6. The set is similar but not exactly identical to the twenty-scene version reproduced in Shi Ke 石可, *Kongzi shiji tu, Lunyu zhenyan yin* 孔子事跡圖. 論語箴言印 (Ji'nan: Qi Lu shushe, 1987).

7. For a list of successive holders of the title, see *Qufu Kongmiao jianzhu*, 443–445. The extensive files and collections amassed by the dukes are now administered by the Archive Office of Confucius Mansion [sic] under the Cultural Relics Administration Committee of Qufu City, Shandong Province (Kongfu wenwu dang'an, Shandong sheng Qufu shi wenwu guanli weiyuanhui); itemized in UNESCO, "A Regular Report," Appendix IV, 100–102.

8. Many attractive publications treat the San Kong; for a couple of recent examples, see *Qufu Kongmiao, Konglin, Kongfu* 曲阜孔廟·孔林·孔府, Chen Chuanping 陳傳平, comp., in *Zhongguo shijie yichan congshu* 中國世界遺產叢書 (Xi'an: San Qin chubanshe, 2004) and the bilingual *Temple and Cemetery of Confucius and the Kong Family Mansion in Qufu/Qufu Kongmiao, Konglin, Kongfu* 曲阜孔廟·孔林·孔府, Kong Deping 孔德平, comp. (Beijing: New World Press, 2007).

9. "San Kong Pijiu youxian gongsi" 三孔啤酒有限公司, Baidu wenku 百度文庫, 2010, accessed August 24, 2010, http://wenku.baidu.com/view/796481da50e2524de5187e7f.html.

10. I stumbled on this shrine in 2001 and surmise from recent tourist photographs posted on the Internet that it is still in business. Its address is 2-12 Gulou bei lu 鼓樓北路, Qufu.

11. The birthday of Confucius began to be regularly celebrated in the early twentieth century; previously, he received regular sacrifices in the second months of spring and fall. Ancient texts record his birth date variously as the twenty-seventh or twenty-eighth day of the eighth month of the lunar calendar. In 1904, the Qing government declared lunar 8/28 a national holiday but changed it to 8/27 in 1910. Lunar 8/27 was reaffirmed as a national holiday in 1931 under the Republic. In 1952, the government in Taiwan fixed the date as September 28 in the Western calendar. For details concerning the evolution of the contemporary observance in Qufu, based on extensive local interviews, see Hongliang Yan and Bill Bramwell, "Cultural Tourism, Ceremony and the State in China," *Annals of Tourism Research* 35, no. 4 (October 2008): 969–989, http://www.elsevier.com/locate/atoures.

12. Yan and Bramwell, "Cultural Tourism, Ceremony and the State in China," 980–981.

13. Yan and Bramwell, "Cultural Tourism, Ceremony and the State in China," 983. The authors suggest that the attendance of representatives of the central government and international bodies made the event a "public cult ceremony" rather than a "civilian cult ceremony."

14. "Descendants Attend Memorial Ceremony for Confucius in Qufu," *China Economic Net*, March 31, 2008, accessed September 28, 2008, http://en.ce.cn/National/pic-news/200803/31/t20080331_15010653_4.shtml; and "Descendants Hold Memorial Ceremony for Confucius in Qufu," *China Economic Net*, April 6, 2009, accessed May 27, 2009, http://en.ce.cn/National/culture/200904/06/t20090406_18719670.shtml.

15. Peter Foster, "Confucius Family Tree Unveiled," *The Daily Telegraph*, September 26, 2009, accessed August 29, 2010, telegraph.co.uk/news/worldnews/asia/china/6230959/Confucius-family-tree-unveiled.html; also "*Kongzi shijia pu*

xuxiu fenpu dianli zai Qufu Kongmiao longzhong juxing" 孔子世家譜續修頒譜典禮在曲阜孔廟隆重舉行, Kongshi zongqin wang 孔氏宗親網, October 19, 2009, accessed December 4, 2009, http://www.Kong.org.cn/Item/Show.asp?m=1&d=585. The genealogy is the first to include female descendants and descendants residing abroad.

16. The Jiajing ritual reform of 1,530 removed images from all temples of Confucius except for the one in his hometown of Qufu; see Deborah A. Sommer, "Destroying Confucius: Iconoclasm in the Confucian Temple," in *On Sacred Grounds: Culture, Society, Politics, and the Formation of the Temple of Confucius*, ed. Thomas A. Wilson (Cambridge: Harvard University Asia Center, 2002), 95–133.

17. For a discussion of who was enshrined and why, see Thomas A. Wilson, *Genealogy of the Way: The Construction and Uses of the Confucian Tradition in Late Imperial China* (Stanford: Stanford University Press, 1995).

18. A third main hall that is also of imperial scale stands at the Wenmiao in Harbin, Heilongjiang, which was actually built in 1926; see *Zhongguo Kongmiao* 中國孔廟, Gao Wen 高文, and Fan Xiaoping 范小平, comps. (Chengdu: Chengdu chubanshe, 1994), 18 and 93, and plates 77–80.

19. For the ritual configuration of the Beijing temple in the late Qing, see Pang Zhonglu 龐鍾璐, *Wenmiao sidian kao* 文廟祀典考 (n.p. 1878), *juan shou.*

20. My description of the inset tablets is based on their configuration as I observed it in August 2001.

21. Perhaps best known today for collating the *Shisan jing zhushu* 十三經注疏, the Qing official edition of the Classics, Ruan Yuan is exhaustively treated in Betty Peh-ti Wei, *Ruan Yuan, 1764–1849: The Life and Work of a Major Scholar-Official in Nineteenth-Century China before the Opium War* (Hong Kong: Hong Kong University Press, 2006).

22. The painting in ink and slight color on silk, 6.5 meters in height, is signed by Wang Hongxi 王宏喜 (b. 1937) and dated early summer 1991. As part of the Jiajing reform, Confucius's title was changed from King of Exalted Culture (Wenxuan wang 文宣王) to Ultimate Sage and First Teacher, which it remained thereafter, except for a brief change in effect from 1645 to 1657; see Thomas A. Wilson, "Ritualizing Confucius/Kongzi," in *On Sacred Grounds: Culture, Society, Politics, and the Formation of the Temple of Confucius*, ed. Thomas A. Wilson (Cambridge: Harvard University Asia Center, 2002), 50–57.

23. Two additional panels contain the title, credits, and introductory label. Fabricated in 1998 by the Jingyi Artistic Sculpture Company (Jingyi yidiao youxian gongsi 精义艺雕有限公司) of Yueqing City 樂清市, Zhejiang, each panel is 2.5 meters high and 1.3 meters wide and covered by glass. A few panels are reproduced online at "Nanjing Confucius Temple," Nanjing Jiwan Technology Co. Ltd., 2000, accessed August 25, 2010, http://www.njfzm.com/fzmen/fzm-morepic.htm.

24. The Nanjing illustrations themselves are based on painted compositions in a widely published Ming album in Qufu, reproduced in *Shengji zhi tu/The Pictures About Confucius' Life* [sic] (Ji'nan: Shandong General Press, 1988).

25. See photos on Shanghai Confucius Temple, accessed August 25, 2010, http://www.confuciantemple.com/english/e-guanyu-wenmiao/wenmiao-jianjie.

htm, 2006. When I visited the temple in 2001, the main icon was flanked by gilded standing figures of disciples Yan Hui and Zengzi, but these were later removed.

26. Idem. I have not been able to ascertain whether the main hall had a figural icon during the Qing dynasty; however, at least one county temple in the region (Kunshan 昆山) restored its icon in the early Qing; see Han Seunghyun, "Shrine, Images, and Power: The Worship of Former Worthies in Early Nineteenth Century Suzhou," *Toung Pao* 95, nos. 1–3 (2009): 177. Another precedent that might be relevant is that the temple of Confucius in Tokyo (Yushima Seido 湯島聖堂) enshrined a small Ming bronze image of Confucius; reproduced in *Kongzi baitu* 孔子百圖, comp. Wang Shucun 王樹村 (Guangzhou: Lingnan meishu chubanshe, 1997), 64, cat. no. 50. A photo of the statue in situ appears in *Rujia tuzhi* 儒家圖誌, Xu Lingyun 許凌雲, comp., *Kongzi wenhua daquan* (Ji'nan: Shandong Youyi shushe, 1994), 439.

27. "Parents Call on Confucius for Exam Good Fortune," *China Economic Net*, June 5, 2008, accessed September 28, 2008, http://en.ce.cn/National/Education/200806/05/t20080605_15735862.shtml. The practice of seeking Confucius's aid for success in examinations or other kinds of personal benefit seems to be quite recent, perhaps prompted by the late Qing movement to make Confucianism a national religion (discussed below).

28. Identified by the inscription as Chen Chun 陳春 of the Zhongwei gongsi 中威公司 (Redland Precast Concrete Products Ltd.), Hong Kong.

29. According to John Makeham, the statue was donated in 1997, although its inscription is undated; *Lost Soul* (Cambridge: Harvard Asia Center, 2008), 307.

30. Cai Wenyi 蔡文怡, "Kongzi shengxiang tantao" 孔子聖像探討, *Guoli lishi bowuguan guankan* 8 (October 1976), 115; reproduced and further discussed in my "Portraits of Confucius: Icons and Iconoclasm" *Oriental Art* 47, no. 3 (2001), 17, 26; also see my " 'Idols' in the Temple," 402, Fig. 11.

31. A possible exception comes up in an anecdote about Confucius seeing a bronze statue by the steps outside the Zhou ancestral temple depicting a man whose mouth was sealed with three strips and whose back bore a cautionary inscription. An illustration is included in the largest versions of the pictorial biography; e.g., see *Kongzi shengji tu* 孔子聖蹟圖, Kongzi wenhua daquan (Ji'nan, Shandong Youyi shushe, 1988), 80. For two late sixteenth-century illustrations of an anthologized version of the story, see my "Squaring History with Connoisseurship: Jiao Hong's *Yangzheng tujie*," in *Art of the Chinese Book*, ed. Ming Wilson and Stacey Pierson (London: Percival David Foundation), 142–143 and figs. 5–6.

32. I have treated this subject in detail in "Pedagogue on the Go: Portraits of Confucius as an Itinerant Teacher," in *Bridges to Heaven: Essays in Honor of Professor Wen C. Fong*, ed. Judith Smith and Dora C. Y. Ching (Princeton: Tang Center for East Asian Art, forthcoming).

33. The origin and significance of this epithet are obscure, but it is often interpreted as referring both to Confucius's travels and his teachings; e.g., see *Kongzi xingjiao tu* 孔子行教圖/*Confucius Journeys through Pictures* (Taipei: Zuanshi chubanshe, 1974).

34. The Nationalist government changed Kong Decheng's title in 1935 from Duke for Perpetuating the Sage to Sacrificing Official for the Greatly Accomplished Ultimate Sage and First Teacher (*Dacheng zhisheng xianshi fengsiguan* 大成至聖先師奉嗣祀官); see Jun Jing, *Temple of Memories: History, Power, and Morality in a Chinese Village* (Stanford: Stanford University Press, 1996), 39. He left Qufu during the Japanese invasion and moved to Taiwan with the Nationalist government, in which he served in various capacities; for an obituary, see Stephen Miller, "Kung Te-cheng (1920–2008): Lineal Descendant of Confucius Fostered Tradition," *Wall Street Journal*, November 1, 2009, http://online.wsj.com/article/SB122550105993889975.html.

35. For a nuanced analysis of Taiwan's "Cultural Renaissance," of which the statues were a small part, see Makeham, *Lost Soul*, 192–207.

36. For example, a colorized rendition of the *Xingjiao* portrayal appears on the cover of the October 1983 issue of *The Journal of Confucius*, the Academy's journal. On the Academy itself, see Makeham, *Lost Soul*, 306.

37. The gilding seems to be fugitive. When I photographed the Beijing Guozijian statue in 2001, the entire inscription was filled in with gold (and the statue had no fence); by my return visit in 2008, all the gilding was gone, and it was surrounded by a picket fence bedecked in red plaques (shown in Fig. 7.10).

38. By November 2004, Tang Enjia had already donated sixty statues of Confucius to mainland sites, which he called "priceless treasures" (*wujia zhi bao* 無價之寶); Zheng Qiao 鄭超, "Quanqiu jiangban baisuo Kongzi sueyuan; shousuo xueyuan benyue Han'guo jiepai" 全球將辦百所孔子學院 首所學院本月韓國揭牌, Xinhuanet.com, November 16, 2004, accessed September 3, 2010, http://news.xinhuanet.com/newscenter/2004-11/16/content_2222750.htm. On Tang's agenda, see Makeham, *Lost Soul*, 306–307.

39. Hsi-yuan Chen, "Confucianism Encounters Religion: The Formation of Religious Discourse and the Confucian Movement in Modern China" (PhD diss., Harvard University, 1999), 88.

40. On the Kongjiao hui, see Chen, "Confucianism Encounters Religion," chapter 3; also Makeham, *Lost Soul*, 278–279; for the contestation over ritual during the Republic, see Rebecca Nedostup, *Superstitious Regimes: Religion and the Politics of Chinese Modernity* (Cambridge: Harvard Asia Center, 2009).

41. Guo Xiaohong, "UNESCO Confucius Prize for Literacy Launched," *China through a Lens*, December 1, 2005, accessed September 1, 2010, http://www.china.org.cn/english/China/150588.htm.

42. "Kongzi daodi zhang shayang; Kongzi biaozhun xiang 6 yue quanqiu fabu" 孔子到底長啥樣 孔子標准像6月全球發布, *Xinhuanet.com*, February 2, 2006, accessed September 4, 2010, http://news.xinhuanet.com/book/2006-02/16/content_4186182.htm.

43. *Analects* 7.38; trans. Raymond Dawson, *Confucius: The Analects*, Oxford World's Classics (Oxford: Oxford University Press, 1993), 27.

44. Li Shan 黎珊, "Kongzi biaozhun xiang quanqiu zhengshi fabu (tupian) 孔子標准像全球正式發布 (圖片)," *Donghai Jiguan jiayuan* 東海《機關

家園》 September 24, 2006, accessed September 1, 2010, http://dh.jgjy.gov.cn/
shownews.asp?news_id=1098.

45. I discuss a broad range of versions and sponsors from the mid-fifteenth
century to the late twentieth in "Varied Views of the Sage: Illustrated Narratives
of the Life of Confucius," in *On Sacred Grounds: Culture, Society, Politics, and the
Formation of the Cult of Confucius*, ed. Thomas A. Wilson (Cambridge: Harvard
University Asia Center, 2002), 222–264.

46. See my "Illustrations of the Life of Confucius: The Evolution, Functions,
and Significance in Late Ming China," *Artibus Asiae* 57, nos. 1–2 (1997): 73–
134.

47. Sima Qian 司馬遷, *Shiji* 史記, Beijing University punctuated and
annotated edition (Beijing: Zhonghua shuju, 1982), 47.1905–1947. The life
of Confucius occupies most of the chapter titled "Master Kong's Hereditary
Household" ("Kongzi shijia" 孔子世家), tracing his ancestry and posterity as if
he were an aristocrat. The title was later adopted for Kong family genealogies,
including the most recent one published in 2009 (see above at note 15).

48. The Beiping minshe's publication, titled *Kongzi Shengji tu*, was a
lithographic edition based on an 1874 woodblock version published by seventy-
second-generation descendant Kong Xianlan 孔憲法蘭 in Qufu; Taiwan reprints
include two under that title (Taipei: Zhongguo wenjiao chubanshe, 1957 and
Wensi chubanshe, 1984); a variant title, *Kongsheng huazhuan* 孔聖畫傳 (Taipei:
Fuxing Zhonghua wenhua chubanshe, 1975); and a bilingual edition, *Kongzi
xingjiao tu/Confucius Journeys through Pictures*. For the "Cultural Renaissance," see
Makeham, *Lost Soul*, 192–207.

49. For the *Kongzi wenhua daquan* series, see note 2. The two items on
pictorial biography are *Kongzi shengji tu* (as in note 31) and the bilingual *Shengji
zhi tu/The Pictures about Confucius' Life* (as in note 24).

50. Selected leaves from the album have most recently been exhibited in
the United States; see Wensheng Lu and Julia K. Murray, *Confucius: His Life and
Legacy in Art* (New York: China Institute Gallery, 2010), cat. no. 4.

51. The Kuiwen'ge was the Qufu temple's library. I saw the recently reprinted
Shengji tu displayed there on my first visit in 1992, and it was still (or again) on
view in 2009. For reproductions of two prints made for the 2010 China Institute
exhibition, and of the two-sided woodblock from which the impressions were
taken, see Lu and Murray, *Confucius: His Life and Legacy in Art*, cat. no. 5.

52. E.g., *Shengji tu* (Wuhan: Hubei jiaoyu chubanshe, 1994); *Kongzi shengji
tu* (Shijiazhuang: Hebei meishu chubanshe, 1996) and a bilingual *Kongzi shengji
tu/The Sage's Traces Pictures of Confucius* [sic], Liu Ying 劉映, comp. (Beijing:
Xianzhuang shuju, 2005); and Wu Jiamo 吳嘉謨, *Kongsheng jiayu tu* 孔聖家
語圖 (1589), Zhongguo gudai banhua congkan erbian 中國古代版畫叢刊二編
(Shanghai: Shanghai guji chubanshe, 1994); there are many more.

53. CCF Deputy Secretary-General Wang Daqian 王大千, quoted in
"Confucius Promoted by Cartoon Imagery," *China Daily*, May 5, 2007, accessed
December 7, 2007, http://www.chinadaily.com.cn/china/2007-05/20/content_
876382.htm.

54. The funds come from the Propaganda Department of the Shandong Provincial Party Committee, the China Confucius Foundation, Shandong Province Broadcast Film & TV Bureau, CCTV, Shenzhen Chongde Film & TV Media; He Dongxian 何東憲, "Daxing donghua pian *Kongzi* jijiang bochu" 大型動畫片《孔子》即將播出, *Jingji ribao* 經濟日報, September 23, 2009, Zhongguo jingji wang 中國經濟網, accessed September 29, 2009, http://paper.ce.cn/jjrb/html/2009-09/23/content_81672.htm#.

55. In brief: after his mother offered a sacrifice on Nishan, a *qilin* 麒麟 brought her an inscribed jade tablet predicting his birth, which was presaged by gods and dragons appearing in the sky on the night before he was born, and the baby's body bore forty-nine auspicious marks, including an inscription on his chest; for annotated illustrations, see *Shengji zhi tu/The Pictures about Confucius' Life*, 1–4.

56. The episode was broadcast in two parts, which can be viewed online on CCTV.com at http://space.tv.cctv.com/video/VIDE1254189206723884 and http://space.tv.cctv.com/video/VIDE1254189206723887.

57. As of mid-summer 2010, CCTV had broadcast just the first two seasons of twenty-six episodes each, taking Confucius from boyhood to middle age.

58. He Dongxian, "Daxing donghua pian *Kongzi* jijiang bochu."

59. Pang Li, "Hu Mei Brings Confucius to the Big Screen," China.org.cn, April 13, 2010, accessed September 1, 2010, http://www.china.org.cn/arts/2010-04/13/content_19800838.htm.

60. "Chow Yun-fat Saves the Third Kowtow for Confucius," *China.org.cn*, January 22, 2010, accessed September 1, 2010, http://www.china.org.cn/wap/2010-01/22/content_19291174.htm; also see photos posted on "Chow Yun-fat Honors Descendant of Confucius," accessed September 1, 2010, *One Asian World*, 2010.

61. "Biopic Movie Stars, Crew Pay Tribute to Confucius," *China.org.cn*, January 22, 2010, accessed September 1, 2010, http://www.china.org.cn/arts/2010-01/22/content_19292257.htm.

62. Ibid.

63. Raymond Zhou, "Confucius Loses His Way," *China Daily*, January 29, 2010, accessed September 2, 2010, http://www.chinadaily.com.cn/life/2010-01/29/content_9396402.htm.

64. David Bordwell, "Confucius Reborn," Observations on Film Art, April 15, 2009, accessed September 1, 2010, http://www.davidbordwell.net/blog/?p=4269. See also the bilingual publication of essays and photos from the film *Fei Mu Kong Fuzi* /費穆孔夫子 *Fei Mu's Confucius* (Hong Kong: Hong Kong Film Archive Publications, 2010). I thank David Bordwell for sending me a copy.

65. The well-known hymn, attributed to Mi Fu 米黻 (1051–1107; also known as Mi Fei [米芾]), is inscribed on a portrait of Confucius on a stone tablet in the Shengjidian; reproduced in Luo Chenglie 駱承烈, *Huaxiang zhong de Kongzi* 畫像中的孔子 (Shanghai: Guji chubanshe, 2003), 26. Its lyrics are simple in the extreme:

Confucius, Confucius, great is Confucius.
Before Confucius, there was no Confucius.
After Confucius, there will be no Confucius.
Confucius, Confucius, great is Confucius.
孔子孔子，大哉孔子！孔子以前，既無孔子。孔子以后，更無孔子。
孔子孔子，大哉孔子！

66. For examples and references, see my more detailed discussion in " 'Idols' in the Temple," 394–397.

67. A quick search on the Internet turns up a 1-*yuan* banknote issued in 1938 by the Chinese Republic (see http://www.banknotes.com/CNJ61.jpg); also, a 100-*yuan* note issued in 1944 by the Japanese-controlled puppet government in Manzhouguo (see http://www.banknotes.com/CNJ138).

68. Zou Le, "Authority Denies 'New Bill' Reports," *Global Times*, August 19, 2010, accessed September 12, 2010, http://china.globaltimes.cn/society/2010-08/565101.html.

69. " 'Official' Image of Confucius Sparks Debate among Scholars," CRIEnglish.com, September 26, 2006, accessed September 1, 2010, http://english.cri.cn/3126/2006/09/26/264@143753.htm.

70. "Confucius Is a Brand Name in Hometown Lottery Promo," *Xinhua English*, February 2, 2010, accessed September 2, 2010, http://english.sina.com/china/2010/0201/302715.html.

71. " 'Official' Image of Confucius Sparks Debate among Scholars."

Comprehensive Bibliography

Sources in Chinese

Beijing chenbao 北京晨报 [Beijing Morning News]. "Shi qinquan haishi 'shuo hao de' de hezuo? Yu Dan Kong Jian wei li fanlian? 是侵权还是'说好的'的合作? 于丹孔健为利翻脸?" *China News*, June 3, 2010. http://www.chinanews.com.cn/cul/news/2010/06-03/2320320.shtml.

Beijing daxue 北京大学 [Beijing University]. "Qianyuan guoxue jiaoshi 乾元国学教室." *Beijing Daxue*, 2005. http://www.qianyuangx.com/pkugx.jsp.

Cai Degui 蔡德贵. *Kongzi vs. Jidu* 孔子 vs. 基督. Beijing: Shijie zhishi chubanshe, 2008.

Cai Wenyi 蔡文怡. "Kongzi shengxiang tantao 孔子聖像探討." *Guoli lishi bowuguan guankan* 國立歷史博物館館刊 8 (1976): 114–118.

Fan Ruiping, ed. *Rujia shehui yu daotong fuxing: yu Jiang Qing duihua* 儒家社会与道统复兴：与蒋庆对话. Shanghai: Huadong Shifan Daxue, 2008.

Fu Peirong 傅佩荣, Guo Qiyong 郭齐勇, and Kong Xianglin 孔祥林. *Kongzi jiu jiang* 孔子九讲. Beijing: Zhonghua shuju, 2008.

Gan Yang 甘阳. *Tong san tong* 通三统. Beijing: Sanlian Publishing, 2007.

Gang Zhong 钟刚. "Kongzi houren Kong Jian bei Yu Dan zhikong qinquan, shouci xiangshu shijian shimo 孔子后人孔健 被于丹指控侵权首次详述事件始末." *Sohu.com*, June 3, 2010. http://yule.sohu.com/20100603/n272542569.shtml.

He Dongxian 何東憲. "Daxing donghua pian 'Kongzi' jijiang bochu 大型動畫片《孔子》即將播出." *TV.Sohu.com*, September 23, 2009. http://tv.sohu.com/20090923/n266945780.shtml.

Hong Ziliang 洪子良, ed. *Xin shenghuo chubu* 新生活初步. Nanjing: Xinshenghuo shushe chuban, n.d.

Jiang Qing 蒋庆. "Zhengzhi de Kongzi yu Kongzi de zhengzhi: huiling jinnian laidui *Zhengzhi Ruxue* de piping 政治的空子与孔子的政治：回应今年来对政治儒学的批评." In *Kongzi yu dangdai Zhongguo* 孔子与当代中国, ed. Chen Lai and Gan Yang, 321–327. Beijing: Sanlian Publishing, 2008.

195

Jin Baoshan 金寶善. "Xin shenghuo yundong yu minzu jiankang 新生活運
　動與民族健康." *Xinyun daobao* 新運導報 117 (June 10, 1947): 22–23.
Kong Lao'er 孔老二. Shanghai: Shanghai Renmin chubanshe, 1974.
Kongsheng huazhuan 孔聖畫傳. Taibei: Fuxing Zhonghua wenhua chubanshe,
　1975.
Kongzi baitu 孔子百圖. Compiled by Wang Shucun 王樹村. Guangzhou:
　Lingnan meishu chubanshe, 1997.
Kongzi shengji tu 孔子聖蹟圖. Comp. Liu Ying 劉映. Beijing: Xianzhuang
　chubanshe, 2005.
Kongzi shengji tu 孔子聖蹟圖. Shijiazhuang: Hebei meishu chubanshe, 1996.
Kongzi shengji tu 孔子聖蹟圖. Taibei: Wenjiao chubanshe, 1957.
Kongzi shengji tu 孔子聖蹟圖. Taibei: Wensi chubanshe, 1984.
"*Kongzi shijia pu* xuxiu banpu dianli juxing 《孔子世家譜》續修頒譜典禮舉
　行." *CRIonline*, September 27, 2009. http://big5.cri.cn/gate/big5/city.cri.
　cn/25364/2009/09/27/3866s2480733.htm.
Kongzi wenhua daquan zongmu tiyao 孔子文化大全總目提要.Jinan: Shandong
　youyi shushe, 1994.
Kuang Yaming 匡亞明. *Qiusuo ji* 求索集. Beijing: Renmin chubanshe, 1995.
Li Ling 李零. *Sangjia gou: wo du Lunyu* 喪家狗: 我读《论语. Taiyuan:
　Shanxi renmin chubanshe, 2008.
Li Shan 黎珊. "Kongzi biaozhun xiang quanqiu zhengshi fabu (tupian)
　孔子標准像全球正式發布(圖片)." *Sina.com*, September 23, 2006.
　http://news.sina.com.cn/c/2006-09-23/211711086974.shtml.
Li Zhenyu 厲振羽. "*Kongzi shi jiapu* xuxiu banpu dianli zai Qufu Kongmiao
　juxing 《孔子世家譜》續修頒譜典禮在曲阜孔廟舉行." *Renmin wang*,
　September 25, 2009. http://culture.people.com.cn/BIG5/22226/169787
　/169788/10116372.html.
Luo Chenglie 駱承烈. *Huaxiang zhong de Kongzi* 畫像中的孔子. Shanghai:
　Guji chubanshe, 2003.
Nanjing Fuzi miao 南京夫子廟. Beijing: Zhongguo gongren chubanshe, 2005.
Pang Zhonglu 龐鍾璐. *Wenmiao sidian tukao* 文廟祀典考. N.p., 1878.
Qufu Kongmiao jianzhu 曲阜孔廟建築. Beijing: Zhongguo jianzhu gongye
　chubanshe, 1987.
Qufu Kongmiao, Konglin, Kongfu. 曲阜孔廟·孔林·孔府. Compiled by Chen
　Chuanping 陳傳平. Xi'an: Sanqin chubanshe, 2004.
Qufu Kongmiao, Konglin, Kongfu. 曲阜孔廟·孔林·孔府. Compiled by Kong
　Deping 孔德平. Beijing: New World Press, 2007.
Ruan Yuan 阮元 et al. *Shisanjing zhushu fu jiaokan ji* 十三经注疏附校勘记.
　Beijing: Zhonghua shuju, 1980 [1935].
Rujia tuzhi 儒家圖誌. Comp. Xu Lingyun 許凌雲. Jinan: Shandong youyi
　shushe, 1994.
Shi Ke 石可. *Kongzi shiji tu, Lunyu zhenyan yin* 孔子事跡圖, 論語箴言印.
　Jinan: Qi Lu shushe, 1987.

Sima Qian 司馬遷. *Shiji* 史記. Beijing: Zhonghua shuju, 1959.

Wang Guangtao 王光燾. *Kongzi xingjiao tu* 孔子行教圖. Taibei: Zuanshi chubanshe, 1974.

Wong Ain-ling 黃愛玲, ed. *Fei Mu Kong Fuzi* 費穆孔夫子. Hong Kong: Hong Kong Film Archive, 2010.

Wu Jiamo 吳嘉謨. *Kongsheng jiayu tu* 孔聖家语圖. Shanghai: Shanghai guji chubanshe, 1994.

Xiao Jizong 蕭繼宗, ed. *Geming wenxian* 革命文獻, vol. 68. *Xin shenghuo yundong shiliao* 新生活運動史料. Taibei: Zhonghua yinshua, 1975.

Xin shenghuo yundong xuzhi 新生活運動須知. Nanjing: N.p., 1935.

Xinhua wang 新华网. "Kongzi daodi Changsha yang: Kongzi biaozhun xiang liuyue quanqiu fabu 孔子到底長啥樣 孔子標準像6月全球發布." *Xinhuanet.com*, February 16, 2006. http://big5.xinhuanet.com/gate/big5/news.xinhuanet.com/book/2006-02/16/content_4186182.htm.

Ye Chucang 葉楚傖, ed., *Xin shenghuo congshu* 新生活叢書. Nanjing: Nanjing zhengzhong shuju kan, n.d.

Yu Dan 于丹. *Yu Dan Zhuangzi xinde* 于丹《庄子》心得. Beijing: Minzhu fazhi chubanshe, 2007.

———. *Yu Dan Zhuangzi xinde* 于丹《庄子》心得. Beijing: Minzhu fazhi chubanshe, 2007.

———. *Yu Dan Lunyu xinde* 于丹《论语》心得. Beijing: Zhonghua shuju, 2006.

Yu Dan 于丹, and Kong Jian 孔健. *Lunyu li: Yu Dan Lunyu Fusang xing* 论语力: 于丹《论语》 扶桑行. Beijing: Xin shijie chubanshe, 2008.

"Zhanlüe guanli: San Kong Pijiu Youxian gongsi 三孔啤酒有限公司." *Shangxue wang*, October 27, 2009. http://www.shangxuewang.cn/news/zlgl/2009/10/0910271619141006.html.

Zheng Qiao 鄭超. "Quanqiu jiangban baisuo Kongzi sueyuan; shousuo xueyuan benyue Hanguo jiepai 全球將辦百所孔子學院首所學院本月韓國揭牌." *Xinhuanet.com*, November 16, 2004. http://news.xinhuanet.com/newscenter/2004-11/16/content_2222750.htm.

Zhongguo chuban gongzuozhe xiehui 中国出版工作者协会, ed. *Zhongguo chuban nianjian* 中国出版年鉴. Beijing: Zhongguo chuban nianjian she, 2008.

Zhongguo Kongmiao 中國孔廟. Compiled by Gao Wen 高文 and Fan Xiaoping 范小平. Chengdu: Chengdu chubanshe, 1994.

Zhongguo shijie yichan congshu 中國世界遺產叢書. Xi'an: San Qin chubanshe, 2004.

Zhou Shang 周尚. "Minzu shengcun yu zhengjie shenghuo 民族生存與整潔生活." *Xinyun daobao* 新運導報 120 (June 1948): 12–13.

Zhongguo gudai banhua congkan 中國古代版畫叢刊. Shanghai: Shanghai guji chubanshe, 1994.

Sources in English

A State of Mind: Life in North Korea. Dir. Dan Gordon and John Battsek. 2003; Princeton: Films for the Humanities and Sciences, 2006. DVD.

Ai, Jiawen. "The Refunctioning of Confucianism in Mainland China: Intellectual Response to Confucianism since the 1980s." *Issues and Studies* 44, no. 2 (June 2009): 29–78.

Bai Xu, Wang Haiying, and Chuai Xianyu. "Statue of Confucius Erected Near Tiananmen Square." *Xinhua News*, January 12, 2011. http://news.xinhuanet.com/english2010/china/2011-01/12/c_13687988.htm.

Balfour, Andrew. "Hygiene as a World Force." *Science* 64, no. 1668 (November 12, 1926): 459–466.

Barr, Michael. *Lee Kuan Yew*. Richmond, Surrey: Curzon, 2000.

Bell, Daniel A. *China's New Confucianism: Politics and Everyday Life in a Changing Society*. Princeton: Princeton University Press, 2008.

———. "The Confucian Party." *New York Times*, May 11, 2009. http://www.nytimes.com/2009/05/12/opinion/12iht-edbell.html.

Berlin, Isaiah. *Four Essays on Liberty*. Oxford: Oxford University Press, 1969.

Bhattacharji, Preeti, Carin Zissis, and Corinne Baldwin. "Media Censorship in China." Council on Foreign Relations, March 7, 2011. http://www.cfr.org/publication/11515/media_censorship_in_china.html.

Billioud, Sebastién. "Confucianism, 'Cultural Tradition,' and Official Discourse in China at the Start of the New Century." Translated by Christopher Storey. *China Perspectives* 3 (2007): 50–65.

Bol, Peter K. *Neo-Confucianism in History*. Cambridge: Harvard University Asia Center, 2008.

Bordwell, David. "Confucius Reborn." *Observations on Film Art*, April 15, 2009. http://www.davidbordwell.net/blog/2009/04/15/confucius-reborn/.

Brendon, Piers. "For China, Will Money Bring Power?" *New York Times*, August 22, 2010. http://www.nytimes.com/2010/08/22/opinion/22brendon.html.

Brownell, Susan. *Training the Body for China: Sports in the Moral Order of the People's Republic*. Chicago: University of Chicago Press, 1995.

"Building Harmonious Society Crucial for China's Progress: Hu." *People's Daily Online*, June 27, 2005. http://english.peopledaily.com.cn/200506/27/eng20050627_192495.html.

Chen, Hsi-yuan. "Confucianism Encounters Religion: The Formation of Religious Discourse and the Confucian Movement in Modern China." PhD diss., Harvard University, 1999.

"China Embraces New Scientific Development Concept: Hu." *People's Daily Online*, April 22, 2006. http://english.peopledaily.com.cn/200604/22/eng20060422_260256.html.

"Chinese Cultural Development Top Priority." *China CSR*, September 21, 2006. http://www.chinacsr.com/en/2006/09/21/748-chinese-cultural-development-top-priority/.

Chow, Elaine. "Avatar Cashing In in China." *The Shanghaiist,* January 11, 2010. http://shanghaiist.com/2010/01/11/avatar_cashing_in_in_china_how_you.php.

"Chow Yun-fat Saves the Third Kowtow for Confucius." *China.org.cn,* January 22, 2010. http://www.china.org.cn/wap/2010-01/22/content_19291174.htm.

Chun, Alan. "An Oriental Orientalism: The Paradox of Tradition and Modernity in Nationalist Taiwan." *History and Anthropology* 9, no. 1 (1995): 27–56.

Complete Opening Ceremony: The Games of the XXIX Olympiad, Beijing, 2008, dir. Dick Ebersol. 2008; New York: Ten Mayflower Productions, 2008. DVD.

Confucius. *The Analects.* Translated by D. C. Lau. New York: Penguin Books, 1979.

———. *The Analects of Confucius.* Translated by Arthur Waley. New York: Random House, 1938.

Croizier, Ralph C. *Traditional Medicine in Modern China: Science, Nationalism and the Tensions of Cultural Change.* Cambridge: Harvard University Press, 1968.

Deng Xiaoping. "Building a Socialism with a Specifically Chinese Character." *People's Daily Online,* June 30, 1984. http://english.peopledaily.com.cn/dengxp/vol3/text/c1220.html.

Deutsch, Francine. "How Parents Influence the Life Plans of Graduating Chinese University Students." *Journal of Comparative Family Studies,* June 22, 2004. http://www.highbeam.com/doc/1G1-122319625.html.

Dikotter, Frank, ed. *The Construction of Racial Identities in China and Japan.* London: Hurst and Company, 1997.

Dikotter, Frank. *The Discourse of Race in Modern China.* Stanford: Stanford University Press, 1992.

Dirlik, Arif. "Confucius in the Borderlands: Global Capitalism and the Reinvention of Confucianism." *boundary 2* 22, no. 3 (Autumn 1995): 229–273.

Du, Fangqin, and Susan Mann, "Competing Claims on Womanly Virtue in Late Imperial China." In *Women and Confucian Cultures in Premodern China, Korea, and Japan,* edited by Dorothy Ko, Jahyun Kim Haboush, and Joan R. Piggott, 219–247. Berkeley: University of California Press, 2003.

Ewing, Kent. "All Hail Hu Jintao." *Asia Times,* September 27, 2007. http://www.atimes.com/atimes/China/II22Ad01.html.

Fan, Maureen. "Confucius Making a Comeback In Money-Driven Modern China." *Washington Post,* July 24, 2007. http://www.washingtonpost.com/wp-dyn/content/article/2007/07/23/AR2007072301859.html.

Farrer, James. *Opening Up: Youth Sex Culture and Market Reform in Shanghai.* Chicago: University of Chicago Press, 2002.

Feng, Tao. "Hu Jintao Proposes Scientific Outlook on Development for Tackling China's Immediate Woes, Challenge." *Chinaview*, October 15, 2007. http://news.xinhuanet.com/english/2007-10/15/content_6883135.htm.

Fewsmith, Joseph. "Promoting the Scientific Development Concept." *China Leadership Monitor* 11 (July 30, 2004). http://media.hoover.org/sites/default/files/documents/clm11_jf.pdf.

Fong, Vanessa. *Only Hope: Coming of Age under China's One-Child Policy.* Stanford: Stanford University Press, 2004.

Foster, Frances H. "Translating Freedom for Post-1997 Hong Kong." *Washington University Law Quarterly* 76, no. 1 (Spring 1998). http://lawreview.wustl.edu/inprint/76-1/761-10.html.

Foster, Peter. "Confucius Family Tree Unveiled." *The Telegraph*, September 25, 2009. http://www.telegraph.co.uk/news/worldnews/asia/china/6230959/Confucius-family-tree-unveiled.html.

———. "China Backs £10m Biopic of Confucius." *The Telegraph*, March 16, 2009. http://www.telegraph.co.uk/news/worldnews/asia/china/4999702/China-backs-10m-biopic-of-Confucius.html.

"Fueled by Filial Piety." *China Daily*, March 10, 2010. http://www.china.org.cn/china/2010-03/10/content_19573827.htm.

Fung, Yiu-ming. "Problematizing Contemporary Confucianism in East Asia." In *Teaching Confucianism*, edited by Jeffrey L. Richey, 157–183. New York: Oxford University Press, 2008.

Gang, Qian. "Looking Back on Chinese Media Reporting of School Collapses." *China Media Project*, May 7, 2009. http://cmp.hku.hk/2009/05/07/1599/.

Gao, Zhihong, "What's in a Name? On China's Search for Socialist Advertising." *Advertising and Society Review* 4, no. 3 (2003). http://muse.jhu.edu/login?uri=/journals/asr/v004/4.3gao.html.

Giddens, Anthony. *Modernity and Self-Identity: Self and Society in the Late Modern Age.* Stanford: Stanford University Press, 1991.

Gluck, Carol. *Japan's Modern Myths: Ideology in the Late Meiji Period.* Princeton: Princeton University Press, 1985.

Goodman, David S. G. "Contending the Popular: Party-State and Culture." *positions: east asia cultures critique* 9, no. 1 (2001): 245–252.

Gu, Edward X. "Cultural Intellectuals and the Politics of the Cultural Public Space in Communist China (1979–1989): A Case Study of Three Intellectual Groups." *Journal of Asian Studies* 58, no. 2 (1999): 389–431.

Guo, Xiaohong. "UNESCO Confucius Prize for Literacy Launched." *China through a Lens*, December 1, 2005. http://www.china.org.cn/english/China/150588.htm.

Hadiz, Vedi R. "The Rise of Neo-Third Worldism? The Indonesian Trajectory and the Consolidation of Illiberal Democracy." *Third World Quarterly* 25, no. 1 (2004): 55–71.

Hall, Donald E., ed. *Muscular Christianity: Embodying the Victorian Age.* Cambridge: Cambridge University Press, 1994.

Han, Seunghyun. "Shrine, Images, and Power: The Worship of Former Worthies in Early Nineteenth Century Suzhou." *T'oung Pao* 95, nos. 1–3 (2009): 167–195.

Hassid, Jonathan. "Controlling the Chinese Media: An Uncertain Business." *Asian Survey* 48, no. 3 (2008): 414–430.

Henke, Frederick Goodrich, trans. *The Philosophy of Wang Yang-Ming.* 2nd ed. New York: Paragon Book Reprint Company, 1964.

Henriot, Christian. *Shanghai 1927–37: Municipal Power, Locality, and Modernization.* Translated by Noel Castelino. Berkeley: University of California Press, 1993.

Hessler, Peter. *Oracle Bones: A Journey through Time in China.* New York: HarperCollins, 2007.

Hobsbawm, Eric, and Terence Ranger. *The Invention of Tradition.* Cambridge: Cambridge University Press, 1983.

Hsu, Francis L. K. *Religion, Science and Human Crises.* London: Routledge and Kegan Paul, 1952.

Hua, Shiping. *Scientism and Humanism: Two Cultures in Post-Mao China (1978–1989).* Albany: State University of New York Press, 1995.

Irokawa, Daikichi. *The Culture of the Meiji Period.* Translated by. Marius B. Jansen. Princeton: Princeton University Press, 1985.

Jacobs, Andrew. "Confucius Statue Vanishes near Tiananmen Square." *New York Times*, April 22, 2011. http://www.nytimes.com/2011/04/23/world/asia/23confucius.html.

Jankowiak, William. *Sex, Death and Hierarchy in a Chinese City: An Anthropological Account.* New York: Columbia University Press, 1993.

Jensen, Lionel M. *Manufacturing Confucianism.* Durham: Duke University Press, 1997.

Johnson, Steven. *The Ghost Map.* New York: Riverhead Books, 2006.

Jordan, David. "Filial Piety in Taiwanese Popular Thought." In *Confucianism and the Family*, edited by Walter H. Slote and George A. De Vos, 267–283. Albany: State University of New York Press, 1998.

Kaufman, Stephen. "China's Government Praised for Easing Media Restrictions." Consulate General of the United States, Shenyang, China May 20, 2008. http://shenyang.usembassy-china.org.cn/uc080520.html.

Kimmelman, Michael. "Abroad: D.I.Y. Culture." *New York Times*, April 18, 2010. http://www.nytimes.com/2010/04/18/arts/18abroad.html.

Kipnis, Andrew B. "Within and against Peasantness: Backwardness and Filiality in Rural China," *Comparative Studies in Society and History* 37, no. 1 (January 1995): 110–135.

Kwok, D. W. Y. *Scientism in Chinese Thought, 1900–1950.* New Haven: Yale University Press, 1965.

Lackner, Michael, and Natascha Vittinghoff, eds. *Mapping Meanings: The Field of New Learning in Late Qing China*. Leiden: E. J. Brill, 2004.

Lam, Oiwan. "China and Hong Kong: Jackie Chan's Comment on Military Parade." *Global Voices Online*, October 8, 2009. http://globalvoicesonline. org/2009/10/08/china-jackie-chans-comment-on-military-parade/.

Lam, Oiwan. "China: Yang Jia Is Dead." *Global Voices Online*, November 26, 2008. http://globalvoicesonline.org/2008/11/26/china-yang-jia-is-dead/.

Levenson, Joseph R. *Confucian China and Its Modern Fate: A Trilogy*. Berkeley: University of California Press, 1972.

Link, Perry, trans. "China's Charter 08." *New York Review of Books*, January 15, 2009. http://www.nybooks.com/articles/archives/2009/jan/15/ chinas-charter-08/.

Liu, Kang. *Globalization and Cultural Trends in China*. Honolulu: University of Hawai'i Press, 2004.

Liu, Xin. *In One's Own Shadow: An Ethnographic Account of the Condition of Post-Reform Rural China*. Berkeley: University of California Press, 2000.

Lu, Guangming. "Memorial Ceremony Held at Confucius Temple to Mark New Semester." *People's Daily Online*, February 21, 2011. http://english. peopledaily.com.cn/9000/907082/7294166.html.

Lu, David John, ed. *Japan: A Documentary History*. 2 vols. Armonk, NY: M.E. Sharpe, 1997.

Lu, Wensheng, and Julia K. Murray. *Confucius: His Life and Legacy in Art*. New York: China Institute in America, 2010.

Lu, Xun. *Selected Stories of Lu Hsun*. New York: Norton, 1977.

———. "A Madman's Diary." Translated by Yang Xianyi and Gladys Yang. In *The Columbia Anthology of Modern Chinese Literature*, edited by Joseph S. M. Lau and Howard Goldblatt, 7–15. New York: Columbia University Press, 1995.

Luke, Timothy W., and Gearóid Ó Tuathail. "Global Flowmations, Local Fundamentalisms, and Fast Geopolitics: 'America' in an Accelerating World Order." In *An Unruly World? Globalization, Governance and Geography*, edited by Andrew Herod, Susan Roberts, and Gearóid Ó Tuathail, 72–94. London: Routledge, 1998.

Macartney, Jane. "Waitress Deng Yujiao Who Stabbed to Death Communist Official Walks Free." *The Times*, June 17, 2009. http://www.timesonline. co.uk/tol/news/world/asia/article6513750.ece.

Makeham, John. *Lost Soul: "Confucianism" in Contemporary Chinese Academic Discourse*. Cambridge: Harvard University Press, 2008.

———. *New Confucianism: A Critical Examination*. New York: Palgrave Macmillan, 2003.

Melvin, Sheila. "Modern Gloss on China's Golden Age." *New York Times*, September 3, 2007. http://www.nytimes.com/2007/09/03/arts/03stud. html.

Metzger, Thomas A. *Escape from Predicament*. New York: Columbia University Press, 1977.

Meyer, Michael J. *The Last Days of Old Beijing: Life in the Vanishing Backstreets of a City Transformed.* New York: Walker and Company, 2008.

Miller, Stephen. "Kung Te-Cheng (1920–2008): Lineal Descendant of Confucius Fostered Tradition." *Wall Street Journal,* November 1, 2008. http://online.wsj.com/article/SB122550105993889975.html.

Milne, R. S., and Diane K. Mauzy. *Singapore: The Legacy of Lee Kuan Yew.* Boulder: Westview Press, 1990.

"Mission to Accomplish: Xu Jialu's Academic Pursuit." *Confucius Institute Online,* September 7, 2009. http://www.chinese.cn/college/en/article/2009-09/07/content_69613.htm.

Moore, Malcolm. "Jackie Chan Says Chinese People Need to Be 'Controlled,'" *The Telegraph,* April 12, 2009. http://www.telegraph.co.uk/news/worldnews/asia/china/5182114/Jackie-Chan-says-Chinese-people-need-to-be-controlled.html.

Moore, Robert L., Eric Bindler, and David Pandich. "Language with Attitude: American Slang and Chinese *Liyu.*" *Journal of Sociolinguistics* 14 (2010): 524–538.

Moore, Robert, and James Rizor. "Confucian and Cool." *Education About Asia* 13, no. 3 (Winter 2008): 30–37.

Moore, Robert L. "Romantic Love in 1950s Rural China: Repressed, Suppressed or Simply Not There?" Paper presented at the Annual Convention of the Society for Anthropological Sciences, New Orleans, Louisiana, February 22, 2008.

———. "Generation Ku: Individualism and China's Millennial Youth." *Ethnology* 64 (2005): 357–376.

———. "Confucian Gravity: The Effect of Perceived Tradition on Talk of Love and Sex among Chinese University Students." Paper presented at the Annual Convention of the American Anthropological Association, Washington, DC, November 28, 2001.

———. "Love and Limerence with Chinese Characteristics: Student Romance in the PRC." In *Romantic Love and Sexual Behavior: Perspectives from the Social Sciences,* edited by Victor C. DeMunck, 72–94. Westport, CT: Praeger, 1998.

Morris, Andrew. *The Marrow of the Nation.* Berkeley: University of California Press, 2004.

Murray, Julia K. "Squaring Connoisseurship with History: Jiao Hong's *Yangzheng tujie.*" In *The Art of the Book in China,* edited by Ming Wilson and Stacey Pierson, 139–157. London: Percival David Foundation, 2006.

———. " 'Idols' in the Temple: Icons and the Cult of Confucius." *Journal of Asian Studies* 68, no. 2 (May 2009): 371–411.

———. "Illustrations of the Life of Confucius: Their Evolution, Functions, and Significance in Late Ming China." *Artibus Asiae* 57, nos. 1–2 (1997): 73–134.

———. "Pedagogue on the Go: Portraits of Confucius as an Itinerant Teacher." In *Bridges to Heaven: Essays in Honor of Professor Wen C. Fong,* edited by Judith Smith and Dora C. Y. Ching, n.p. Princeton: Tang Center for East Asian Art, forthcoming.

———. "Portraits of Confucius: Icons and Iconoclasm." *Oriental Art* 47, no. 3 (2001): 17–28.

———. "The Hangzhou *Portraits of Confucius and 72 Disciples (Shengxian tu)*: Art in the Service of Politics." *The Art Bulletin* 74 (March 1992): 7–18.

———. "Varied Views of the Sage: Illustrated Narratives of the Life of Confucius." In *On Sacred Ground: Culture, Society, Politics, and the Formation of the Temple of Confucius*, edited by Thomas A. Wilson, 222–264. Cambridge: Harvard University Press, 2002.

Nakayama, Shigeru. *Academic and Scientific Traditions in China, Japan and the West*. Translated by Jerry Dusenbury. Tokyo: University of Tokyo Press, 1984.

Nandy, Ashis. *Return from Exile*. Delhi: Oxford University Press, 1998.

Nedostup, Rebecca. *Superstitious Regimes: Religion and the Politics of Chinese Modernity*. Cambridge: Harvard University Asia Center, 2010.

"The New 11th Five Year Guidelines." *China.org.cn*, November 9, 2005. http://www.china.org.cn/english/features/guideline/157519.htm.

The New Life Movement. Nanking [Nanjing]: The New Life Movement National Headquarters, 1948.

Nylan, Michael, and Thomas A. Wilson. *Lives of Confucius: Civilization's Greatest Sage through the Ages*. New York: Doubleday, 2010.

Nylan, Michael. *The Five "Confucian" Classics*. New Haven: Yale University Press, 2001.

Okakura, Kakuzo. *The Book of Tea*. Champaign, IL: NetLibrary, 1906.

Oldstone-Moore, Jennifer. "The New Life Movement of Nationalist China: Confucianism, State Authority and Moral Formation." PhD diss., University of Chicago, 2000.

Owen, D. R. G. *Scientism, Man and Religion*. Philadelphia: The Westminster Press, 1952.

Pa, Chin. *Family*. 2nd ed. Prospect Heights, IL: Waveland Press, 1964.

Palmer, David. *Qigong Fever: Body, Science and Utopia in China*. London: C. Hurst & Co., 2007.

Paltiel, Jeremy T. "Confucianism Contested: Human Rights and the Chinese Tradition in Contemporary Chinese Political Discourse." In *Confucianism and Human Rights*, edited by Wm. Theodore deBary and Tu Wei-ming, 222–264. New York: Columbia University Press, 1998.

Pang, Li. "Hu Mei Brings Confucius to the Big Screen." China.org.cn, April 13, 2010, http://www.china.org.cn/arts/2010-04/13/content_19800838.htm.

"Parents Call On Confucius For Exam Good Fortune." *People's Daily Online*, June 5, 2008. http://english.people.com.cn/90001/6424741.html.

Paulette. "Chow Yun-fat Honors Descendant of Confucius." *One Asian World*, January 16, 2010. http://www.oneasianworld.com/2010/01/chow-yun-fat-honors-descendant-of-confucius/.

Peerenboom, R. P. *China Modernizes: Threat to the West or Model for the Rest?* New York: Oxford University Press, 2007.

Porter, Roy, ed. *The Cambridge History of Medicine*. Cambridge: Cambridge University Press, 2006.

Pyle, Kenneth B. *Japan Rising: The Resurgence of Japanese Power and Purpose*. New York: Public Affairs, 2007.

Qufu City Cultural Relics Administration Committee. "World Heritage: A Regular Report on the Implementation of the Convention for the Protection of World Cultural and Natural Heritage, Part II: Preservation Status of the Specific World Heritage; Treaty Signatory State: The People's Republic of China; Name of Property: Confucius Temple, Confucius Forest and Confucius Mansion in Qufu." UNESCO World Heritage Centre, September 2, 2002. http://whc.unesco.org/archive/periodicreporting/apa/cycle01/section2/704.pdf.

"Reactions To Jackie Chan 'Control' Comment & Translation." *chinaSMACK*, April 28, 2009. http://www.chinasmack.com/more/chinese-reactions-translation-jackie-chan-controlled-comment/.

Reporters Without Borders, "China." *Reporters Without Borders*, September 9, 2010. http://en.rsf.org/report-china,57.html.

Reuters. "China: A Stealth Move to Make an Underwater Claim." *New York Times*, August 26. 2010. http://www.nytimes.com/2010/08/27/world/asia/27briefs-BEIJING.html.

Rogaski, Ruth. *Hygienic Modernity Meanings of Health and Disease in Treaty-Port China*. Los Angeles: University of California Press, 2004.

Rosen, Stanley. "Contemporary Chinese Youth and the State." *Journal of Asian Studies* 68, no. 2 (May 2009): 359–369.

Rossabi, Morris. *Modern Mongolia: From Khans to Commissars to Capitalists*. Berkeley: University of California Press, 2005.

Rozman, Gilbert. "Can Confucianism Survive in an Age of Universalism and Globalization?" *Pacific Affairs* 75, no. 1 (Spring 2002): 11–37.

Schell, Orville. "China: Humiliation & the Olympics." *New York Review of Books* 55, no. 13 (2008): 30–33.

Selden, Mark. *The Yenan Way in Revolutionary China*. Cambridge: Harvard University Press, 1971.

Shaw, Thomas. "'We Like to Have Fun': Leisure and the Discovery of the Self in Taiwan's New Middle Class." *Modern China* 20, no. 4 (1994): 416–445.

Smith, Patrick. *Japan: A Reinterpretation*. New York: Pantheon Books, 1997.

Sommer, Deborah A. "Destroying Confucius: Iconoclasm in the Confucian Temple." In *On Sacred Grounds: Culture, Society, Politics, and the Formation of the Cult of Confucius*, edited by Thomas A. Wilson, 95–133. Cambridge: Harvard East Asian Monographs, 2002.

Soseki, Natsume. *Kokoro*. Translated by Edwin McClellan. Chicago: Regnery Gateway, 1957.

Spence, Jonathan. *The Gate of Heavenly Peace: The Chinese and Their Revolution, 1895–1980*. Harmondsworth: Penguin Books, 1981.

"Steady Course towards Scientific Development." *China.org.cn*, December 2, 2005. http://www.china.org.cn/english/China/150700.htm.

Sun Liping. "The Biggest Threat to China Is Not Social Turmoil but Social Decay." *China Digital Times*, March 10, 2009. http://chinadigitaltimes.net/2009/03/sun-liping-孙立平-the-biggest-threat-to-china-is-not-social-turmoil-but-social-decay/.

Sun, Anna. "The Fate of Confucianism in Socialist China." In *State, Market, and Religions in Chinese Societies*, ed. Fenggang Yang and Joseph B. Tamney, 229–253. Leiden: Brill, 2005.

Tanizaki, Jun'ichirō. *In Praise of Shadows*. Translated by Edward G. Seidenstricker. Stony Creek, CT: Leete's Island Books, 1977.

Tu, Wei-ming. "Implications of the Rise of 'Confucian' East Asia." *Daedalus* 129, no. 1 (2000): 195–218.

———. *A Confucian Perspective on Human Rights*. Singapore: UniPress, 1996.

———. "Cultural China: The Periphery as Center." *Daedalus* 120, no. 2 (1991): 1–32.

Vogel, Ezra. *The Four Little Dragons: The Spread of Industrialization in East Asia*. Cambridge: Harvard University Press, 1991.

"Waitress Stabs Government Official Trying to Rape Her." *chinaSMACK*, May 18, 2009. http://www.chinasmack.com/more/waitress-stabs-government-official-during-rape-attempt/.

Wang, Hui. *The End of the Revolution: China and the Limits of Modernity*. London: Verso, 2009.

Wang, Hui, and Theodore Huters. *China's New Order: Society, Politics, and Economy in Transition*. Cambridge: Harvard University Press, 2003.

Wang, Jing. *High Culture Fever: Politics, Aesthetics, and Ideology in Deng's China*. Berkeley: University of California Press, 1996.

Wang, Juntao. "Confucian Democrats in Chinese History." In *Confucianism for the Modern World*, ed. Daniel Bell and Chae-bong Ham, 69–89. Cambridge: Cambridge University Press, 2003.

Wang, Liang. "The Confucius Temple Tragedy of the Cultural Revolution." In *On Sacred Grounds: Culture, Society, Politics, and the Formation of the Cult of Confucius*, ed. Thomas A. Wilson, 376–400. Cambridge: Harvard East Asian Monographs, 2002.

Wang, Xin. "Seeking Channels for Engagement: Media Use and Political Communication by China's Rising Middle Class." *China: An International Journal* 7, no. 1 (March 2009): 31–56.

Wei, Betty Peh-T'i. *Ruan Yuan, 1764–1849: The Life and Work of a Major Scholar-Official in Nineteenth Century China Before the Opium War*. Hong Kong: Hong Kong University Press, 2006.

Wen, Chihua. *The Red Mirror: Children of China's Cultural Revolution*. Boulder: Westview Press, 1995.

Wilson, Thomas A., ed. *On Sacred Grounds: Culture, Society, Politics, and the Formation of the Cult of Confucius.* Cambridge: Harvard East Asian Monographs, 2002.

Wilson, Thomas A. "Ritualizing Confucius/Kongzi: The Family and State Cults of the Sage of Culture in Imperial China." In *On Sacred Grounds: Culture, Society, Politics, and the Formation of the Cult of Confucius*, ed. Thomas A. Wilson, 43–94. Cambridge: Harvard East Asian Monographs, 2002.

———. *Genealogy of the Way: The Construction and Uses of the Confucian Tradition in Late Imperial China.* Stanford: Stanford University Press, 1995.

Wright, David Wright. *Translating Science: The Translation of Western Chemistry into Late Imperial China, 1840–1900.* Leiden: Brill, 2000.

Xinhua. "Confucius Is a Brand Name in Hometown Lottery Promo." *Xinhua English*, February 2, 2010. http://english.sina.com/china/2010/0201/302715.html.

———. "Biopic Movie Stars, Crew Pay Tribute to Confucius." *China.org.cn*, January 22, 2010. http://www.china.org.cn/arts/2010-01/22/content_19292257.htm.

———. "Senior Official Calls for Inheriting, Displaying Confucianism." *Gov.cn: Chinese Government's Official Web Portal*, September 25, 2009. http://www.gov.cn/english/2009-09/25/content_1425935.htm.

———. "More Patriotic Education Urged Ahead of National Day." *China Daily*, August 17, 2009. http://www.chinadaily.com.cn/china/2009-08/17/content_8577338.htm.

———. "Descendants Hold Memorial Ceremony for Confucius in Qufu." *China Economic Net*, April 6, 2009. http://en.ce.cn/National/culture/200904/06/t20090406_18719670.shtml.

———. Confucius Promoted by Cartoon Imagery." *China Daily*, May 5, 2007. http://www.chinadaily.com.cn/china/2007-05/20/content_876382.htm.

———. "'Official' Image of Confucius Sparks Debate among Scholars." *CRIEnglish.com*, September 26, 2006. http://english.cri.cn/3126/2006/09/26/264@143753.htm.

———. "CPC Sets Moral Yardstick For Officials." *China.org.cn*, April 5, 2006. http://www.china.org.cn/english/government/164570.htm.

Xu, Janice Hua. "Building a Chinese 'Middle Class': Consumer Education and Identity Construction in Television Land." In *TV China: A Reader on New Media*, ed. Ying Zhu and Chris Berry, 150–167. Bloomington: Indiana University Press, 2009.

Yan, Hongliang, and Bramwell, Bill. "Cultural Tourism, Ceremony and the State in China." *Annals of Tourism Research* 35, no. 4 (2008): 969–989.

Yan, Yunxiang. *Private Life under Socialism: Love, Intimacy, and Family Change in a Chinese Village, 1949–1999.* Stanford: Stanford University Press, 2003.

Yang, Guobin. *The Power of the Internet in China: Citizen Activism Online.* New York: Columbia University Press, 2009.

Young, Nick. "The Cultural Crusades." *New Internationalist,* June 1, 2009. http://www.newint.org/features/2009/06/01/culture/.

Yu, Dan. *Confucius from the Heart: Ancient Wisdom for Today's World.* Translated by Esther Tyldesley. New York: Atria Books, 2009.

Zhang, Wei-Bin. *Singapore's Modernization: Westernization and Modernizing Confucian Manifestations.* Huntington, NY: Nova Publishers, 2002.

Zhang, Xiaoling. "Seeking Effective Public Space: Chinese Media at the Local Level." *China: An International Journal* 5, no. 1 (March 2007): 55–77.

Zhang, Yongle. "The Future of the Past: On Wang Hui's *Rise of Modern Chinese Thought.*" *New Left Review* 62 (March/April 2010): 47–83.

Zhao Yong. "Why Are We Always Correcting Yu Dan's Mistakes?" *Danwei,* May 8, 2007. www.danwei.org/scholarship_and_education/yu_dan_defender_of_traditional.php.

Zheng, Yongnian, and Sow Keat Tok. *"Harmonious Society" and "Harmonious World": China's Policy Discourse under Hu Jintao.* China Policy Institute Briefing Series, no. 26. Nottingham: University of Nottingham China Policy Institute, 2007.

Zhou, Raymond. "Confucius Loses His Way." *China Daily,* January 29, 2010. http://www.china.org.cn/arts/2010-01/29/content_19328023.htm.

Zhu, Ying. *Television in Post-Reform China: Serial Dramas, Confucian Leadership, and the Global Television Market.* London: Routledge, 2008.

Žižek, Slavoj. "Economic Emergency." *New Left Notes* 64 (August/September 2010): 85–95.

Zou, Le. "Authority Denies 'New Bill' Reports." *Global Times,* August 19, 2010. http://china.globaltimes.cn/society/2010-08/565101.html.

Index